Learning 2D Game Development with Unity®

A Hands-On Guide
to Game Creation

Matthew Johnson

James A. Henley

Addison-Wesley

Upper Saddle River, NJ • Boston • Indianapolis • San Francisco
New York • Toronto • Montreal • London • Munich • Paris • Madrid
Capetown • Sydney • Tokyo • Singapore • Mexico City

Many of the designations used by manufacturers and sellers to distinguish their products are claimed as trademarks. Where those designations appear in this book, and the publisher was aware of a trademark claim, the designations have been printed with initial capital letters or in all capitals.

The authors and publisher have taken care in the preparation of this book, but make no expressed or implied warranty of any kind and assume no responsibility for errors or omissions. No liability is assumed for incidental or consequential damages in connection with or arising out of the use of the information or programs contained herein.

For information about buying this title in bulk quantities, or for special sales opportunities (which may include electronic versions; custom cover designs; and content particular to your business, training goals, marketing focus, or branding interests), please contact our corporate sales department at corpsales@pearsoned.com or (800) 382-3419.

For government sales inquiries, please contact governmentsales@pearsoned.com.

For questions about sales outside the United States, please contact international@pearsoned.com.

Visit us on the Web: informit.com/aw

Library of Congress Cataloging-in-Publication Data

Johnson, Matthew (Computer programmer)
  Learning 2D game development with Unity : a hands-on guide to game creation / Matthew Johnson, James A. Henley.
    pages   cm
  Includes index.
  ISBN 978-0-321-95772-6 (pbk. : alk. paper)—ISBN 0-321-95772-5 (pbk. : alk. paper)
  1. Computer games—Programming. 2. Unity (electronic resource) I. Henley, James A. II. Title.
  QA76.76.C672J64 2015
  794.8'1526—dc23
                                                                          2014037406

Unity, Unity Free, Unity Pro, and the Unity Web Player are registered trademarks of Unity Technologies.

Adobe®, Flash®, and Photoshop® are registered trademarks or trademarks of Adobe Systems Incorporated in the United States and/or other countries. THIS PRODUCT IS NOT ENDORSED OR SPONSORED BY ADOBE SYSTEMS INCORPORATED, PUBLISHER OF Adobe® Flash® and Photoshop®.

The Kenney logo and the Made with Kenney Logo belong to Kenney.nl, Netherlands, used with permission.

Mac® is a trademark of Apple Inc., registered in the U.S. and other countries.

Linux® is the registered trademark of Linus Torvalds in the U.S. and other countries.

DirectX, Direct3D, and Visual Studio are either registered trademarks or trademarks of Microsoft Corporation in the United States and/or other countries.

ISBN-13: 978-0-321-95772-6
ISBN-10: 0-321-95772-5
Text printed in the United States on recycled paper at RR Donnelley in Crawfordsville, Indiana.
First printing, December 2014

Editor-in-Chief
Mark L. Taub

Executive Editor
Laura Lewin

Development Editor
Songlin Qiu

Managing Editor
John Fuller

Senior Production Editor
Kesel Wilson

Copy Editor
Barbara Wood

Indexer
Jack Lewis

Proofreader
Melissa Panagos

Technical Reviewers
Reshat Hasankolli, II
Sheetanshu Sinha

Editorial Assistant
Olivia Basegio

Cover Designer
Chuti Prasertsith

Compositor
Shepherd, Inc.

❖

*First and foremost, a big thanks to my friends and family
for supporting me throughout this process. You pushed me
to start this book and then begged me to finish it!*

*To my late father, who taught me to inspire
and entertain others with my talent and
wild imagination: I am forever your biggest fan.*

*Last, to the love of my life and best friend, Jessica:
without you this book would have been just
more dust in the wind of my ideas. Thank you for
all of your guidance and wisdom, and for believing
that I could accomplish this. I love you always and forever.*
—*Matthew Johnson*

*For my wonderful wife, who brought me tea
whenever I locked myself in my office to write
and tolerated being temporarily widowed by this book.*
—*James A. Henley*

❖

Contents at a Glance

Contents

Preface

Why Write This Book?

Since there are hundreds of books on game design and quite a few about using the Unity game engine, you might be asking, "Why even write another book on Unity?" We wanted to write a book about game development with a 2D approach, using an engine that is most widely known for being 3D. There are a bunch of Unity books covering 3D mesh and building game worlds, and fancy game mechanics, but there is really not much in the way of anything about a 2D platformer.

Another goal was to show a simplistic and inexpensive approach to creating your own game. Creating games is tough enough with the amount of time and effort you have to put into it, and rising costs are something no indie developer wants to deal with. Every element of this book uses free software and assets to build the game!

Last, we wanted to write our book around a small game project. Using simple approaches to scripting and asset creation, we wanted to create a game that even someone new to Unity and game development could easily pick up and tackle. Every aspect of the project is covered in the book with clear explanations, examples, and images!

Who Is This Book For?

This book is for those who want to learn more about the process of creating a game and all of the different parts that are involved, from having an initial idea, planning and designing, to the final steps of building and deploying the game to share with others.

This book is also for those who are new to Unity and the new 2D tools that have recently been integrated. We will touch on creating sprites and sprite atlases, applying 2D physics, and adding game scripts, audio, and animations. Almost every aspect of Unity is touched on and explained in detail.

Why Did We Choose to Use Unity?

The core of any game development is the game engine. It needs to handle all of the rules, tasks, and mathematics thrown at it. It also needs to be able to grow and evolve with new technology and the needs of the consumers playing the games.

While it's possible to develop your own game engine, starting with a well-structured foundation allows you to focus on creating your game content and letting the game engine do the dirty work. There are a dozen great game engines that are capable of this, but Unity excels where others have failed.

Having started out as a great 3D game engine, Unity has blossomed into an end-all development tool for creating games that you can then push to just about every platform available. As time went on, the need for more 2D game tools became obvious, and Unity jumped onboard, creating some of the most intuitive and easy-to-use 2D tools available.

Another reason is how accessible Unity is. While the Pro version has some really great additional features, they are tailored more to teams or people looking to really fine-tune every aspect of their game. We will cover a few of the Pro features, but the free version will work great for us.

What Will You Need?

So what will you need to develop your game? After you have purchased this book, and assuming you have a computer to work on, there is nothing else to buy. All of the assets we will use to create our game are accessible to anyone and readily available on the Internet, the obvious being the Unity engine, which is easily downloadable from their Web site (we cover this in the Introduction).

For the game sprites we were lucky enough to get assets from a great game artist, Kenney Vleugels. We are including these with the ancillaries for this book, but check out all of the amazing resources and game assets on his Web site, www.kenney.nl. He continually adds more and more assets and will even create specific assets at your request.

Last, all of the scripts for our game will be created within the chapters. We will be providing the final scripts along with the project files, but we recommend you follow along and create them for yourself. Having a good grasp of even simple scripting will take you a long way toward creating a game that is truly unique and completely yours.

Register your book at informit.com/title/9780321957726 to access assets, code listings, and video tutorials on the companion website.

How Much Scripting Is Involved?

While we don't dig down into the trenches of writing complex code behaviors, we do cover a lot of the basics and create quite a few scripts throughout this book. Learning a little programming can go a long way in any profession but is highly recommended for game design. Even tests and debugging are helpful and require just a very basic level of scripting knowledge.

How Is the Book Organized?

Our goal for this book was to have those reading it start from the beginning and work their way through it until the very end. Readers can build upon what they learned in previous chapters and continually come back to elements they have already built. With these building blocks, we hope that at the end, you will have the confidence and skill to either continue building on the example project or start your own game design.

However, we know this is not the case. There will be those who have an understanding of the game development process and are looking for a game authoring engine upon which to build their idea and designs. So we have broken each chapter down into individual lessons. That way those who are looking to learn about a specific mechanic or process can easily jump ahead.

We encourage even those with a general understanding of Unity to read through all of the chapters, as we cover many elements of the Unity engine, both old and new. We have provided notes, tips, and figures throughout to help reinforce or reiterate a specific lesson, so look for these as well.

Here is a summary of each chapter:

- Chapter 1, "Setting Up the Unity Development Environment"

    This chapter will familiarize readers with the Unity interface, provide them with an understanding of a Project's hierarchy, and begin to build the initial Project for the game that will be created throughout this book.

- Chapter 2, "Understanding Asset Creation"

    In this chapter readers will start to build the foundation of the game by importing the assets we will use for the game Project. They will get an understanding of how the Unity engine uses GameObjects on which everything in Unity is built. This chapter will break down how Components are the nuts and bolts of a GameObject and how to utilize them to build upon each other for complex behaviors. Last, this chapter will touch upon using third-party assets and packages and how to bring them into our game environment.

- Chapter 3, "Creating 2D Sprites"

    In this chapter we will dive into the new tools and features added for building 2D gameplay. We will discuss the sprite editor, as well as some Pro-only features and how we can work around them.

- Chapter 4, "Building the Game World"

    In this chapter we will take all of the existing prefabricated GameObjects and start building the world our player will live in. We will learn to use the Transform tools to place our GameObjects, and we will learn about sorting our sprites for layering and depth. Finally, we will go over grouping sprites and the parent-child relationship, and how keeping these organized and named correctly will keep our Scene View and Hierarchy easy to manage.

- Chapter 5, "The Basics of Movement and Player Control"

    This chapter will teach a basic understanding of creating scripts and functions to drive input and control the physical behaviors of our GameObjects. We will discuss the basic scripts for controlling user input and building upon these for all the necessary mechanics of our game. We will briefly discuss the Unity native programming languages and the pros and cons of each. This chapter will also discuss error handling and basic debugging of scripts.

- Chapter 6, "Adding Animations to Our Scene"

  This chapter will go into setting up and creating the animations for the GameObjects and sprites. It will discuss creating animations with base transform versus frame animations and the benefits of both methods. We will then discuss creating 2D sprite behaviors with the Animator State Machine. Here we will begin to create the mechanics for the characters for our game.

- Chapter 7, "Setting Up Player Physics and Colliders"

  This chapter will discuss adding physics for both 2D and 3D GameObjects. It will discuss setting up GameObject collision and knowing which one is best to maintain game performance. We will also discuss setting up the forces for our GameObjects and creating dynamic physics.

- Chapter 8, "Creating and Applying Gameplay Systems"

  This chapter will discuss the creation of key gameplay elements such as picking up collectibles, checkpoints, and respawning. Readers will be taught about Unity's trigger system and the code methods that it uses. We will also include some design theory related to these systems.

- Chapter 9, "Creating Hazards and Crafting Difficulty"

  This chapter will discuss the creation of some basic enemy types and the underlying code that makes them work. We will add damage scripting and teach the player how to hook enemies into spawning logic. This chapter will also touch on some of the design theory related to difficulty and tuning.

- Chapter 10, "Creating the Menus and Interface Elements"

  In this chapter we will create the basic menus for getting into and out of our game as well as the game interface elements that will make up the on-screen player information and statistics. We will discuss basic input for menu selections and game screens.

- Chapter 11, "Applying Effects to the GameObjects"

  This chapter will guide the reader in adding the final polish to the game assets by adding animations, effects, and audio Components. It will discuss an overview of the Unity particle system, adding audio listeners and effects to our non-character gameplay elements.

- Chapter 12, "Organization and Optimization"

  We will go over final tips and recommendations for game optimizations and compressions for deploying to the various platforms. We will also look into some final organization tips for file handling and future revisions.

- Chapter 13, "Bringing It All Together"

  In this chapter we will wrap things up. We will package up our game and discuss publishing the game with the Unity Web Player and other platforms. This chapter will briefly detail best practices for monetizing a game and advice for a successful published game. We will then look at publishing the game to the Web.

- Chapter 14, "UGUI"

  Chapter 14 is a bonus chapter for the upcoming UGUI system in Unity 4.6. We will take an in-depth look into setting up a new UGUI interface and getting acquainted with the Components and new Rect Transform Component.

Conventions Used in This Book

The book uses a few conventions for explaining best practices and for sharing useful information that is relevant to learning Unity.

- Figures

  Figures are used to explain a process or approach that needs a visual example to clarify the information. These are used throughout the chapters as assets and levels are generated to show the game design process taking shape.

- Notes

  Notes are used to share additional information with the reader that does not fit exactly into the context but should be explained along with it.

- Tips

  Tips are used to share workflows or information not generally known that can help with a specific task or problem.

- Warnings

  Warnings are used to signify caveats about established rules or situations in which the game may behave in unexpected ways. These will help you sidestep some of the potential pitfalls of the game development process.

- Code listings

  Code listings are used throughout the book and are the bread and butter of the game development process. Code listings contain elements of a script or the entire script that the reader can copy and use or use as a guide when approaching a specific function. Later chapters use code listings to update gameplay to add additional mechanics and features that help polish the gameplay.

- Exercises

  At the end of almost every chapter are exercises for readers to complete. These are based on the content of that chapter. After reading the chapter, they should have gained a solid understanding of the information and should be able to use it to complete more gameplay elements. The exercises are built to be easily completed yet require a little bit of discovery and trial and error.

Supplementary Materials

The project development covered within this book will help you build a fully realized game Project, complete with all of the sprites, audio, and script assets that we show. The objective is to help you learn how to create all of these from scratch, but we do understand that you might get stuck or confused about specific processes.

For this reason, we have provided a Web site to grant you access to the entire contents of the Project we will make throughout the book. All of the Scenes, packages, assets, and scripts will be available to you to follow along with, or to reference in case you need a little extra help.

We have provided a series of video learning modules for you to watch and to follow along with as well. These are designed to show the UnityProject coming together, with audio commentary that explains our methods and approach to the game design. The videos recapitulate the book's contents, but sometimes a visual explanation is warranted.

Register your book at informit.com/title/9780321957726 to access assets, code listings, and video tutorials on the companion website.

Acknowledgments

Matthew Johnson

Thank you to Laura Lewin for taking a chance on me, and for not flying to Florida to strangle me. I know the urge was there and was warranted.

Thank you to Olivia Basegio for all of your support and guidance. You truly made this experience enjoyable and as pain-free as you could.

Thank you to Songlin, Reshat, and Sheetanshu, whose wisdom truly made this book that much better. Your suggestions and feedback always seemed to be spot-on.

Thank you to Kenny Vleugels for your great artwork and for making it easy to access it. You are a godsend to game developers everywhere.

Last, to my colleague and friend James Henley: a thousand times over, thank you. Thank you for all of your insight, humor, and hard work. Most importantly, thank you for your understanding and patience in helping me see this book through. Without you stepping in to take the helm, it would never have seen the light of day.

James A. Henley

Foremost, I would like to offer my sincerest thanks to K2, without whom I would not have become the kind of developer that I am today. Years of design theory discussions, feedback, and soundboarding have been integral to my growth as a developer.

I would like to express my great appreciation to the publisher, who provided me with both the opportunity and the means to share some of my knowledge and experience. In particular, I'd like to thank Laura and Olivia for taking the time to answer my questions, no matter how mundane, as well as Songlin, Reshat, and Sheetanshu for their hard work as editors and the many excellent suggestions they made.

I would also like to thank my stream regulars for sticking by me despite the many interrupted or canceled casts this book caused.

Finally, I wish to thank you, the reader, for having the courage to pursue the dream that is game development.

Thank you all.

About the Authors

Matthew Johnson is a principal 3D artist at Firebrand Games in Merritt Island, Florida. He graduated with a BFA from the International Academy of Design, where he trained in computer animation before going on to study animation at Animation Mentor.

Matthew has been in game development for the past seven years working on more than a dozen AAA racing games, such as NASCAR, Hot Wheels, and the Need for Speed series. He has helped publish titles on almost every platform, including PC, Wii U, iOS, Android, and Steam.

In his spare time Matthew enjoys spending time with his wife and two kids and, when he finds time, pursuing his love for photography.

James A. Henley is an experienced game developer who has worked on several major titles and franchises, including Mass Effect, Dragon Age, Star Wars, and Skylanders, over the past decade. He originally entered the industry via the Neverwinter Nights modding community, where he was able to indulge his desires to craft content, tell stories, and write code all at the same time. He turned that love into a job opportunity at BioWare, where he spent three years with the Edmonton studio and five more with the Austin studio in a variety of design roles before briefly working for Activision.

Currently, James is working as an independent developer on [TITLE REDACTED] and is actively live streaming to share his love of games and game design in an interactive fashion. He may or may not also be a mad scientist. Analysis has proven inconclusive.

Introduction

Welcome to the exciting world of Unity and game development! We hope you are reading this because you want to learn what we have found to be an exciting and rewarding career with indie game development.

Between the two of us, we have over a decade of game development experience and hope to share our insights with you. Both of us have a strong passion for video games and immersing ourselves in hundreds of different worlds and stories. While game development can take a lot of time and effort, seeing someone else play your creation is well worth it! Imagine an idea you have for a new game that you would love to create. Now imagine creating it and then being able to share it with millions of others. Exactly!

We have created this learning guide to get you up to speed quickly with Unity to create your very own platform game from start to finish. This guide may not cover every little detail of Unity as we are focused on a 2D development platform, but we feel that after reading this you can go on to create your own game and dig deeper into Unity, building on what you learn here.

Introduction to Unity

Let's go over the steps needed to get Unity up and running on your machine. We will then take a look at creating a workflow for organizing your files and recommended steps to avoid problems further along in development. Finally, we will describe the basics of the Unity interface, file menus, and navigation. By the end, we hope you will have a grasp of the Unity user interface and some solid principles for creating your Projects. So let's get started!

Downloading and Installing Unity

Before we dive headfirst into the game development aspects of this book, we need to get our Unity environment up and running. You can download the latest Unity release at their Web site: http://unity3d.com/unity/download. While writing this book, we used version 4.5.1. You may end up with a newer version depending on when you bought the book, but as long as it is 4.5.0 or above, you will be able to follow along.

While on the Unity download page, take a look at the System Requirements as well as the License Comparisons pages. The System Requirements page lists the general requirements for Windows or OS X–based machines, along with those requirements needed to publish to the various development environments. If you have a fairly recent Operating System such as Microsoft Windows 7/8 or Apple OS X 10.5 (Leopard) or newer, you will be fine.

The License Comparisons page gives you a full rundown of the features available with the free versus paid versions of Unity, as well as the add-ons to Unity Pro for building your game to their respective platforms. Unity Pro comes with a host of added features that make game creation and debugging a lot easier and even more exciting.

Note

While there are a few Unity Pro features we could benefit from in our game development, you will not need them to follow along in this guide. We will, however, mention a few of these in later chapters just to discuss their advantages for those with access to Unity Pro.

Component Installs

Once you have downloaded and begun the installation, Unity will pause and prompt you with the Choose Components screen (see Figure I.1). The items listed here are additional resources and add-ons that you may wish to install along with the Unity

Figure I.1   Unity Choose Components screen

engine. We recommend installing all of them as they will be helpful in your journey developing Unity Projects and games.

Example Project

Angry Bots is a feature-rich Unity Project developed by the minds at Unity Technologies. While it is a fun and immersive game experience, it is of greater significance as a tool for developing your own games. All of the assets are easily viewable in the engine as well as the scripts, Components, and animations. While the features and scope of Angry Bots are beyond what we cover in this guide, we highly recommend looking it over, especially if you are designing any type of 3D game experience.

Note

The Unity Asset Store also carries a bunch of old and new example Projects like this. There are quite a few built by the Unity Technologies team. There is a very good "2D platformer" Project available from them that we highly recommend checking out. We will discuss more about the Unity Asset Store and downloading Projects, packages, and assets in Chapter 2, "Understanding Asset Creation."

Unity Development Web Player

The Unity Development Web Player will be a vital part of our game development workflow. The Web Player allows you to quickly see what your published game will look and run like on your computer hardware. In later chapters we will see it in action. The Web Player will also be used to publish our game to HTML code for playing through a Web browser such as Firefox or Chrome. This is useful for allowing others to run and test your game from their computers or devices and to get valuable feedback. As we wrap up things in Chapter 13, "Bringing It All Together," we will go over building for HTML and packaging your game for the Web Player.

MonoDevelop

While we can get so far with our game assets and animations, it's the core mechanics and gameplay events that create the true experience for the gamer. You can have a hero and a villain character with combat animations, but without gameplay scripts, you won't be able to move them or have them interact. We can do all of this and more by making a few simple scripts. MonoDevelop is the IDE that allows you to build those runtime events and scripts for Unity. It is by far the most important of the add-ons you can install. If you are fairly new to scripting and Unity, this is a must for creating your game. We will go into MonoDevelop in a lot more depth as we go along, but for now just continue by hitting Next.

Once everything has installed, open Unity by clicking the Unity icon on your desktop. From here you will be given a Unity Activation screen. Click the Register button and finish the registration authorization. Once this is done, you should get a screen for the Project Wizard.

> **Note**
>
> By registering you will be given the option of a 30-day evaluation of Unity Pro and access to the Unity mailing list for upcoming news and updates. Again, we will not have to worry about any of the added Pro features here, but after finishing this guide, if you wish to dive deeper into them, you will be able to update to either the 30-day evaluation or the full version by purchasing Unity Pro.

Project Wizard

The final step (before we see all of the beauty that is the Unity Editor!) is to create our Project. A good way to understand a Project is to think of it as being like building a house. Without having the right pieces such as the walls, doors, and a roof, and if it's not constructed in an organized and methodical manner, things could get unorganized, messy, and come falling down. A Project in Unity can be viewed in the same way: we want to keep it as simple and easy to comprehend as we can for both us and others who are on our team.

Open Project Tab

There are two tabs in the Project Wizard, the first being the Open Project tab (see Figure I.2). Here we can choose an existing Project if we have one. You will use only one Project for each game you are creating. With the house scenario we described, the Project is your house and you really only need one, right? For now we do not have a preexisting Project, so just click over to the Create New Project tab.

Figure I.2   The Project Wizard—Open Project tab

> **Tip**
>
> We personally like to create a sandbox Project, a second Project that we use for testing game-play scripts. We also use it to test assets so that we won't have to scrap them if we don't need them in our game Project. By importing and then deleting assets in your Project, you can accidentally leave unused assets, or more importantly remove assets or code, that can break your game. Again, keeping our Project clean and clutter-free is vital.

Create New Project Tab

On this tab we will set up the Project that we will use for the duration of this guide and our game. Under Project Location, select the path and name for your Project. By default Unity will name your Project "NewUnityProject" without you entering anything. To follow along we have named our Project "LearningUnity" (see Figure I.3). We have also set up the preference defaults for 2D as we will be building a 2D platform game. You can switch the Unity preferences between 2D and 3D, but Unity will open with a few features defaulted to a 2D setup like this.

Packages

Below the Project Location is a list of packages that come preinstalled with Unity. Packages are collections of assets and GameObjects from a Unity Project that get bundled and exported. You can then take them into other Projects and use them there. This can be very useful for reusing scripts and certain elements rather than having to remake them.

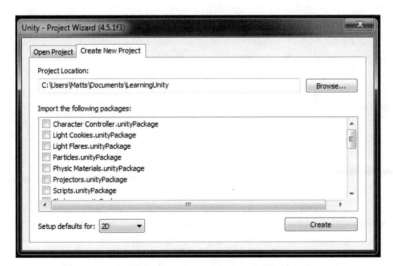

Figure I.3   The Project Wizard—Create New Project tab

Some of these do require a Unity Pro license, but most of them are available in the free version. These packages are very helpful when you're starting out and can get you up and running quickly for testing simple gameplay ideas and mechanics. While we will not be using any of these to start, note that they are here and available to use in your Projects. We will revisit these packages in Chapter 2, "Understanding Asset Creation."

Setting Our Project

One of the most important skills you can have in game development is an understanding of asset management and Project structure. In Chapter 2, "Understanding Asset Creation," we will go more into the asset management side, but here we will cover the Project structure side.

Project Structure

Project structure refers to the hierarchy of files that are used in a Project, how they are named, and their ordered layering. Having a firm grasp of how you keep your Hierarchy organized and named will help you from the beginning of a Project through to the final build so that your game runs at its optimal frame rate. It also allows you to know what is needed in your deliverable game so that there are no unwanted files or folders that could bloat your game. Chapter 12, "Organization and Optimization," will go deeper into optimizing your game for best results, but understand early on that there will be limits on the file size of your game that you cannot exceed. Each device and publisher is different, and you must follow their guidelines when publishing your game.

The best way to understand the Project structure is the house analogy we made earlier. The staple of a house is its name. Some call it "home" or "pad." The point is, the name is the base, just as our Project base should have a name. When we started in the New Project window, we named it "LearningUnity." This is the name we will use throughout, and it best describes what the Project is about.

Your Unity Project is an extension of your Windows Explorer or Finder on Mac. Just as you can create folders, move files in and out, and rearrange things, you can do the same with your Unity Project. Anything you add into your Project will almost instantly be updated and appear in your Explorer Project path and vice versa. This is so important to remember; as we mentioned earlier, adding and deleting files can produce some unintentional consequences.

> **Note**
>
> While it may seem simple to rename or delete a file, remember that Unity has underlying data connections to the files and there may be unintended results.

Folder Organization

When you first build your Unity Project, you will see that it comes with some pre-made folders: Assets, Library, Project Setting, and a Temp folder. The Library, Project Setting, and Temp folders all contain files related to Unity and creating assets for your game. Stay clear of these and most certainly do not delete them.

As we build our Project, we will be creating an abundance of assets, such as models, sprites, scripts, and Materials. Keeping these assets in a neat and organized manner will simply make things easier as your Project continues to grow. At this point we have yet to import anything, but here is an example template for a folder structured for Unity:

```
Assets/
        Materials/
        Meshes/
                Actors/
                        GoodGuy
                        BadGuy_A
                        BadGuy_B
                Props/
                        GarbageCan_Clean
                        GarbageCan_Dirty
        Plugins/
        Prefabs/
                Actors/
                        GoodGuy
                        BadGuy_A
                        BadGuy_B
        Scenes/
                Chapter_1/
        Scripts/
```

File Naming Conventions

Another valuable tool to have in your workflow toolbox is an understanding of how to use namespaces. Namespaces (not the scripting ones) are a means of keeping your file names simple and short and easy to read and understand at a later point in time. Not only can it become difficult for you and others to find a file if there is no structure, but it can be just as frustrating if the files do not have a clear and concise naming convention.

For example, what if we lazily named two scripts "script_1" and "script_2"? It may be easy to remember just these two, but imagine having dozens, or several hundred, of them. We're pretty sure that if we went to bed for the night and then reopened Unity the next day, we would most likely forget what these two scripts contained, let alone a hundred or so of them! Having a concise naming convention in your work can help you stay focused and organized. It works just as well in 2D and 3D packages.

We have compiled a list of some of the best practices to use when dealing with namespaces inside of Unity:

1. Start with the most descriptive word, followed by an underscore. An asset named alienShip.png is not bad; however, char_enemy_alienShip.png is much clearer.

2. Folders take up very little hard drive space. Use as many as you need, for example, Assets/_meshes/_characters/_enemy/alienShip.fbx.

3. Try to use namespaces for linked assets. If you use alienShip.fbx for your mesh, try to use alienShip.cs for the script and alienShip_death.anim for its death animation. Folder management will keep them organized.

4. While we will cover asset labels more in Chapter 2, "Understanding Asset Creation," they are definitely worth mentioning here. As a sort of internal file system, this simple tool will make locating assets quick and painless.

> **Note**
>
> While these recommended guidelines work for some, they may not feel right to you. Use your best judgment when setting up your Project and when naming your files. The best advice is having a plan in place from the start. As the Project grows and more files are added, understanding your workflow will be key.

From here on we will dive into Unity and game design to start creating our 2D platform game. We have a long road ahead of us, but as they say, "It's all about the journey and not the destination." So let's move on to Chapter 1, "Setting Up the Unity Development Environment," and get a look at what the power of Unity can do.

> **Tip**
>
> Take a look through the Unity documentation and learning resources provided on their Web site. Unity provides a bunch of their own learning videos, follow-along tutorials, and tips, and the Unity Community and Forum pages are just as valuable.
>
> The Unity Manual is one of your greatest assets when creating games, so remember you always have this available to you as well. You can access the Unity Manual, along with links to their Community, Forum, and Answers pages, from the Help menu inside of Unity. Here are the links to the Internet Web pages for all of this information:
>
> - Unity Documentation: http://unity3d.com/learn/documentation
> - Unity Tutorials: http://unity3d.com/learn/tutorials/modules
> - Unity Forums: http://forum.unity3d.com/
> - Unity Answers: http://answers.unity3d.com/

Setting Up the Unity Development Environment

As we will see in this chapter, the folks at Unity Technologies really understand how to design the most effective interface for their users. At first glance, it may not appear as though there is a lot to it, but that is where Unity shines. By starting with a clean slate, you are able to build your game and know what each element is from the start. Now let's take a look at the interface, see how to build workspaces and Layouts, and learn how to navigate in Unity.

Welcome Screen

When you first open Unity, you will be greeted with the Welcome To Unity screen (as seen in Figure 1.1). Here you will find an endless amount of free help in the form of

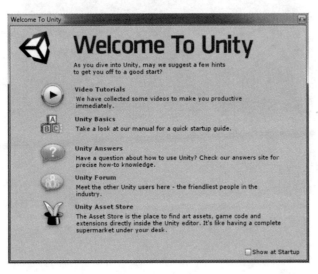

Figure 1.1   The Welcome To Unity screen

tutorials, Unity Answers, the Unity Forum, and of course the quick startup guide. The guides and tutorials are another shining example of the support and passion put into Unity. The Unity community is a strong, highly intelligent, and helpful group, all with the same goal of creating a fun experience. We can close this screen for now, but do not neglect its resources.

The Unity Interface

Now that we have made it through the installation process, set up our Project, and gone over a few ground rules, it's on to mastering the Unity game engine! You get past the Welcome Screen and . . . it doesn't look like much, does it? But as you will soon see, this interface will soon be populated with all sorts of information.

Figure 1.2 shows the Unity interface. This is the light gray color from the Unity free version. If you are using the Unity Pro version, you may see the dark gray color.

Menus

Many of Unity's common tasks and commands, such as opening Scenes, creating GameObjects and Components, and accessing the various windows and Layouts, can be accessed through the Unity menu. Figure 1.3 shows the menu bar and all of the different options. Let's take a brief tour of what each of these menus and submenus contains.

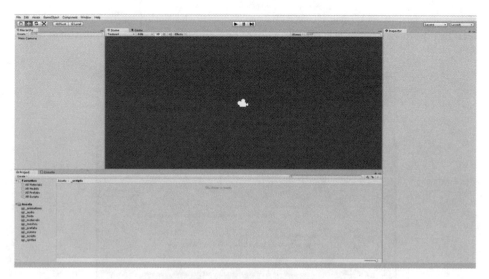

Figure 1.2   The default Unity interface

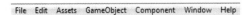

Figure 1.3   The menu bar

Figure 1.4   The File menu

File Menu

The File menu (shown in Figure 1.4) holds basic commands for starting or saving a new Unity Scene or Project. This is also where you access the options for building your game Project to the various platforms and then running it. We will go more into the Build Settings in Chapter 13, "Bringing It All Together."

- **New Scene**: Creates and loads a new, empty Scene in the existing Project.
- **Open Scene:** Loads an existing Scene from a file browser. It will prompt you if the Scene you are trying to load is not part of the current Project.
- **Save Scene:** Saves the Scene that is currently loaded. This will prompt you for a name if the Scene has not yet been saved to the hard drive.
- **Save Scene as:** Allows you to save the currently loaded Scene with a file browser.
- **New Project:** Opens the Project Wizard to start a new Project, completely devoid of any existing content.
- **Open Project:** Opens the file browser to allow you to load a preexisting Project.
- **Save Project:** Saves any changes to the currently loaded Project.
- **Build Settings:** Opens the Build Settings screen to allow you to set options for building your Scenes and Project before publishing your game.

- **Build & Run:** Builds and runs your game based on the options that have been preset. The Build Settings screen will open if there are no preset settings or if there are no Scenes added to build from.

Edit Menu

Figure 1.5 shows the Edit menu. This menu houses tools for editing elements of your Scenes and Projects. Basic commands such as Undo, Copy, and Paste are here, along with some settings to emulate network and graphic environments.

- **Duplicate:** Duplicates a currently selected item in the Scene or Project Browser.
- **Delete:** Deletes a currently selected item in the Scene or Project Browser.
- **Frame Selected:** When pressed while over the Scene View, moves the current camera to focus and center on a selection.
- **Lock View to Selected:** Locks the current camera to the currently selected object. This is useful when a GameObject plays a transform animation that translates it through the Scene.

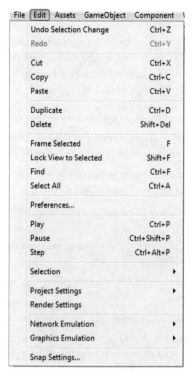

Figure 1.5   The Edit menu

- **Find:** Highlights the search field for the currently selected window if applicable. Useful for finding a specific object in the Scene View, Hierarchy, or Project Browser when dealing with a large number of assets.

- **Select All:** Selects all assets from the current active panel.

- **Preferences:** Brings up the Unity Preferences window to allow you to set custom settings for the Editor, External Tools, and Hotkeys.

- **Play:** Allows you to go into game mode to play and test your game in real time.

- **Pause:** Pauses the active game state at its current point in time.

- **Step:** Continues the game after a pause and runs through to the next breakpoint that is set.

- **Selection:** Allows you to create a quick selection set for a number of assets in the Scene View. Useful for quickly and easily selecting a large number of things in your game, such as point lights in your Scene.

- **Project Settings:** A submenu of Project-specific parameters you can set to affect the overall settings of your game. An example is the Audio submenu that controls the volume and stereo output for your game.

- **Render Settings:** Adjustable settings to control the atmospheric effects of your game, such as fog, ambient lighting, and the Skybox.

- **Network Emulation:** Various types of network settings to emulate the connection speed of your game played over a network. This is useful for emulating a player who may not have an optimal network connection.

- **Graphics Emulation:** Allows you to emulate lower graphic specs of popular platforms to more accurately reflect how the game will look on a particular device.

- **Snap Settings:** A tool for setting the units of the snap tool when aligning objects to specific points on the grid.

Assets Menu

The Assets menu, shown in Figure 1.6, has tools for creating or importing assets and scripts, and then syncing them to the most recent version in the Project.

- **Create:** Holds a list of Project resources, such as prefabricated GameObjects, folders, and fonts.

- **Show in Explorer:** Opens the file browser on your machine to the location of the asset.

- **Open:** Opens the asset and the program associated with its extension. For example, opening a TIFF file might open a 2D imaging editor such as Adobe Photoshop.

Figure 1.6   The Assets menu

- **Delete:** Deletes the asset from the Project as well as the hard drive. This method is somewhat safer than removing an asset from the file browser.

- **Import New Asset:** Opens the file browser to allow you to browse and find an asset that does not live in the current Unity Project.

- **Import Package:** A drop-down to import a custom or preinstalled package. A package is a set of assets bundled together for easier distribution.

- **Export Package:** Allows you to take a set of GameObjects selected from the Hierarchy, or Project View, then bundle and export them for use in another Project.

- **Find References In Scene:** When applicable, shows which GameObjects have a linked reference to the selected asset.

- **Select Dependencies:** When applicable, shows a list of assets dependent upon the selected asset.

- **Refresh:** Synchronizes the selected asset with any recent edits made outside of Unity.

- **Reimport:** Reimports the selected asset from scratch. Very useful if your Project works over a Version Control System.

- **Reimport All:** Same as Reimport, but with all assets in the entire Project.

- **Sync MonoDevelop Project:** Syncs your Project with the MonoDevelop Editor to allow real-time interoperability between the two.

GameObject Menu

The GameObject menu (shown in Figure 1.7) is where you will spend most of your time in the menus. It includes all of the base objects that become the building blocks for everything you create. We will gain a better understanding of GameObjects in Chapter 2, "Understanding Asset Creation."

- **Create Empty:** Creates an empty Transform node. Use this to build a GameObject from just a Transform that you can customize with the Components you want.

- **Create Other:** A drop-down list of premade GameObjects such as GUI elements, lights, and simple 3D primitives. We will examine this list extensively in Chapter 2, "Understanding Asset Creation."

- **Center On Children:** Takes the parent of the currently selected GameObject and centers its Transform at coordinates determined to be in the "middle" of all of its child GameObjects' Transform coordinates.

- **Make Parent:** Takes the currently selected child object and moves it up the hierarchy to become the parent chain.

- **Clear Parent:** Removes the hierarchy chain from the selected object and places it at the root of the Project Hierarchy.

- **Apply Changes To Prefab:** When enabled, takes a modified, instanced Prefab in the Scene and updates the master Prefab to match. Once applied to the master Prefab, this action cannot be undone.

- **Break Prefab Instance:** Breaks the link of the selected object to its original and does not allow you to pass updates or accept changes from the master Prefab.

- **Move To View:** Takes the selected GameObject and repositions it to the center of the current view.

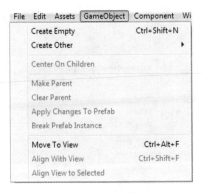

Figure 1.7   The GameObject menu

- **Align With View:** Aligns the position of the selected GameObject to match that of the camera. This is helpful for setting the position of lights.
- **Align View to Selected:** Does the opposite of Align With View as it will match the camera to the selected GameObject's Transforms.

Component Menu

Components are the internals of your GameObjects and create their unique behaviors. Without Components your hero cannot move and his gun cannot fire. We will explore Components more in the next chapter, but know that they are built onto your existing GameObjects to give them life. Figure 1.8 shows the Component menu and its contents.

- **Add:** Here you can attach a Component to a selected object, whether from the Project Browser, Hierarchy, or Scene View. Using this just opens a floating Component menu that is independent of the menu bar.
- **Mesh:** Deals with the visibility and rendering of a mesh object.
- **Effects:** Deals with creating real-time effects such as fire, snow, or the flashbang from a fired gun.
- **Physics:** These are for 3D objects to control weight, collision, and kinematics.
- **Physics 2D:** Similar to Physics, but these are for 2D GameObjects. We will get into these heavily in Chapter 7, "Setting Up Player Physics and Colliders."
- **Navigation:** For dealing with artificial intelligence (AI) navigation paths and obstacle detection.
- **Audio:** For adding sounds and audio effects to your game.
- **Rendering:** Deals with rendering aspects of your Scene, such as cameras, lights, and occlusions. Most 2D Components can be found here as well.
- **Miscellaneous:** Uncategorized Components such as animations and the Animator Component, both of which we will be using extensively in Chapter 6, "Adding Animations to Our Scene."

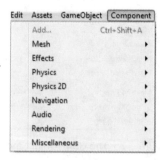

Figure 1.8   The Component menu

Window Menu

The Window menu (see Figure 1.9) allows you to set up workspace configurations, so you can decide which windows you wish to have open and how they are laid out. In later chapters we will discuss each of these windows in more depth.

The only one we should mention now is the Layouts drop-down. The predesigned Layouts let you customize the interface to work best for you. Use preexisting Layouts or rearrange the interface and then save your newly customized Layout.

> **Note**
>
> While all of the options in Figure 1.9 appear to be available, this is only because it shows the Unity Pro version. The Profiler, Sprite Packer, and Navigation windows are Pro features. The Asset Store and Version Control require additional tools and plug-ins for integrating team development.

Help Menu

Last but certainly not least is the Help menu (see Figure 1.10). Here you can access various tools that will guide you in getting the most out of Unity. You can access the Unity Manuals, utilize Web resources, and report issues here as well. This is also where you find the Welcome Screen we saw back when we first opened Unity.

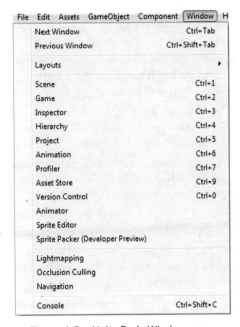

Figure 1.9   Unity Pro's Window menu

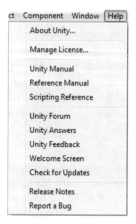

Figure 1.10   The Help menu

- **About Unity:** Used to check which version of Unity you are currently running.
- **Manage License:** Used for updating your free or Pro trial versions to a full copy of Unity Pro.
- **Unity Manual:** A great resource for learning everything about Unity and its features.
- **Reference Manual:** An invaluable guide for learning all of the available Components that you can connect to your GameObjects.
- **Scripting Reference:** Detailed documentation for scripting gameplay methods with the Unity API. We will touch on this a little more in Chapter 5, "The Basics of Movement and Player Control."
- **Unity Forum:** A great, if not the best, resource for resolving issues outside the Unity documentation. Also a great source for finding assets and Projects and collaborating with like-minded Unity developers.
- **Unity Answers:** A more professional and deeper community for finding answers to difficult problems. Its voting system helps in finding those answers that best resolve common issues.
- **Unity Feedback:** Good for giving feedback to Unity Technologies and requesting additional features you might like to see in future updates.
- **Welcome Screen:** The initial Welcome Screen we were shown when Unity first opened. Most of it is covered here in the Help menu with the exception of Tutorials.
- **Check for Updates:** Used to check for updated versions of Unity.

- **Release Notes:** A detailed list of updates and revisions from the current Unity version you are using.
- **Report a Bug:** Used to report critical errors or crashes you may experience when developing in Unity.

Toolbar

The toolbar shelf runs along the top of the Unity interface, just below the menu bar. Although there are just a few tools here, they will be widely used throughout our game development, so let's get to know them.

Transform Tools

The Transform tools are how you will manipulate your GameObjects in the Scene View. Being able to lay out your game Scenes, place items in the world, and alter their size and position is vital to making an immersive experience. Figure 1.11 shows the Transform tools.

- **Hand tool:** Used to move the camera around in the Scene View
- **Translate tool:** Used to move an object in 2D and 3D space while in the Scene View
- **Rotate tool:** Used to rotate an object on its axis
- **Scale tool:** Used to scale the object based on its axis

Transform Gizmo Toggles

Figure 1.12 shows the Transform Gizmo toggles. These toggles allow you to fine-tune controls when transforming your GameObject in the Scene View. Toggling them on and off affects the object's manipulators and how it transforms in 3D space.

- **Pivot:** The Transform handle is placed at the selected object's pivot point.
- **Center (pivot toggled):** The Transform handle is placed at the selected object's center.

Figure 1.11   Transform tool icons

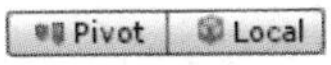

Figure 1.12   Transform Gizmo toggles in Object mode

- **Local:** The selected object will transform using its local space coordinates.
- **World (local toggled):** The selected object will transform using world space coordinates.

Game View Controls

The Game View controls (shown in Figure 1.13) are for testing your game at its current state. We discussed these in conjunction with the Edit menu tools earlier. Having them here along the toolbar makes them easier to access, since you will use them quite often.

Layers and Layout Drop-Downs

The Layers drop-down is a great tool for Project organization and also to customize relationships in your game. GameObjects can be placed into Layers that are similar in nature, allowing you to control what is visible to the camera. Another feature is being able to turn on and off Layers that contain assets. You may want to hide some elements of your game to view less clutter when working on other aspects of the game. Figure 1.14 shows the Layers and Layout drop-downs.

We discussed Layouts earlier in the context of the Window menu. The Layout drop-down is simply a quicker means of switching Layouts without having to dig through the Window menu.

Hierarchy

The Hierarchy (see Figure 1.15) is a textual list of all the GameObjects in the current Scene. As you add elements to your game, including any GameObjects added programmatically, this list will grow. The Hierarchy is also a great tool for parenting GameObjects. Parenting is a linked-style method of transforming GameObjects. An example would be a train and its caboose. When you move the train, the caboose follows. The train would be the "parent" of the caboose.

Inspector

The Inspector gives a detailed description of a selected GameObject and anything attached to it. Whenever you add a Component to a GameObject, such as a Material or script, it will show up attached to that object in the Inspector. Here you can tweak all of the Transform properties for the GameObject as well as its Components. We will

Figure 1.13   Play, Pause, and Step icons

Figure 1.14   The Layers and Layout drop-downs

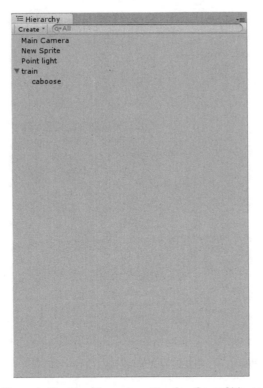

Figure 1.15   The Hierarchy with a few GameObjects

learn more about the Inspector in the next chapter. Figure 1.16 shows the Inspector with our Main Camera properties.

Project Browser

The Project Browser (Figure 1.17) is the visual window into your files. As we discussed in the "Project Structure" section of the Introduction, the Project Browser is an extension to your Windows Explorer files. All of the assets you import into your Project will be found here. Organization and naming are key to finding files.

As your Project grows, it will inevitably become more and more difficult to dig through dozens of folders, subfolders, and assets to find a specific one. Luckily there is a really nice search feature in the Scene View for this. The Project Browser search bar (Figure 1.18) can help you find an asset quickly and easily.

You can simply type in the name of the asset, but even that may still yield tons of results. Searching for an asset named "prop_" may give hundreds of results for other assets with the same namespace.

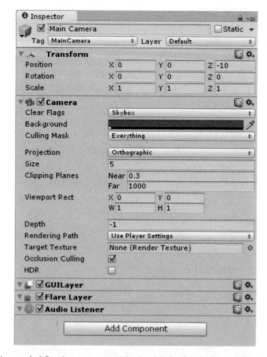

Figure 1.16   Inspector with the Main Camera properties

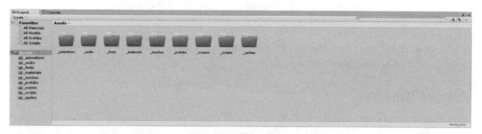

Figure 1.17   Project Browser with the Assets folder

Figure 1.18   Project Browser search bar

To the right of the search input field are three icons to help define your search: Search by Type, Search by Label, and Save Search.

- **Search by Type:** This allows you to first specify a specific type, such as a script, material, or texture.
- **Search by Label:** You can use this to sort by a specific label that has been tagged to the asset. An example would be a label for "Weapon," which would bring up a search list of any asset tagged with that label. We will discuss labels in the next chapter.
- **Save Search:** Allows you to save a search with a custom name. This creates a folder in the Favorites tab that you can then rename and to which you can add specific assets for accessing quickly.

Scene View

The Scene View is where you will spend the most amount of time in the Editor. All of the creation happens here. Here you can create GameObjects by dragging them into the Scene View or Hierarchy, or create them from the Create menu. Figure 1.19 shows the default Scene View with a generated Unity cube placed in the Scene.

Across the top portion of the Scene View is the Scene View control bar. This control bar holds a number of invaluable tools for working in the Scene View:

- **Draw mode:** Allows you to select from a drop-down list of styles in which to view your game. These are mostly used for debugging or selection purposes.
- **Render mode:** Allows you to choose from four render modes that help with debugging texture issues.

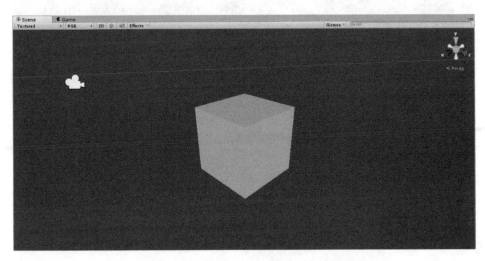

Figure 1.19   Scene View with default cube GameObject

- **2D/3D toggle:** Toggles the Scene View between a free-moving 3D and locked 2D axis.

- **Lighting toggle:** Toggles lighting on and off.

- **Audio toggle:** Toggles the audio for the Scene View on and off.

- **Effects drop-down:** Sets certain types of effects on and off such as the Skybox or Animated Materials.

- **Gizmos drop-down:** A drop-down that allows you to decide which Scene View Gizmos are viewable. An example would be a light that was placed in the Scene. Turning off the lighting Gizmo would hide the light icons.

Game View

Last but certainly not least is the Game View (as seen in Figure 1.20). Once we have created a few GameObjects and have added them to the Scene, we can start to test our game to see how things are looking and playing. Based on your rendered cameras, Unity will quickly compile and build your game and play it back in the Game View.

Running across the top of the Game View is the Game View control bar. Here you can control a real-time view of your game with a couple of options for the aspect type, visibility, and stats to display. Let's take a quick look at these now.

- **Aspect drop-down:** Allows you to select a few different screen aspect ratios for viewing your game. Aspects ratios are the width and height of the screen to mimic different size formats such as 4:3 (native) or 16:9 (wide-screen).

Figure 1.20   Empty Game View

- **Maximize on Play:** Allows you to maximize the screen so the Game View takes up the full extent of the monitor. Really helpful for when you have two monitors and can run the Game View on the second monitor.
- **Stats:** Allows you to view real-time stats while your game is in play. This can be very helpful when debugging sluggish playback performance.
- **Gizmos toggle:** Allows you to display iconic Gizmos just as the Gizmo toggle from the Scene View will. Good for viewing things such as where colliders or lighting might be while in gameplay.

Summary

This chapter was an introduction to the Unity interface and finding your way around the different views. We first opened Unity and were brought to the Welcome Screen. Remember that this can be a valuable tool for finding information or for help in troubleshooting a specific action or issue.

We looked at the menu bar and what each drop-down consisted of. This menu contains all of the commands and tools for building and running your game Projects.

Last, we looked into the different interface views inside of Unity. Each view has a special purpose, and knowing your way around the views lets you focus on creating content instead of finding commands.

In the next chapter we will begin importing our assets and packages and setting the rest of our Project to begin creating gameplay. We will start to build our GameObjects and behaviors and discuss working in a 2D view.

Exercises

Now that we have a little knowledge of the Unity interface, let's perform a few steps and commands. After doing these few exercises, you will be ready to move on to Chapter 2, "Understanding Asset Creation."

1. Create a new Project titled "2D_Platform_Game." Do not worry about importing any packages at this time.

2. In the Project window, create a new folder titled "_scenes."

3. Create a new Scene. Save it with the name "Test_Level" into the new _scenes folder we just made.

4. Under Preferences > General, uncheck the Always Show Project Wizard checkbox. This is a global Unity setting and will not save with the Project.

5. Create a new folder titled "_GUI," which we will use to place our GUI elements in a later chapter.

6. From the GameObject menu, create a new sprite. Rename this new sprite "Player."

7. With the Player GameObject selected, attach an Animator Component to it either through the Component menu or in the Inspector.

8. From the Inspector, manually set the Transform positions for X, Y, and Z to a 0 value.

9. Save your new Scene and new Project.

On to the next chapter!

2

Understanding Asset Creation

Now that we have a basic understanding of the Unity interface, let's begin to prepare our assets and integrate them into our Project. Remember that assets can be any combination of art, scripts, or even a plug-in brought into Unity and used in your Project. Characters, animation, audio files, even textures are all good examples of assets. Just as we made rules for setting up our Project, it is equally important to take measures when creating assets.

In this chapter we will import the assets we have set up for our Project and look at ways we can optimize them for the various platforms; we will also cover some best practices for file formats and compressions. After this we will start to add these to our game by creating GameObjects, adding some simple behaviors called Components, and creating our first sprite.

So with that, let's get started!

File Formats

Before we import our assets, let's take a look at the types of formats Unity can handle and how they can be used. Unity supports most file types, including native formats in both 2D programs such as Illustrator and Photoshop and 3D packages like 3ds Max and Maya. This means you can have an interoperable workflow, create the asset in your program, save the file to disk, and instantly see your updates in Unity.

3D Formats

Unity accepts a number of 3D formats; Table 2.1 lists the popular ones. FBX and OBJ are the most widely used formats as they can be exported from a number of different packages. While this list does show native 3D software support such as Maya and 3ds Max, Unity will import these using the software's FBX exporter.

Table 2.1   **Popular 3D Supported Formats**

3D Package	Mesh	Textures	Animations	Skeletons
3ds Max	Yes	Yes	Yes	Yes
Blender	Yes	Yes	Yes	Yes
Cinema 4D	Yes	Yes	Yes	Yes
FBX	Yes	Yes	Yes	Yes
Maya	Yes	Yes	Yes	Yes
Modo	Yes	Yes	Yes	No
OBJ	Yes	No	No	No
SketchUp Pro	Yes	Yes	No	No

2D Formats

Unity also supports a lot of the popular 2D formats, including Photoshop's PSD format. Unfortunately, it does flatten the PSD layers upon import into Unity. We will mostly be using 2D formats in this book, and later we will review some Import Settings for optimizing our assets. Here are some of the more popular 2D image formats that Unity supports:

- BMP
- GIF
- JPG
- PNG
- PSD (Adobe Photoshop Data file format)
- TGA
- TIFF

Importing Our Assets

There are a few methods for adding assets to a Unity Project. We can import assets and assign them to our Project, or even start from premade assets available from inside of Unity. Let's take a look at these.

Importing from Inside Unity

Importing an asset inside of Unity is as simple as going to the Assets menu and then to the option Import New Asset. You can also right-click while the mouse is over the Project window, and then select Import New Asset. The advantage of doing this from the Project window is that if you have a folder set up and open, the new asset will be added inside that folder. This is helpful when you're importing a large number of assets at one time.

Importing Premade Assets from the File Browser

Dragging and dropping files or copying and pasting them into the Unity Project folders is another method of bringing assets into your Project. This works in the same way as importing them from inside of Unity, only through your system's file browser.

> **Warning**
>
> Remember that this is an acceptable way of adding assets and files to your Project, but be advised not to shuffle them or delete them. Unity attaches information to these files (meta-data) as well as connections to other assets and GameObjects. It is a much safer approach to make these types of changes within the Unity Editor.

Creating New Assets

Unity also offers a list of premade assets that you can create and add to your Project from the Assets menu (shown in Figure 2.1). These assets are specific to Unity

Figure 2.1   The Assets menu—Create

Projects, and you will use most of them in your games. Use them to quickly create scripts, animations, Materials, as well as other important assets you can assign to your GameObjects. Let's take a look at some of these.

- **Folder:** Creates a new folder inside your Project.
- **Javascript/C# Script/Boo Script:** Scripting languages for customization of runtime behaviors.
- **Shader/Compute Shader:** Small scripts for handling rendering of objects, such as shadows and lighting.
- **Prefab:** A master GameObject that drives all instantiated copies of it. Any changes to it will be propagated down to the copies. We will discuss this in depth a little later.
- **Material:** When this Component is added to a GameObject, it controls the overall appearance, such as color, highlights, and reflection.
- **Cubemap:** A rendered reflection of the environment. This is used to fake real-time reflections, which can be very costly to your game's frame rate.
- **Lens Flare:** Mimics a camera's sensor for allowing light back into the camera.
- **Render Texture (Pro feature):** Very costly, but allows real-time rendering effects such as a dynamic shadow, reflections, or live playback of the game.
- **Animator Controller:** Used for creating an Animation State Machine that controls multiple actions on a single GameObject. An example would be a walk, run, or idle animation for a character.
- **Animation:** Creates a single animation that can then be linked to the GameObject.
- **Animator Override Controller:** Allows you to override certain animations to make a character's actions unique over the base Animator Controller.
- **Avatar Mask:** Allows you to control specific areas of a character in an animation, such as when carrying an item and locking the hands.
- **Physics Material:** Lets you add specific properties to a physics object and control how the object is affected by collision.
- **Physics2D Material:** Just like the 3D, but constrained to the X and Y values. We will cover this further in Chapter 7, "Setting Up Player Physics and Colliders."
- **GUI Skin:** Allows you to control a selection of GUI Styles for your game.
- **Custom Font:** Allows you to create custom parameters for an additional font resource for your game.

Importing Packages

Another method of importing assets is through Unity's own Packages format. Packages are containers of assets that are bundled and exported together for use in another Project. A good example would be a weapon that has materials and textures, custom animations, and scripts. Being able to easily save these out and drop them into another Project might be beneficial. A package is also a good way to add assets to the Unity Asset Store as well as to receive them.

Unity Packages

Unity comes with a bunch of premade packages already installed on your hard drive (see Figure 2.2). These can be very helpful for starting a Project; it is very beneficial for designers and programmers to have artwork in place so they don't have to wait for an art team to create assets.

Custom Packages

Another option may be to use assets created by another developer and made available for you to use. Packages contain a collection of assets and GameObjects that you can import into your Project, allowing you to quickly design, test features, or even

Figure 2.2   The Assets menu—Import Packages

use the assets as final elements in your game. Just as there are a few ways to import a particular asset into a Project, there are a few ways to import custom packages as well. Drag the package into the Unity Project window, and it will automatically begin unpacking with a prompt asking you which assets you wish to install. You can also use Assets > Import Package > Custom Package from the menu toolbar, or right-click in the Project window.

We are going to use a premade asset package for our Project. These assets were created by Kenny Vleugels, a game artist and developer. We have packaged them to allow us to import them more easily into our Project.

1. Launch Unity and select the LearningUnity Project we made in Chapter 1, "Setting Up the Unity Development Environment."

2. Right-click in the Project window and select Import Package, and then Custom Package.

3. Find the Chapter2_projectFiles for this chapter, and inside that will be a _packages folder.

4. Select the platformerGraphics_KennyV.unitypackage and select Open.

5. Once Unity has decompressed the package, the Importing Package window (Figure 2.3) will prompt you to select the package assets to import. Click the All button at the bottom left and then click Import at the bottom right.

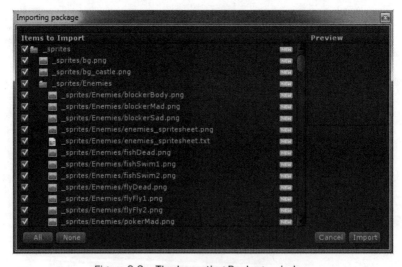

Figure 2.3   The Importing Package window

6. Once the unpacking is completed, the platformerGraphics package will create a folder called "_sprites" with all of the 2D assets we will need for our game.

7. Take a look and get acquainted with these sprites. We will get into creating sprite sheets and 2D layering in greater detail in Chapter 3, "Creating 2D Sprites."

GameObjects

A GameObject sits at the root of all the assets in your game. Without a GameObject, your asset cannot exist. Think of a GameObject as being the driver of a car. Even with a great car, a powerful engine, and a tank full of gas, without a driver, the car cannot get very far. We need that driver to control our car, or in our case drive our assets.

Once a GameObject is created, we can attach various behaviors (called "Components") to it. Another good way of thinking about it is like the foundation of a house. We can create a foundation, and then build upon it with walls, windows, and doors. The walls, windows, and doors are the "Components" or details that help define it.

Our First GameObject

When we made our LearningUnity Project, Unity created our first GameObject for us in our Scene called Main Camera. In order to view and play our game, it must have a camera to render the game assets for us to see and interact with. Just as a movie uses a camera to record the actors and scenes, we use a camera to view our characters and levels.

In our Scene View, there should be an icon that resembles an old-fashioned film camera from the side. Select the Main Camera by either clicking this camera icon in the Scene View or by clicking the Main Camera text in the Hierarchy window. We can tell that our Main Camera GameObject is selected by the colored Transform Gizmo handles that are visible in the Scene View (Figure 2.4). We can also note what is selected by the information displayed in the Inspector window.

The Inspector window (Figure 2.5) has a lot of information about our Main Camera GameObject such as its Transform values, the Camera Component settings, and a couple of camera-specific Components such as the GUI Layer and Audio Listener. We will get into Components and adding them shortly.

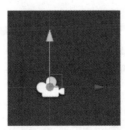

Figure 2.4   Main Camera with Transform Gizmo

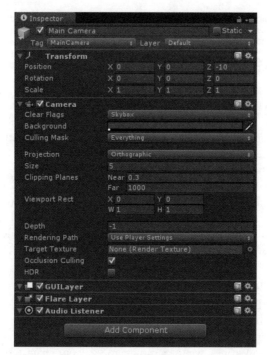

Figure 2.5   Inspector with our Main Camera attributes

Creating a GameObject

To create a GameObject, click on the GameObject menu and select Create Empty or click the Create Other drop-down and select from Unity's premade GameObjects. An empty GameObject will be empty, except for a Transform Component. The Transform Component is automatically attached to any GameObject and cannot be removed. Figure 2.6 shows the GameObject menu and its contents.

Let's create an empty GameObject that we will build upon for our first game sprite in Chapter 3, "Creating 2D Sprites":

1. Left-click the GameObject menu and select Create Empty (or use Ctrl + Shift + N for the hotkey). This will create an empty GameObject in our Scene.

2. Let's rename this by either left-clicking once (if selected) in the Hierarchy window or by double-clicking the name from the Inspector. Rename this GameObject "Player."

3. In the Inspector, under the new Player name is the Tag Manager. Let's click where it says "untagged" and change this to "Player." For now, just know that anything we wish to affect only the Player GameObject can easily use the "Player" tag to do this.

Figure 2.6　The GameObject menu—Create Other

4. Next to this is the Layers Manager. This is more for design and rendering, but it's helpful for isolating certain elements as well. Click where it says Default and Select Add Layer . . . . This will bring up the Tags & Layers Manager (see Figure 2.7).

5. Let's assign the Player GameObject to its own unique layer. Next to User Layer 8, enter the text "Player."

Note

A **tag** is a string identifier that can be applied to GameObjects so that certain script functions can find them during runtime. The same tag can be applied to a single unique GameObject, such as the Player GameObject, or several discrete GameObjects, such as enemies or collectibles.

Now we have our first GameObject: our player. In our Scene View, it doesn't look like much. That is because we have created a foundation for our player, but we haven't created any of the walls for it. In the case of a character, we haven't added the images of our player or any of his animations or scripts. This is where attaching the necessary Components will help us.

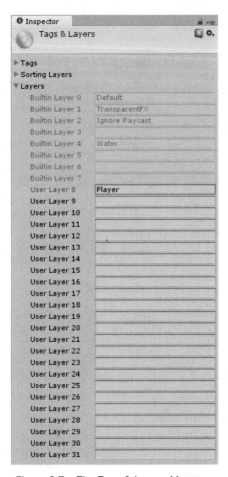

Figure 2.7   The Tags & Layers Manager

Components

Components are the "guts" of a GameObject. They are the details of our house such as the walls, the front door, or the windows. Without them, we merely have a slab of concrete. Adding these elements will give it life. For a GameObject, adding a Component will help define its properties such as appearance or behavior.

Just about every asset (with the exception of a Prefab) can be used as a Component in your game. Sprites, scripts, animations, and effects all need a GameObject to exist in the Scene. We attach all of these elements as Components.

If we look back at Figure 2.4, we see that our Main Camera has five Components that are often used to create our game elements: Transform, Camera, GUI Layer, Flare Layer, and Audio Listener.

- **Transform:** Controls the position, rotation, and scale of our camera. Without this our camera could not exist in 3D space.

- **Camera:** The actual Camera Component. This helps define the characteristics of our camera settings such as what the camera can and cannot see and how it will render these elements.

- **GUI Layer:** Allows us to add UI and HUD (heads-up display) elements such as menus, timers, and counters.

- **Flare Layer:** Allows us to use lighting elements to create realistic lens effects, like those of a real camera lens.

- **Audio Listener:** Allows us to hear in-game audio and sound effects. We need this on one of our cameras.

Creating a Component

Just as for assets and GameObjects, we have a couple of ways of adding a Component to a GameObject (remember that we must create our GameObject first). Click the Component menu and then select from one of the submenus available. This will assign the selected Component to the currently selected GameObject. We can also do the same thing by clicking the Add Component button inside the Inspector with our GameObject selected.

Another method is to drag and drop an asset into the Hierarchy window or Scene View. Unity will automatically define which type of GameObject and Component this should be according to its Import Settings. While this method is available, we suggest creating Components from the menu or inside the Inspector as this structured work-flow lets you know which Components are being added.

Assign a Component

Let's build onto our Player GameObject by assigning our first Component. We already have the Transform Component to determine its point in 3D space but nothing to define the look of it. As our game will be a 2D platformer, it makes sense that we should create our player as a sprite.

1. If not already selected, make sure you have the Player GameObject selected. Again, you can check the Hierarchy or Inspector to make sure of this.

2. Click the Add Component button at the bottom of the Inspector and select Rendering > Sprite Renderer. In the Inspector, the Sprite Rendered Component should now be attached to our Player GameObject.

3. We can now add our sprite asset to our new Component. In the Inspector, click the small target icon to the right of the Sprite Element. This will bring up a Select Sprite window (see Figure 2.8).

4. Click the Assets tab and in the search field above this, type "p1_stand." You will see our p1_stand player sprite. Left-click the p1_stand sprite and then close the window.

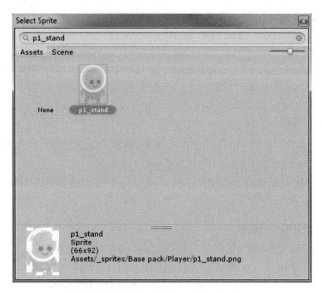

Figure 2.8   The Select Sprite window

5. We have now attached our sprite asset to our Player GameObject. We can verify this by seeing the p1_stand text in the Sprite Element in the Sprite Renderer. Also we can see that our sprite now appears in the center of our Scene View as well as the Game View. We have added the first graphic for our game!

Prefabs

One last area to discuss in this chapter is Prefabs. Prefabs are listed under assets, act more like GameObjects, but are truly one of the best resources you can have in your game. A Prefab is a master entity of a GameObject. When it is attached to a GameObject, all of the instanced copies made from it will inherit its settings. This means that if we make copies of this, say, as a pickup in the game, anything we do to the master Prefab will automatically update in the game. This is essential when duplicating a lot of elements in your game Scene.

Let's turn our Player GameObject into a Prefab. Even though there would be no real reason to make duplicates of the main character in the game, having all of your GameObjects as Prefabs is another organizational and workflow tool to keep your Scene as organized and optimized as possible. Whenever you do need to add a model to your game, you can simply drag and drop an existing Prefab and it will have all of its custom Components and attributes attached to it.

1. In the Project Window select the Assets >_prefabs folder.

2. Right-click and choose Create > Prefab. This will create a Prefab asset in the _prefabs folder.

3. Rename this new prefab "Player."

4. Select the Player GameObject from the Hierarchy window and drag and drop it on the Player Prefab we just made. You will know it linked if the text on the Player GameObject in the Hierarchy is now blue. Your Player object is now a Prefab.

Summary

In this chapter we got a good introduction to creating and importing assets for our Project. We also imported our sprite package with all of the game sprites we will use for our game. These came packaged in preexisting folders all named for easy searching. Having a valid workflow and structure is key to staying organized and not wasting valuable time searching through folders when we want to add something into our Project.

Next, we created our first GameObject and got an understanding of how to add it to our Scene. We also learned how we can use Unity's premade GameObjects to quickly build pieces of our game for early game design and development. We also covered our Main Camera GameObject and its Components and how they are necessary to view and hear our game.

Last, we covered Components and adding them to our Player GameObject. Components are the internals of our GameObjects and help define all of the characteristics of each element we see, hear, and interact with in our game.

Chapter 3, "Creating 2D Sprites," will take us into fleshing out more of the entities for our game such as enemies, props, and backgrounds, getting them ready for applying movement and interaction with other sprites.

Exercises

Now that we have our Player GameObject, let's set up a few more elements to prepare for Chapter 3, "Creating 2D Sprites":

1. Select the Player Prefab from the _prefabs folder.

2. In the Inspector, make sure you have selected the Player GameObject and select Add Component.

3. Select Miscellaneous > Animation Component. This will attach a blank Animation Component to our Player GameObject. We will go into this in the next chapter, but we can assign this as we will be using it for our player.

4. Select the Player GameObject from the Hierarchy to ensure that the new feature has been added to the GameObject already in our Scene.

5. Now we need to save our Scene. Choose File > Save Scene As . . . , make sure you are under the Project > _scenes folder, and save this as "Test_Level."

On to the next chapter!

3

Creating 2D Sprites

Now that we have cleared the hurdles of installing Unity, gotten a basic grasp of the Unity interface, and understand asset creation, we can start to tackle the next step: creating sprites.

In this chapter we will gain an understanding of setting up our assets as sprites. We will look at creating sprite sheets, slicing those sheets into multiple sprites, and setting their size for our game resolutions. We will look at a "Pro only" feature for packing multiple sprites onto a single sheet, but also ways we can do the same thing using the free version.

Last, we will take a look at setting the priorities of our sprites and how layering them can make our game feel as though it has depth and dimension. So what are you waiting for? Let's get into Unity!

> **Note**
>
> We mix the terms *sprite sheet* and *atlas* throughout the chapter, but both refer to the same thing: a single asset that holds multiple sprites. Once Unity has tagged an asset as a multi-sprite, it can then be used as a single GameObject.

Working in 2D

To begin, let's make sure we are working in the correct workspace. By default, Unity is a 3D game engine. This means it works in 3D space with an X-axis (left to right), Y-axis (up and down), and then an additional Z-axis (front to back).

Since our game is a traditional 2D side scroller, we will not need a true Z-axis plane, but we still require a Z-depth. Z-depth refers to elements that appear to be at different depths and sizes. Using this will make our game appear not to have everything on the same focal plane and will allow us to fake the third dimension of objects in front of and behind one another. There are a couple of ways to have our GameObjects appear to be in front of and behind one another, but first let's look at a couple of settings to make sure we are working in 2D mode.

2D Behaviors

When we imported our assets, Unity set all of our images up to be rendered as sprites. This was because we set the Project's workspace to 2D. We can check this by going to

Edit > Project Settings > Editor and setting the Default Behavior Mode. Now any-time we import a texture, Unity will automatically assume we want to use it as a sprite. Figure 3.1 shows the Default Behavior Mode correctly set to 2D.

Having the images in our Project set to 2D will allow us to combine multiple images onto single sheets. This gives us a few benefits for our workflow and our organization:

- Fewer sprites to manage (we can have all of the character animations on a single sheet).

- Fewer draw calls (having multiple sprites on one sheet means only that one image is drawn).

- All animation calls, Physics Colliders, and scripts on a single GameObject will help with performance and rendering at runtime.

Warning

Using Sorting Layers to render one GameObject in front of another will add an extra draw call. This is the case even if they share the same sprite sheet. This is due to the render buffer having to "draw" the first image and then the second overtop the first one.

2D Workspace

Another necessity is making sure our view is set to 2D. This way we do not have to worry about positioning objects in the Z-axis and can rely on a 2D plane (X- and Y-axes) and sorting to design our game.

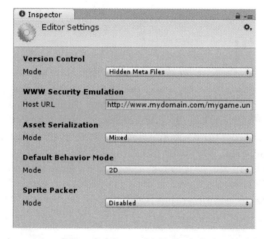

Figure 3.1   Inspector—Editor Settings with Default Behavior Mode set to 2D

Figure 3.2   Scene View control bar—2D workspace view toggled on

Running along the top of the Scene View is the Scene View control bar (Figure 3.2). When we built our Project, we defaulted the workspace to 2D. This should have toggled our Scene View to 2D. You can easily check and swap from 2D to 3D in the Scene View by either left-clicking the 2D toggle button or by simply hitting the number 2 key (in the horizontal number keys that run along the top) on your keyboard.

Building Our Sprites

With our assets set to draw in 2D, we can now make a few more adjustments to set them to the best quality we can get. Seeing as our game is based around our Player GameObject, this would be the best place to start. Having the main GameObject set correctly will help ensure that we are building the rest of our game elements the right way.

1. Open the 2D_Platform_Game and load the Test_Level Unity Scene.

2. Select the Player GameObject from the Hierarchy.

3. In the Inspector, click the small target icon to the right of the p1_stand reference name. The p1_stand is a single sprite. While this would work for some instances, we should use a sprite sheet for our player.

4. Select the p1_spritesheet atlas directly above our current asset. Our Scene View will have a bunch of character images on it. Not to worry, though; we just need to set up our asset as a sprite sheet.

5. In the Project Browser, tunnel down to the Assets > _sprites > Player folder and left-click the p1_spritesheet asset we just assigned to our Player GameObject.

6. Once again in the Inspector, we should have the Import Settings for the p1_spritesheet. Set the Sprite Mode from Single to Multiple, and then click Apply under the Settings. Now our Scene View shows only a single sprite.

Import Settings

Now that our Player GameObject has the correct atlas assigned and showing as a single sprite, let's look at a couple of other settings for the sprite sheet that we need to adjust. The Inspector should still show the Import Settings for the p1_spritesheet. If you need to load this again, you can find it in the Project Browser (see step 5 in the "Building Our Sprites" section). Figure 3.3 shows the Inspector with the Import Settings for the p1_spritesheet.

Figure 3.3   Inspector—Texture Import Settings

We won't go into great detail about all of the settings in the Texture Import Settings, but let's get a basic understanding of sprites before we adjust a few of them.

- **Texture Type:** Has multiple settings for different texture assets, such as a 3D texture, GUIs, sprites, and more.
- **Sprite Mode:** Used to set the sprite as a single element or for use as multiple sprite elements. We set this to Multiple for our p1_spritesheet asset.
- **Packing Tag:** Lets you assign sprites with a tag that will then be assigned to the same atlas.
- **Pixels To Units:** Sets the sprite's resolution based on its pixel size in comparison to Unity's unit settings.
- **Filter Mode:** Sets how the texture is rendered as it becomes larger or smaller by the 3D transformation.
- **Max Size:** The largest resolution at which a texture can be used. Set when the asset is imported.
- **Format:** The quality of the texture based on its bit depth.

We need to change a couple of the default values for our Project: the Texture Type and Pixels To Units value.

Updating the Format will adjust the resolution of the sprites in the game. Setting this will give the sprites a better compression ratio, but also a possible reduction in the quality of the image resolution. You have to weigh the pros and cons of each.

- **Compressed:** Most compressed format. Less color information, but smaller files. With a 256 × 256 texture the file would save at 32KB.

- **16 bits:** Holds more color information. Has a lot more than Compressed, but not as much as Truecolor. A 256 × 256 texture would save at 128KB.
- **Truecolor:** The least amount of compressed color information, but with the most cost. A 256 × 256 texture will save at 256KB.

Pixels To Units

The Pixels To Units value lets you set the scale of the sprite in relation to the units in Unity. Setting this to more closely match the dimensions of your sprites will give you a more accurate resolution. This will also allow us to use Unity's tool to create our levels more quickly and with more ease. We will go into creating our environments in the next chapter. For now, let's explain Pixels To Units a little more.

In Figure 3.3 we can see that the Pixels To Units value is set at 100. This says that every 100 pixels will be equivalent to 1 unit in Unity. Our Player GameObject is roughly 92 pixels tall. We can check this by looking at the single sprites for our p1 character in the Project Browser, or by opening our p1_spritesheet in the Sprite Editor and selecting one of these sprites. Let's set our p1_spritesheet to the 92 pixels setting:

1. Select the p1_spritesheet and check that it is loaded in the Inspector.
2. Adjust the Pixels To Units value from 100 to 92. As the actual dimensions of the sprites are closer to 92 pixels, this will give us a more accurate scale.
3. Set the Format from Compressed to Truecolor. This will give our sprites a higher overall quality. Luckily we are not loading the output with a lot of content to drag down our frame rate, so we can afford the expense for a slight increase in quality.

Sprite Editor

We have already set the Texture Type to Sprite and the Sprite Mode to Multiple. This allowed us to use a previously generated sprite sheet that was composed of multiple sprites. When we did this, it added the Sprite Editor button (Figure 3.4).

The Sprite Editor allows you to slice the sheet of sprites into multiple elements. This way each element can become an individual sprite that you can then use in your game as a static sprite or for a multi-sprite animation.

There are three methods for slicing your sprites: **Manual**, **Automatic**, and **Grid**. Each one has its own set of controls to allow precise slicing. Automatic will usually be good enough, but let's look at all three.

Manual Slicing

Slicing using Manual lets you choose the dimensions of each sprite. This is most useful when you wish to crop a certain sprite or if you need to create a bigger sprite based on more of the image. Set the sprite bounds by clicking on the sprite and then adjusting its points on the rectangle. Figure 3.5 shows properties for the Manual Slicing window.

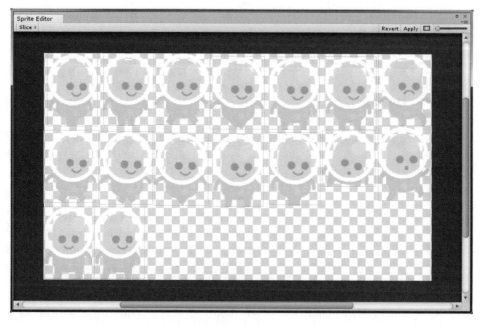

Figure 3.4   Sprite Editor loaded with the p1_spritesheet

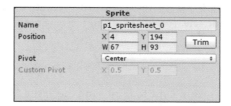

Figure 3.5   Sprite Editor—Manual Slicing

Automatic Slicing

> **Tip**
>
> Be wary of "floating" pixels that are slightly transparent and given their own sprite bounds. If this happens, you can edit the individual sprite with Manual Slicing. Simply select the bounds of the sprite in question, and you can then move and scale the bounds to fit the needed area.

Using Automatic mode (Figure 3.6), Unity will slice the sprites based on their surrounding transparency. Automatic will usually give you a decent result quickly.

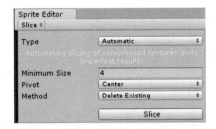

Figure 3.6   Sprite Editor—Automatic Slicing

Grid Slicing

Grid Slicing allows you to set a width and height pixel size to separate the sprites. Use Grid Slicing when all elements of the sprite sheet are to be sliced to the exact same dimensions. Figure 3.7 shows the Grid Slicing window.

Automatic Slicing will work well enough for the sprites for this Project. A minimum size of 4 will work fine as well. The only other setting we need to worry about is the Pivot drop-down. The Pivot drop-down lets you set the location of an individual sprite's pivot point. This is the position or origin from which the sprite will translate.

There are ten different positions where we can place the pivot point, including Center (which each sprite defaults to), Custom for creating our own, and Bottom. We will need to set ours to Bottom so any type of movement or rotation will make it appear as though it is happening from the sprite's feet. Let's go through the steps to prepare our sprite sheet for use:

1. With the p1_spritesheet still selected, left-click the Sprite Editor button to open its window.
2. Left-click the Slice drop-down in the upper left corner. This will give you the Slicing Types.
3. Set the Type to Automatic, change the Pivot to Bottom, and leave the rest at the default settings.

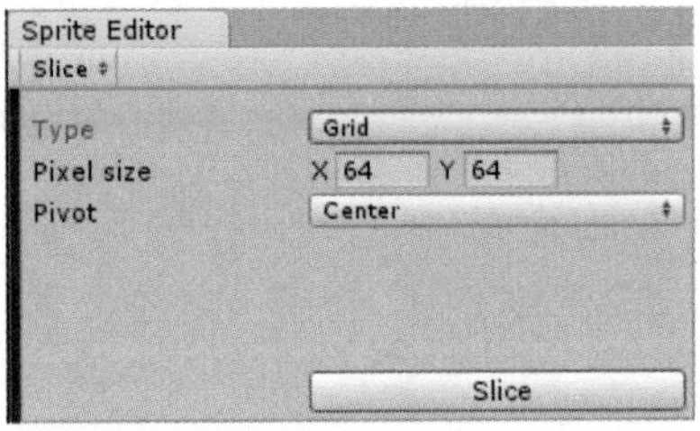

Figure 3.7   Sprite Editor—Grid Slicing

4. Left-click the Apply button from the upper right and then close out of the window.

5. Now would be a good time to save our Scene and Project files.

Sprite Packing

Our sprite assets came with our character sprites already built into a single sprite sheet. This made it simple for us to just set the type to Multiple and then use the Sprite Editor and Automatic to slice them. Having a prefabricated sprite sheet is easier, but sometimes you might have sprites only as separate assets. Sprite Packing lets you create that sprite sheet with multiple assets inside of Unity.

> **Note**
>
> The information in this Sprite Packing section is very handy to know, as you will inevitably have to atlas your own sprites. Luckily the assets with this Project have already been atlased onto sprite sheets that we can use. But this information will come in handy when you have to pack your own sprites in future projects.

Packing Tag

We briefly covered the Packing Tag in the Texture Import Settings of the p1_spritesheet. The Packing Tag lets you define a name so that you can pack all the sprites that share the same name. You could create a Packing Tag for a bunch of sprites called "tiles" and then use that tag for creating your sprite sheet.

Sprite Packer

Unity has a built-in tool for packing multiple sprites into a single sprite sheet called the Sprite Packer (Figure 3.8). Unfortunately, this is a Unity Pro feature, so we will just briefly discuss it for the benefit of those of you who have access to the Sprite Packer tool.

When you open the Sprite Packer window, it will show an empty canvas. Select a sprite asset that has been given a Packing Tag, and left-click the Pack button in the Sprite Packer. This will pack any of the sprites into a single sprite sheet. There are a couple of settings for the Sprite Packer window:

- **Pack:** Takes a selected sprite with a Packing Tag and packs all sprites to a single atlas.

- **Repack:** If you make any changes to the Packing Tags (by adding or removing tags), use Repack to update them.

- **View Atlas:** If you have too many sprites for the texture size that has been set, you can view multiple atlas sheets with this drop-down.

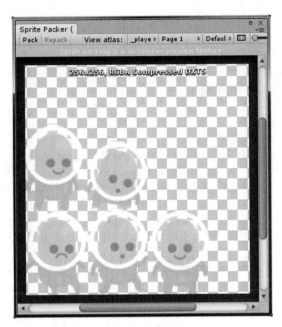

Figure 3.8   Sprite Packer—using the separate p1 assets as an example

- **Packing Policy:** This is how Unity packs and assigns your sprites to the atlas. The Default Packing Policy should be sufficient.

Additional Sprite Packing Resources

If you are just using the Unity free version, there are still a few options for you to use sprite sheets. Keep in mind that all of these resources require access to additional software outside of the Unity Editor.

Texture Packer

Texture Packer is a third-party tool for packing multiple sprites into a single atlas. There are free and paid versions, but the free version should be sufficient. The only real drawback is that it creates smaller sprite sheets. You can download it from the link here: www.codeandweb.com/texturepacker/download

Adobe Photoshop

Another option for packing sprites is the manual approach. Using a 2D software tool such as Photoshop, you can composite the images together and then bring the result into Unity. This approach will let you control the size and placement of the individual sprites along with the image size. Remember to use transparency spacing between each sprite so it's easy and quick to slice them once back inside Unity.

Adobe Flash

Adobe Flash is another great tool that allows you to import elements or even create your own. Another great feature is creating your sprites to be used as frames for an animation. You can then bring all of these into the Generate Sprite Sheet tool inside of Adobe Flash to export your final sprite sheet before importing it into Unity.

Summary

In this chapter we got our first look at setting our Project to work in 2D instead of Unity's default 3D mode. We looked at how we could set this after the Project had been created and how we can bounce back and forth from 2D to 3D in the Scene View.

We started getting into 2D sprites and sprite sheets. We set our Player sprite sheet to Multiple so Unity understands that it contains multiple resources. We then opened the Sprite Editor and learned to slice our sprites as well as set the pivot position for each sprite in the atlas.

Last, we looked at creating custom packed sprites. This is a Unity Pro feature, so we also looked at a few ways of using third-party applications to build our own sprite sheets.

In the next chapter we will use our sprite elements to start building our first game level. We will go over some rules and ideas for starting out in level design and some Unity-specific tools for laying out our GameObjects, setting the sprite priorities for layering them, and monitoring our GameObjects in the Hierarchy view.

Exercises

Let's set up our tiles_spritesheet the same as our Player sprite sheet. This will be the main one for creating our playable level in the next chapter.

1. Select the tiles_spritesheet asset in the Project Browser. You will find it under the Assets > _sprites > Tiles folder.

2. Left-click and in the Inspector change the Sprite Mode from Single to Multiple. Change the Pixels To Units value from 100 to 70.

3. Change the Format from Compression to Truecolor. Click Apply.

4. Open the Sprite Editor window and slice the sprite sheet using Automatic. Set the Pivot to Bottom Left.

5. Click Slice and then Apply and close the window.

6. Drag the tiles_spritesheet into the Hierarchy window. A GameObject will appear in our Scene View that looks like a box with an exclamation point in it.

7. Let's change the name. Left-click and then at the top of the Inspector window, change the name to "boxItemAlt."

8. In the Inspector, make sure the values for Position and Rotation in the Transform Component are all set to 0.

9. Back in the Hierarchy window, left-click and drag the boxItemAlt GameObject into the _prefabs folder in the Project Browser. This will make it a Prefab GameObject.

10. Save the Scene and the Project files.

Building the Game World

In this chapter we will begin building the game world in which our main character will move around. We will need to discuss level design and planning the game design. We will explain how having a solid idea in place will keep you from designing without reason and wasting a lot of time "winging it."

We will then look at Unity's Transform tools and the differences between working in 2D and 3D. We will go over the Hierarchy window and how we can use grouping and parent-child relationships to keep things organized and easy to use. Last, we will look at a few other settings to help us more easily build our Scene. By the end, we will have a full level for our character to explore. So with that, let's get to it!

Level Design 101

Having at least a basic understanding of level design theory, and some knowledge of its rules and principles, will go a long way when you're creating your game environments. Becoming a great level designer takes a lot of practice and patience, and professional level designers have years of experience. By no means are we even remotely in the same ballpark as them, but we do know a few basic rules that will help us create something that can be fun and entertaining to play.

Setting the Scene

One of the best things to have when putting anything together is a detailed set of instructions. Most times they list the tools you will need to do the job and describe step by step where to begin and how to get all the way through to the final piece. Creating a fun and challenging game level is no different. You will need to know what enemies to encounter, which items to collect, and what puzzles to complete. Having a "road-map" of sorts that lists all of these things will go a long way toward helping you achieve your design.

We have a few things in place to help us; we know that we are creating a 2D-side platform game, and we already have the game sprites we will use to build our levels.

But there are still a few questions we should ask ourselves before we jump into Unity and start throwing down sprites:

- What is the end goal? What are we trying to achieve other than going from point A to point B?

- Will this level be easy or hard to complete? Are the puzzles in it fairly easy or complex to solve?

- Where in the overall game does this level take place? Where are we in the timeline of the story?

- Does this level take place in the daytime or nighttime? What are the weather conditions? Is it bright sunshine or overcast and snowing?

- How has our hero progressed to this point in the game? Do they have new weapons, skills, or upgrades?

- What are some challenges or experiences the user has encountered prior to this point in the game that we may be able to build upon in this new level?

Answering these questions first will help us set some rules and standards, so that we are designing the level we feel will give the user a fun and enjoyable experience.

Creating a Roadmap

Once we have all of the answers to these questions, we can create our level. We suggest putting pen to paper, as they say, to rough out an idea of what it should look like first, before jumping into Unity. This will help us understand things like the distance over a gap, or where to place that hidden gem the player has to find.

We have gone ahead and created that roadmap (Figure 4.1), mapping out the conflicts, puzzles, and behaviors we will create. We will try to explain the theory behind the layout and how we answered those earlier questions. Again, our ways of level design may not be the best or the most effective, but we took what we know and applied it here.

The main objective of our game is getting our hero through the level to enter the door to the castle. Original idea, right? In doing so, the player has completed the puzzle and can move on to the next challenge. But there are some gameplay mechanics we will be adding along the way to make it slightly more challenging.

Figure 4.1   Sketched level design

When planning this, our approach was that this would be the first level encountered in the game. That will make it fairly easy for us to map out the details and complexity since this is just a demo for learning the technique. The level will take place in the daytime, it will be fairly simple to solve, and it is designed with the idea that the user has played these types of games before.

A few additions are needed to make this design unique. We tried to use the tools and assets given to us to make something a little different, and we think they work well. We are using some art that has already been created to make this a little easier for us. Now let's take a look at a few rules of level design we might want to take into consideration before fleshing out our level.

> **Note**
>
> Usually all game design, mechanics, and encounters have been solved before asset creation, so you or the art team is making only the art that is needed. Working out all of the design ahead of time will eliminate changes, roadblocks, and issues down the road. Everything should have been planned in advance.

- Players should start out by simply learning the mechanics of moving our hero left and right, along with performing some basic jumping. The first few game screens will be free of enemies to allow players to practice these moves.

- The first obstacle our players will encounter is designed to test their learning curve without any serious repercussions. We want them to succeed, but should they fail, the hero will not lose health or die.

- Our first contact with an enemy is a slow one that weakens our hero only slightly. Its purpose is to set up an encounter so that players learn how they will interact with enemies later on.

- There will be a few simple puzzles for the player to solve. They will use colors to help guide the player toward the solution, for instance, "Find a blue key to open a blue lock."

- Players will know they have succeeded once the castle door opens. To present this, the last puzzle will be placed within viewing distance of the door so that players can see this transition.

Adding Details

Now that we have the basic design and gameplay elements laid out, we can look for ways to liven up the world. It should be noted that this step comes well after the level has been completely designed. All significant changes should be addressed and the level should be signed off. Making things "look pretty" can wait till the end; otherwise you might end up with something that looks great but plays terribly. As the saying goes, it's "icing on the cake." Let's make sure the cake is good first.

Details can have a role in the overall feel and layout of a game and can affect game-play just like anything else. But didn't we just say that adding details should come after the level design is done? What we mean is that the initial questions have been answered, and we have set the tone and the way we want the level to play out.

A good example of adding details that help the gameplay might be a dirt path to lead the player. Another example might be a waterfall to guide the player downward. Think of ways you can add subtle details to guide the player. We want the levels to be somewhat challenging but also enjoyable, and we want to give the player enough help to actually solve them.

Getting around Our Scene

Up to this point we haven't used the Scene View much for our Project. We did a lot of the legwork: bringing in our assets, building our sprite sheets, and creating our GameObjects. But now we really need to get in and get dirty (so to speak). We should first get comfortable with moving around in the environment. Although we are not dealing much with the concept of 3D depth, we should know how to view our GameObjects and Scene in both 2D and 3D space. Let's get familiar with Scene navigation and object manipulation by creating a test Scene where we can move around:

1. Start by creating a new Scene.
2. In the Scene View control bar, toggle the workspace from 2D to 3D.
3. Create a Cube GameObject by going to the GameObject menu > Create Other and selecting Cube.
4. Reset the Cube's Transform values all to 0. With the Cube selected, in the Inspector, right-click the gear icon to the right of the Transform Component and select Reset.

> **Tip**
>
> If you lose focus of a GameObject, or wish to center your view on a particular GameObject, you can reset the camera by selecting the object and tapping the F key. This will center the camera's focus point to that of the selected object. Note that this needs to be done with the mouse pointer over the Scene View.

Scene Gizmo

To begin, it helps to know how 3D space works. Take a look at the little colored Gizmo in the top right corner of the Scene View. This is the Scene Gizmo (Figure 4.2).

In 3D space, there are three different axes that determine the direction you are fac-ing or the direction in which an object is moving. The red (X-axis), green (Y-axis), and blue (Z-axis) axes on the Scene Gizmo help clarify this. An easier way to under-stand this concept is that the X-axis runs left to right, the Y-axis runs up and down,

Figure 4.2   The Scene Gizmo

and the Z-axis moves front (near) to back (far). We will get a better understanding of this in just a bit when we move our cube around in 3D space.

Perspective versus Isometric

Our Main Camera works in **perspective view**. This means that we can see our cube object in our Scene with multiple converging angles (perspective viewpoints). Most likely if you haven't moved your view around, you will see two sides of the cube running off into a two-point perspective view.

Isometric view refers to the camera having equal projection of all three axes. This makes your Scene appear as though it has very little depth. We will see more of this isometric relation when we start laying down our objects using a 2D orthographic mode for the camera. Figure 4.3 shows an example of perspective and isometric cameras. Notice how the objects on the left appear to have depth and foreshortening, while the objects on the right appear flat and almost as though they exist on the same plane.

Camera Controls

There are a few different methods for getting around in 3D space inside Unity. If you come from any type of 3D background or have played a third-person-style game, you will easily grasp this concept.

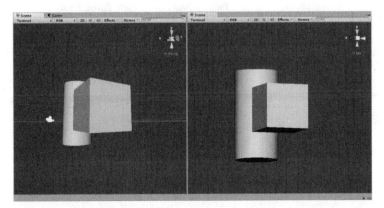

Figure 4.3   A perspective camera (left) and an isometric camera (right)

Arrow Keys

One method of moving around in the Scene View is using the arrow keys on your keyboard. If you are at all familiar with moving around in a third-person game, the arrow keys work the same way: up and down to move you forward and back, and left or right to pan the camera sideways.

WASD Movement

This is the movement that exactly replicates most PC-style games. While the arrow keys method is very similar, this one uses the W, A, S, and D keys for movement while using the mouse to direct the camera for that movement. To enable the WASD keys, you must first hold down the right mouse button.

Mouse Shortcut

The mouse movement is the most efficient method as you can still easily move about in the Scene but also keep the Transform tools for manipulating the GameObjects. While this method is most effective with a three-button mouse, you can use a two-button (no scroll wheel) or even a one-button mouse (most common for Macs or trackpad users). Table 4.1 gives shortcuts to help clarify this.

Hand Tool

Another method is to use the Hand tool (Figure 4.4). You can access it by tapping the Q key on the keyboard. In this mode, you are able to control the camera movements simply by using the mouse.

By holding down the Alt or Ctrl keys, you can orbit or zoom the camera respectively. Also, holding down Shift while using these will increase how fast the camera orbits and zooms.

Table 4.1 **Mouse Movement for One, Two, or Three Button Mouse**

Action	One Button	Two Button	Three Button
Move	Alt+Ctrl(Cmd) and click-drag	Alt+Ctrl(Cmd) and click-drag	Alt and middle click-drag
Orbit	Alt and click-drag	Alt and click-drag	Alt and click-drag
Zoom		Alt and right click-drag	Alt and right click-drag or use the Scroll wheel

Figure 4.4 Transform tools with the Hand tool selected

Manipulating Objects in Unity

We now have a level that we have fleshed out using paper and pen, and we can start to bring these ideas into Unity. But before we do that, let's check a few settings in Unity and make sure we are prepared to replicate our paper level design in the editor. Making sure we can "copy" things from our design to Unity in an almost one-to-one fashion will save us a lot of time and frustration.

Let's start by opening our 2D_Platform_Game Project. We have gone ahead and updated all of the sprites and made Prefabs for all of the GameObjects we will be using in our game. Go ahead and grab the Project files for Chapter 4 if you want to follow along.

Transform Tools

In order for us to lay down our GameObjects, we need to know how to move them around in Unity. We need to be able to position, rotate, and scale our objects and place them exactly where we need them. We also need to know the key differences between working in 2D and 3D and how we can still attain depth in our game.

Translate

You will mostly make use of the Translate tool when positioning your GameObject. In Figure 4.5 you can see the X-, Y-, and Z-axes just like the Scene Gizmo has. In fact, in 3D mode, you will see that the Translate Gizmo and Scene Gizmo match. This is because in world space we will move along these axes.

The Translate button can be found next to the Hand tool in the Transform toolbar. See Figure 4.4 if you do not remember this. You can also access the Translate tool by tapping the W hotkey on the keyboard.

Simply left-click and drag on one of the colored arrows, and your object will move along that axis. Moving along the direction the arrow points will move the object in a positive direction, and negative in the opposite.

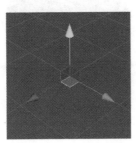

Figure 4.5   Default Translate tool display

> **Note**
>
> The red, green, and blue colors are used to tell us what direction that axis is facing. Red indi-cates the direction for the X-axis. Green is used for up and down or the Y-axis. Blue is for the Z-axis.

Rotate

Tapping the E key will bring up the Rotate tool. This will let you rotate the object along its pivot point. The colored circles again indicate the axes, but the object will rotate around an axis. This tool is very handy for setting an object at a certain angle. Figure 4.6 shows the Rotate Gizmo.

Scale

The last tool is the Scale tool (Figure 4.7). Scale means to increase or decrease the size of an object in relation to its actual size. Using the axis handles will scale the object only in that one axis. This can be handy if you want to adjust the appearance of an object, such as making a cube into a rectangle or a sphere into an ellipse.

Figure 4.6   Default Rotation tool display

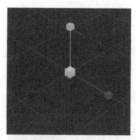

Figure 4.7   Default Scale tool display

Note

Clicking on an individual axis will affect only the object in that axis. Affecting all axes at once is different for each tool. To translate in all three axes, hold Shift and then left-click and drag from the center of the Translate Gizmo. For rotation, select anywhere inside the white circle, but not on a colored circle. With scale you simply left-click and drag within the white cube of the Scale Gizmo.

Z-Depth

Positioning our objects with the Translate tool will help us set up our level and accurately position objects in the Scene. But in a 2D setup this will only help us to place them along the X-axis (horizontal) and Y-axis (vertical). This will work for most everything, but we will want to have some depth to our levels. We want to have some dimension and balance to our world so it doesn't appear flat. Sprites like clouds moving behind our player and allowing the player to walk in front of hills will help add a touch of realism, even though it is 2D.

In a 2D game using Unity, we can still control the Z-depth using the selected sprite's Sorting Layer and Order in Layer attributes. These can be found on the Sprite Renderer of your Sprite GameObject. Figure 4.8 shows an example of this on our Player GameObject.

Sorting Layer

The most effective way we have of sorting our sprites is by using Sorting Layers. Sorting Layers work very similarly to 2D editing package layers. You separate elements into layers, and then place those layers above or behind one another to determine what draws in front of the next. The only difference with Unity is that it draws from bottom to top, with the top being drawn first, and then the next layer down over that. See Figure 4.9 for the Sorting Layers we will set up.

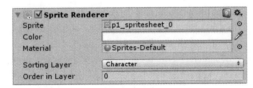

Figure 4.8   Sprite Renderer Component of our Player GameObject

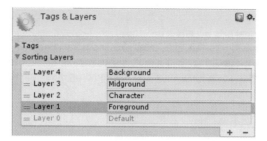

Figure 4.9   Tags & Layers window—Sorting Layers

> **Note**
>
> Sorting Layers are under the Tags & Layers Manager. We discussed where to find these back in Chapter 1, "Setting Up the Unity Development Environment," but as a quick reminder, they are to the right along the toolbar. Choose the drop-down arrow and select Edit Layers to customize these.

Let's add a couple of Sorting Layers for the Player GameObject and Scene elements we will be adding:

1. With the Tags & Layers Manager open, click the drop-down to reveal the default Sorting Layer.

2. Click the + icon to add a new layer. Rename this "Foreground."

3. By default Unity will create new layers below the selected one. Left-click and drag over the Layer 1 text and move this above the Layer 0 slot.

4. Create the remaining three layers for Character, Midground, and Background.

Order in Layer

Another way of layering sprites is with the Order in Layer attribute in the Sprite Renderer. While we could make a bunch of Sorting Layers for each of our sprites, this can be tedious, very hard to work with, and costly for our game. You may have a sprite sheet that consists of elements that you wish to have sort with one another, but you need the entire sheet to sort with other elements. For this we use Order in Layer.

The only difference from a visual standpoint is that Order in Layer sorts based on a value. The higher the value, the later the sprite will draw, with higher values above everything else. You may also find as you create the game that you need to assign a sprite lower than 0. You can use negative values if needed.

Settings

We covered the Pixels To Units measurements for our sprites back in Chapter 3, "Creating 2D Sprites." This ensures that the size of all of our game elements is comparable to that of our player, so that all of the GameObjects will be in scale with one another. Once we have our worlds built, enemies placed, and props added, this will make sense, but first we have to build these things.

Another benefit of setting the Pixels to Units size is that it will uniformly align all of the tile sprites, allowing us to easily snap the ends of one tile to the next.

Grid

The grid in our Scene View will help us "snap" pieces of our levels together easily. When we set the Pixels To Units size for the tile sprites (70), it made them equal to their actual dimensions (70 pixels by 70 pixels). This means our tile will fit exactly into a 1 × 1 Unity grid. Now we can easily "snap" one piece to the next.

Snap Settings

The Snap Settings (Figure 4.10) work in relation to the grid units. Snap Settings allow you to position, rotate, and scale your objects with precise measurements. This tool will become invaluable when we start building our level.

- **Move X (Y and Z):** The number of units the object will move when using snapping
- **Scale:** The percentage an object will scale in size
- **Rotation:** The degree of rotation the object will make

While we do not have to adjust the Snap Settings, it is helpful to know where to locate them. They can be found under the Edit menu (Edit > Snap Settings).

> **Tip**
>
> By holding the Ctrl key and then left-clicking and dragging the tiles, you can easily snap them to each other with precision. This is one method that helps you build your game levels quickly. We also set the pivot point of each sprite to its bottom left, making snapping painless.

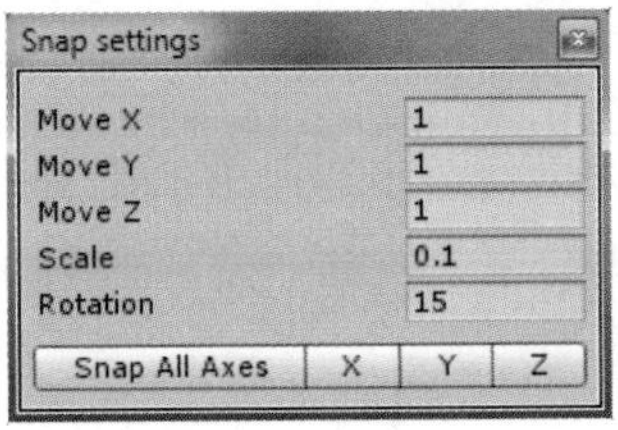

Figure 4.10   Snap Settings with default values

Our First Level

Taking what we have learned from this chapter and our level design concept, let's start building our first level! Find the Chapter 4 project files for the book, and open up the First_Level Scene file. The Project has all of the sprites we will need set up as Prefab objects.

Positioning GameObjects Manually

From the Project window, go to Assets > _prefabs and select the grassMid Prefab. Left-click and drag, then drop this into the Scene View or Hierarchy to add our first piece. Let's adjust the placement by setting the Prefab's Transforms. With the Prefab selected, go to its Transform Component in the Inspector and reset its Position values (the X-, Y-, and Z-values) to 0, 0, and 0 respectively. We have placed our fist sprite! Figure 4.11 shows the Prefab with the correct placement.

Using the Snap Settings to Position GameObjects

We can also use the Snap Settings tool described previously in this chapter. This will snap the GameObject with precise values. From the Project Browser, pull in another Prefab asset to make our current ground a little more solid:

1. Find the grassCenter Prefab and drag it into the Scene View, trying to roughly place it below the grassMid Prefab.

2. Open the Snap Settings window by going to Edit > Snap Settings.

3. With the values for Move X, Move Y, and Move Z all set to 1, click the Snap All Axes button.

4. The grassCenter Prefab should now be snapped below the grassMid Prefab and sitting in world space at 0, −1, 0 in X, Y, and Z respectively.

Using Grid Snapping to Position GameObjects

Last, we can precisely position a GameObject by using the grid snap option. This takes the pivot point of the sprite as the position from which it snaps to place it exactly where you intend. You can do this with multiple selected tile sprites as well.

1. Select both the grassMid and grassCenter GameObjects.

2. Duplicate the GameObjects by tapping Ctrl + D. Notice that you now have two of each object in the Hierarchy window.

3. Select one of the grassMid and one of the grassCenter Prefabs from the Hierarchy window.

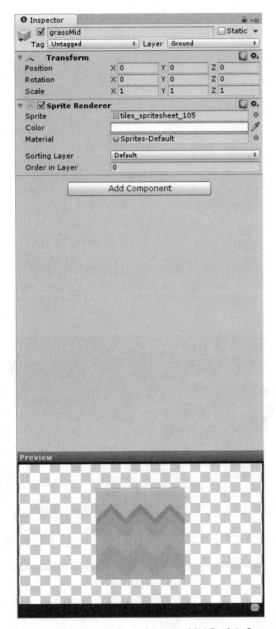

Figure 4.11   Inspector window with grassMid Prefab Component

4. Hold Ctrl and left-click and drag the tiles one snapped unit to the right in the Scene View. You will now have four sprites to make up the first part of our ground-floor tiles.

5. Continue duplicating and positioning these from left to right, until you have a complete ground surface.

6. You should have something that resembles Figure 4.12.

Note

Most often when you duplicate an object a second time, it will spawn from the original GameObject instead of the current one. It is best to deselect and then select the new GameObject before duplicating again. You could also duplicate the number of times you need and then select them individually.

Efficient Level Design

Now that we have the initial ground for our first screen, we will want to duplicate it for the next screen. While it did not take a lot of time to create the first ten, having a quicker solution would make things easier on our level designer! We could simply select

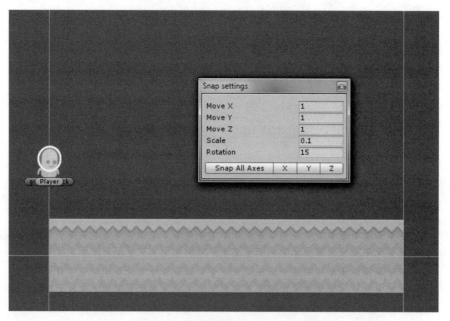

Figure 4.12   Scene View with our initial GameObjects laid out

all 20 grassMid and grassCenter GameObjects, duplicate them, and position them; let's see if we can find a more efficient way:

1. Create an empty GameObject by going to GameObject > Create Empty.

2. Double-click on the name or right-click and select Rename. Let's rename our GameObject "Screen1."

3. Reset the Screen1 GameObject by resetting its Transform values. Remember the gear icon to the right of the Transform text? Click the drop-down and select Reset.

4. Select all of the grass Prefabs up to this point in the Hierarchy.

5. In the Hierarchy window, left-click and drag them to the Screen1 GameObject and release. They will now be parented under Screen1.

6. With the Screen1 GameObject selected, go to Edit > Duplicate to create another instance of the tiles we have already placed. Rename this new one "Screen2."

7. Using our grid snapping technique, move the Screen2 group to the right 10 units. The Transform values for Screen2 should be 10, 0, 0 in X, Y, and Z.

> **Note**
>
> Another useful way to make sure your tiles are aligned is with the Snap Settings. Marquee (left-click and drag) a section of tiles or select them in the Hierarchy window. With the tiles selected, open the Snap Settings and click the Snap All Axes button. This will ensure that any tiles are snapped exactly to the absolute grid values. This is a very good technique for cleaning up tiles whose Transforms may have moved slightly.

Adding Sorting Elements

We covered Sorting Layers earlier in the chapter. Now let's set up a couple of instances of them and see how we can add some simple depth and details to our level. Learning how to do this early will help when you have finished the level design and want to add details, and it may give you ideas for adding your own variations.

We will first add a fence GameObject to the foreground so that our Player GameObject will walk behind it. Then we will add water and a ledge. With the ledge sorted to be in front of the water, it will appear as though there is some depth in our Scene. These details will go a long way toward giving the game life.

1. Select the fence Prefab from the _prefabs folder. Place this roughly at the end of the first screen, just above the ground.

2. Duplicate this and move it to the right, into the second screen. Make two more copies of this, placing them to the right.

3. Use the Snap All Axes tip from earlier to make sure these are lined up correctly. Your Scene should resemble Figure 4.13.

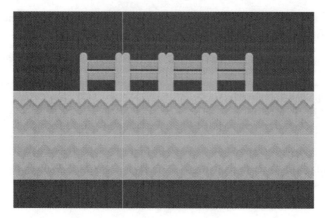

Figure 4.13   Scene View with the newly placed fence GameObjects

4. Make sure to place the first fence Prefab we added to our Scene under the Screen1 parent GameObject. Place the last three under the Screen2 version. This keeps our Hierarchy clean, and we will be able to find elements later on much more easily.

Last, we need to make sure we set the sorting for these, so our Player GameObject will walk behind them. We could do this on a per-object level, but that would take more time as well as make things less consistent. Doing this to the master Prefab in the _prefabs folder will instantly update any of these we have added to our Scene.

Select the fence Prefab in the _prefabs folder and look at its properties in the Inspector. Select the drop-down for the Sorting Layer and change it from Default to Foreground. Now our fence tiles will sort in front of our Player GameObject.

Now let's add the ledge and water. For this we will sort our sprites going back into the Scene. To make our Scene look slightly more realistic, we will change the end of our ground pieces to a ledge and add water:

1. Remove the last grassMid and grassCenter GameObjects from Screen2 by selecting them in the Scene View or Hierarchy and hitting the Delete key.

2. From the _prefabs folder again, select the grassCliffRight Prefab and drag it into the Scene View. Place this roughly at the end of the tiles for Screen2.

3. Select the liquidWater Prefab and place it directly below the ledge sprite.

4. Last, select the liquidWaterTop_mid Prefab and place it directly over the grassCliffRight GameObject.

5. Let's set the Sorting Layer for the water so it draws behind the ledge sprite. Again, let's do this in the Prefab so that any instance of the water will automatically sort correctly. Select the water Prefabs and in the Inspector, set the sorting to be Background.

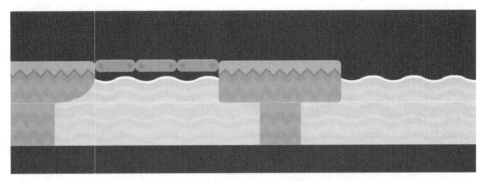

Figure 4.14   Our ledge and water GameObjects placed

6. Finally, we need to make sure the GameObjects are positioned precisely. Select the grassCliffRight and the two water GameObjects and hit the Snap All Axes button again.

7. Your Scene should resemble Figure 4.14. We have gone ahead and added a few additional sprites for Screen3, including an island and a bridge, as well as finished out the water. Remember to use your Sorting Layer and Order in Layer attributes to set the priority of the sprites. See the First_Level_Final Scene file if you get stuck.

Continuing On

Now that we have a basic understanding of adding Prefabs to our tiles, positioning and snapping them, and sorting our sprites, we can continue. We leave you here to carry on and finish the rest of the level design. You are free to use the design we laid out at the beginning of the chapter or to make your own. Most of what we will be adding in the next few chapters can be done with any variation of the design, but we will show you a few select GameObjects and enemies we have chosen.

Feel free to finish this one and keep this chapter handy should you need to review any information. We have also included the final level completely laid out in the Project files for this chapter. This Unity Scene file is in the Chapter 4_projectFiles > _scenes folder and is named First_Level_Final. If you run into any roadblocks, check the Inspector and Hierarchy windows.

Summary

In this chapter we learned a great deal of information on designing the first part of our level. We had a brief overview of level design and reviewed a few simple principles to make our level slightly more enjoyable.

After this we dug into Unity and using the Scene View and camera controls to navigate our Scene. Using a variety of methods, you should now be able to easily move around to view and place your GameObjects in world space.

We went into great detail on the Unity Transforms and Transform Components. This is how we will position, rotate, and scale the elements of our game. We went into 2D projections and Z-depth and how we will use sorting and ordering to added depth and priority to our sprites in the game.

Finally, we started building our first level, adding Prefabs, and setting up sorting and some organization for our Scene. We set a few attributes in the master Prefab and saw how this will directly update all instances in our Scene. From here you are left to carry on and finish the design of your level.

In Chapter 6, "Adding Animations to Our Scene," we will start bringing our characters and Scene elements to life. We will learn how to add a series of complex behaviors and how we can make things move realistically in a short amount of time and with little effort. With that, let's get moving!

Exercises

1. Finish up the Scene, adding elements such as grass, clouds, and props. Remember to set the position with the Snap Settings tool, and set the priorities for the sprites.

2. Set the Sorting Layers in the master Prefabs themselves in the _prefabs folder. This will ensure that all instances we add to our Scene carry them over.

3. Let's add some simple collision for our ground GameObjects. Select grassMid and grassCliffRight in the _prefabs folder.

4. In the Inspector, click the Add Component button and select Physics 2D > Box Collider. This will add a Collider Component for our ground sprites that our Player GameObject will then be able to interact with.

5. The colliders are added, but centered to the pivot of our GameObjects. We need to have the collision cover the bounds of the sprite. Make sure that grassMid and grassCliffRight are still selected from the _prefabs folder.

6. Under the Box Collider Component, find the attribute for Center and set its values in X and Y to 0.5. This will move the collision to center exactly around our sprites.

7. Don't forget to save your Scene!

The Basics of Movement and Player Control

When developing a game, it is often best to start with simple building blocks from which you can build greater functionality and complexity. You must consider what is at the root of your game's experience. We're developing a 2D platformer, so our root is clearly **movement**. Bearing that in mind, we will begin constructing the basics of movement and building on them as we continue through later chapters. If you can make movement feel good in a test level (often referred to as a "white box level"), you're on the right path!

This chapter will also introduce the MonoDevelop–Unity IDE and discuss some of its error-handling tools and how to make use of them to debug your code.

Coding in Unity3D

True to its flexible form, Unity3D supports three separate scripting languages. Scripts can be used to create Components to add to your GameObjects, controlling their behaviors or providing them with expanded functionality. These scripts can reference one another, can manipulate GameObjects and other Components, and can even be used to modify Unity's editor in order to improve your workflow.

The Three Languages

The three scripting languages supported by Unity3D are

- Boo
- C#
- JavaScript (not Java; there's a difference)

> **Note**
>
> Unity's version of JavaScript is known as UnityScript, but even within the toolset it is referred to as JavaScript. There are some differences between the two languages, the details of which can easily be found online.

Choosing the "Right" Language

With three languages at your disposal, you may be wondering which is the right one for you. This honestly comes down to a matter of personal preference. If you have prior experience with one of these languages, that is likely the language you will want to work with.

That being said, it's worth noting that the most-used language is C#, which boasts a lot of online support and a large Unity community, followed fairly closely by JavaScript. Boo is used significantly less than either of these languages, and you may have quite a bit more difficulty finding relevant tutorials or answers to your questions in the Unity community if you use it. It is similar to Python, however, so people with prior experience with that language may wish to delve into it.

Ultimately, however, the "right" language is whichever one lets you get the job done quickly and comfortably. For the purposes of this book, we will be developing our scripts in C#. We're going to assume a rudimentary understanding of syntax here as teaching the language from scratch is outside our scope. JavaScript users can find JavaScript versions of the final scripts in the Appendix.

> **Note**
>
> The Unity Asset Store (www.assetstore.unity3d.com) contains some interesting options for developers in need of non-code solutions, but it is highly recommended that you take the time to learn a scripting language. It will greatly expand what you can accomplish both with and without those solutions. Unity has excellent starter tutorials here: http://unity3d.com/learn/tutorials/modules/beginner/scripting

Making the Player Go

We have a Player GameObject but there's nothing to make it "go" at this point. We're going to remedy that by creating a custom character controller so that our player can perform basic movements such as running and jumping. We'll also touch briefly on some of the necessary physics required to make this work, but that will be covered in greater detail in Chapter 7, "Setting Up Player Physics and Colliders."

Different Ways of Handling Movement

There are a number of considerations when looking at character control in your game, such as movement style, acceleration, and air control. Let's take a look at these, shall we?

Discrete Tile Movement versus Smooth Tile Movement

Some 2D games operate on a purely tile-based system in which the player is always centered on a given tile. Any input typically moves the player to an adjacent tile, assuming nothing is blocking the way. The magnitude of the input is irrelevant as it is handled in a binary fashion (i.e., you are either moving or not moving).

Smooth movement, conversely, takes input from the player and translates the location in much smaller values. In this system, it is possible to end your movement with the player touching more than one tile, and magnitude typically affects the player's speed. This is the more common of the two systems and is the one that we'll be employing here.

Character Acceleration

In addition to movement, we need to consider the rate at which a player accelerates when they begin moving. Think of it like a car accelerating from 0 to a maximum speed of 60 mph; do we want the player to reach that speed slowly? Quickly? Maybe somewhere in between?

This touches on a very subjective element of game design: the role of realism. Realism is not always fun, but that doesn't mean your fun can't be realistic. It's important to understand how the realism you're adding to your game influences the player's experience.

Let's consider acceleration. The slower the acceleration, the less precise control a player is going to be able to exert over their character. In our case, we're making a 2D platformer, so we *want* to give the player a maximum amount of control over their character to better enable them to work their way through the world. To that end, we're going with rapid acceleration in our game.

Air Control

When the character is airborne, how much control are we going to allow the player to exert? There are three common styles in 2D platformers that we will discuss here: zero control, reduced control, and full control.

In a **zero control** system, once the character jumps, the player cannot alter their trajectory or velocity at all. This means they are fully committed to the action they've undertaken, whether they like it or not. This forces the player to constantly gauge and assess jumps before making them. This air control model is represented in Figure 5.1 by the unbroken line.

In a **reduced control** system, the character maintains full velocity if they continue traveling in the direction that they were originally jumping but may change directions at a cost to velocity. This allows the player a degree of corrective control while still forcing them to assess jumps beforehand. This air control model is represented in Figure 5.1 by the longer dashed line.

In a **full control** system, the player's control over their character's velocity remains absolute regardless of adjustments to their direction mid-jump. This allows players a level of control in the air that matches the control they have on the ground. It also

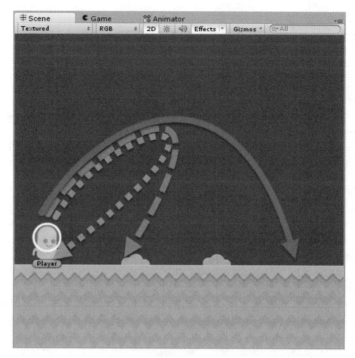

Figure 5.1   Traditional air control models

allows for some jumping tricks that would make the laws of physics weep. This air control model is represented in Figure 5.1 by the shorter dashed line.

Given our goal of providing the player with full control, we'll go ahead and use a full air control system.

> **Tip**
>
> Iteration is the father of quality. Making a decision now doesn't mean you can't tweak it later on to find the gameplay experience that you're looking for. Never be afraid to experiment!

Creating and Hooking Up Our PlayerController

We've discussed the degree of control that we want to give our player, so now it's time to actually make that happen. We'll do this with a PlayerController Component that we'll begin scripting now by taking the following steps:

1. Open the First_Level Scene file.

2. Select the Player GameObject.

3. Click the Add Component button and choose New Script.

4. Name the script PlayerController and ensure that the language is set to CSharp.

5. In the Project Browser, select the newly created script and move it to the _scripts folder.

6. Drag and drop the PlayerController script onto our Player GameObject.

You've just added our controller Component to the player! Soon, this will allow the player to move around, but right now it doesn't do anything for us. It's going to need some custom code for that to happen, which means it's time to introduce the MonoDevelop-Unity IDE.

The MonoDevelop-Unity IDE

This is the tool in which you'll be writing your scripts for Unity. Unity does support other external editors, such as Microsoft Visual Studio, but we'll be using MonoDevelop-Unity for the purposes of this book, as seen in Figure 5.2.

The Document Editor pane is where you'll spend most of your time, for obvious reasons. The panel on the left is the Solution Explorer, in which you'll find your scripts. Along the right-hand side, you'll find panels for a variety of useful tools such

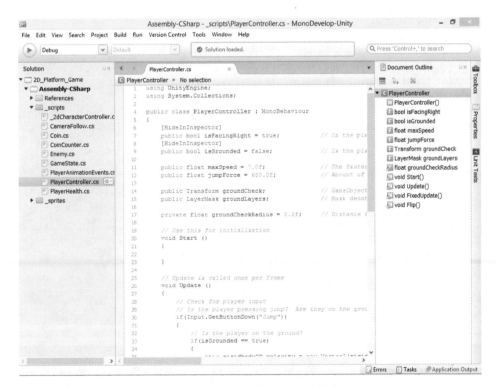

Figure 5.2   The MonoDevelop-Unity IDE

as script templates and unit tests, though exploration of these is outside the scope of this book's goals.

> **Tip**
>
> While we aren't going to examine the extra tools, the Document Outline panel can be useful for jumping around quickly within your script. It's self-explanatory and worth keeping open.

Initial Script Setup

We'll begin by preparing some of the variables we'll use to help our character get around. Open the PlayerController script and fill in the script shown in Listing 5.1. We'll elaborate on the contents momentarily.

Listing 5.1   **Basic Script Setup**

```
public class PlayerController : MonoBehaviour
{
  [HideInInspector]
  public bool isFacingRight = true;
  [HideInInspector]
  public bool isJumping = false;
  [HideInInspector]
  public bool isGrounded = false;

  public float jumpForce = 650.0f;
  public float maxSpeed = 7.0f;

  public Transform groundCheck;
  public LayerMask groundLayers;

  private float groundCheckRadius = 0.2f;

  void Start()
  {
  }

  void Update()
  {
  }

  void FixedUpdate()
  {
  }
}
```

> **Tip**
>
> Public variables can be externally accessed by other scripts. These variables also show up in the Inspector, allowing a developer to change them manually. This may not be the behavior we want and can clutter the Inspector with unnecessary options. [HideInInspector] solves this problem by allowing you to have public variables that are not shown in the Inspector.

> **Note**
>
> FixedUpdate() is a standard Unity method that is called at a set rate during runtime. This makes it ideal for controlling our character as the consistent updates will make the movement smooth.
>
> The Update() method—also a standard Unity method—is called whenever possible during runtime. It occurs more frequently than FixedUpdate() but not at a consistent rate. It's well suited for catching player input in the form of button presses, when players want immediate feedback.

Table 5.1 breaks down what purpose each of these variables will ultimately serve in our controller Component.

Filling In Our Properties

After saving the script, return to the Unity window. You'll notice that there's a brief pause as Unity recompiles the script. If there are any compiler errors, you'll find them in the Console, as indicated in Figure 5.3. If this happens, verify that your script matches our PlayerController script.

Click on the Player GameObject and find our PlayerController Component. If everything compiled correctly, the Component will now be populated with several property fields. The "Max Speed" and "Jump Force" properties will have initial values

Table 5.1   **PlayerController Variables**

Variable	Type	Purpose
isFacingRight	Bool	Tracks player facing direction so that we can flip the sprite accordingly
isGrounded	Bool	Tracks whether the player is touching ground
maxSpeed	Float	The maximum speed of player movement
jumpForce	Float	The amount of vertical force applied to the player when they jump
groundCheck	Transform	A GameObject from which we will check to see if the player is touching ground
groundLayers	Layer mask	The list of layers the game considers to be "ground"
groundCheckRadius	Float	The distance out from the *groundCheck*'s center that we will test for ground

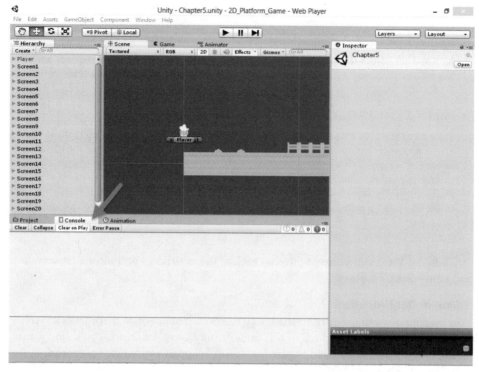

Figure 5.3　Unity Console

already set—these were public variables to which we assigned values in the script—but our "Ground Check" and "Ground Layers" properties have no values yet. We need those in order for our character to tell when they're touching a surface we consider to be ground, so let's fill those out and, while we're at it, add a missing piece we'll need shortly:

1. With the Player GameObject selected, click and drag the groundCheck GameObject from the Hierarchy window into the "Ground Check" property in the Inspector.

2. Click the drop-down menu for Ground Layers and select Ground.

3. Click the Add Component button on our Player GameObject and add a Rigidbody 2D from the Physics 2D category.

4. Check the Fixed Angle box on the Rigidbody 2D Component you just added; if you don't, the player is going to roll around once they can move!

Tip

> **Tip**
>
> As an alternative to clicking and dragging, you can also click the circular icon by a property to open an asset selection window.

Implementing Basic Lateral Movement

We've filled in the data, but nothing would happen if we started the game. We've told the GameObject how fast it can move and when it should consider itself to be grounded, but there still isn't anything that tells it how to move. We're going to expand our PlayerController script by adding the code in Listing 5.2 to our `FixedUpdate()` method.

Listing 5.2   The **`FixedUpdate()`** Method of PlayerController

```
void FixedUpdate()
{
  float move = Input.GetAxis("Horizontal");
  rigidbody2D.velocity = new Vector2(move * maxSpeed, rigidbody2D.velocity.y);
}
```

Let's break down what we're doing here.

At a fixed interval, we're getting the value of the `Horizontal` input (a value range of −1 to 1), and we're going to assign a new velocity to the player's Rigidbody 2D Component.

That velocity is a `Vector2` wherein the first value represents X velocity and the second represents Y velocity. The X velocity is the `Horizontal` input multiplied by our *maxSpeed* variable (giving us a value range of −7 to 7), while the Y velocity is whatever the existing Y velocity happens to be; that's not a value we're trying to change.

Save the script and return to Unity. Start the game and run around using the A and D keys!

> **Tip**
>
> By default, you can also move using the appropriate analog stick if you have a gamepad hooked to your computer.

Setting the Player's Facing

You may have noticed that the sprite is always facing to the right, no matter what direction you're moving in. Rather than have separate sprites for left and right facing, we're going to use a simple code trick to flip the sprite we're already using. Update the PlayerController script with the lines in Listing 5.3.

Listing 5.3   **Handling Player Facing**

```
void FixedUpdate()
{
  isGrounded = Physics2D.OverlapCircle
    (groundCheck.position, groundCheckRadius, groundLayers);

  float move = Input.GetAxis("Horizontal");
  this.rigidbody2D.velocity =
    new Vector2(move * maxSpeed, rigidbody2D.velocity.y);

  if((move > 0.0f && isFacingRight == false)
    || (move < 0.0f && isFacingRight == true))
  {
    Flip ();
  }

void Flip()
{
  isFacingRight = !isFacingRight;
  Vector3 playerScale = transform.localScale;
  playerScale.x = playerScale.x * -1;
  transform.localScale = playerScale;
  }
}
```

Our change adds a new method, Flip(), to the script. This method inverts the value of the isFacingRight bool and then flips the Transform of the Player GameObject along its X-axis. What once was a positive value is now a negative, and vice versa.

We call the Flip() method in our FixedUpdate() loop but only if certain criteria are met. If the player's move value is positive, they are moving to the right, while a negative value implies movement to the left. If the script detects that the player is moving right but facing left, or is moving left but facing right, it will call into our method to flip the sprite's facing to properly match the direction of travel.

Implementing Basic Jumping

Our character can now move laterally, but platformers are all about running and jumping! Let's add some vertical mobility to our character by expanding our PlayerController script with a few simple lines of code, as seen in Listing 5.4.

Listing 5.4   **FixedUpdate() Method of PlayerController**

```
void Update()
{
  if(Input.GetButtonDown("Jump"))
```

```
  {
    if(isGrounded == true)
    {
      this.rigidbody2D.velocity = new Vector2(rigidbody2D.velocity.x,0);
      this.rigidbody2D.AddForce(new Vector2(0, jumpForce));
    }
  }
}


void FixedUpdate()
{
  isGrounded = Physics2D.OverlapCircle
    (groundCheck.position, groundCheckRadius, groundLayers);

  float move = Input.GetAxis("Horizontal");
  this.rigidbody2D.velocity =
    new Vector2(move * maxSpeed, rigidbody2D.velocity.y);
}
```

In the FixedUpdate() method, we've added a Physics2D check that will set our isGrounded bool to true or false. This check creates a circle based on the provided parameters and returns true if it contacts any layers that match the provided mask. Refer to Table 5.2 for an explanation of the variables used in this check. The check is going into FixedUpdate() rather than Update() because it's the more stable of the two locations for physics-related code due to the more reliable and consistent rate at which this function is called by Unity.

In a nutshell, if the check touches anything in the "ground" layer within a range of 0.2 units, it will return true.

We run this check because we need to know if the player is in contact with the ground in the event that they attempt to jump, given that you can't jump while airborne (yet, but we'll visit that in a later chapter). This variable will also become extremely valuable to our animation setup in Chapter 6, "Adding Animations to Our Scene."

Table 5.2   **Anatomy of Our Ground Check**

Variable	Type	Purpose
groundCheck.position	Vector3	Coordinates reflecting the location of our groundCheck GameObject
groundCheckRadius	Float	Radius of the overlap circle that is created
groundLayers	Layer mask	Our list of layers that represent "ground"

Now we need to capture the player's input, so it's time to fill out our `Update()` method in the PlayerController script. Enter the code found in Listing 5.5.

Listing 5.5 **Update() Method of PlayerController**

```
void Update()
{
  if(Input.GetButtonDown("Jump"))
  {
    if(isGrounded == true)
    {
      this.rigidbody2D.velocity = new Vector2(rigidbody2D.velocity.x,0);
      this.rigidbody2D.AddForce(new Vector2(0, jumpForce));
    }
  }
}
```

We're now able to capture some input from the player so that they can jump. The logic breaks down as follows:

1. We check to see if the player is pushing the Jump button. If not, nothing happens.

2. We check to see if the player is grounded. If not, nothing happens.

3. We adjust the player's velocity so that their X-axis speed is unchanged but their Y-axis speed is zeroed out. This prevents the player from gaining additional jump height when running up an incline.

4. We apply a physics force to the player. It has no X-axis power (we're not pushing the player sideways) and contains our *jumpForce* float variable for Y-axis power.

Save your script and return to Unity. After the script compiles, start the game up and you'll find that the spacebar now allows you to jump! We'll be making adjustments to our world's gravity in Chapter 7, "Setting Up Player Physics and Colliders," but feel free to play around with the numbers now to get a feel for how that physics impulse affects your height.

> **Note**
>
> There are many ways to shorthand code. For example, the following two lines are the same:
>
> ```
> if(isGrounded == true)
> if(isGrounded)
> ```
>
> Similarly, both of these lines also present the same logic:
>
> ```
> if(isGrounded == false) )
> if(!isGrounded)
> ```
>
> This kind of shorthand is considered industry standard, but for the purposes of syntactical clarity for the new user, we will refrain from using shorthand code in this book.

Setting Up a Basic Follow-Cam

You may have noticed that you can run and jump your way clean off the screen at this point. We're going to set up a very basic camera for the time being to prevent that from happening.

1. Drag the Main Camera GameObject onto the Player GameObject in the Hierarchy view to parent it to the player.

2. Select the Main Camera.

3. Change its Transform information so that it has the following values: X: 0, Y: 1, Z: −10.

Save the Scene and run the game. The camera now follows the player as they move! This is because the camera has become a child object of the Player GameObject, and children maintain a position relative to their parent whenever it moves. In Chapter 11, "Applying Effects to the GameObjects," we'll expand upon the camera with a script to give it polished, smooth movement.

Introducing the Input Manager

You may be wondering what the `"Horizontal"` and `"Jump"` strings we've been using in our code refer to. These are references to the names of inputs located within the Project's Input Manager, where you control the various input settings of your game. Let's open it now and take a look:

1. Open the Edit menu and select Project Settings > Input.

2. Click on Horizontal to expand it.

3. You should see a window like that shown in Figure 5.4.

This is what we were referencing when we used the `"Horizontal"` string in our script earlier. As you can see, there's a bit more to it than just a name. Let's break down the purpose of all these properties:

- **Size:** The total number of inputs. Increase the value to add new ones.
- **Name:** String used to refer to this input in code.
- **Descriptive Name:** Name the user will see for this input in a key binding Setup menu.
- **Descriptive Negative Name:** Name seen by the user in the Setup menu for the negative version of this input.
- **Negative Button:** Button pressed for movement in a negative axial direction.
- **Positive Button:** Button pressed for movement in a positive axial direction.

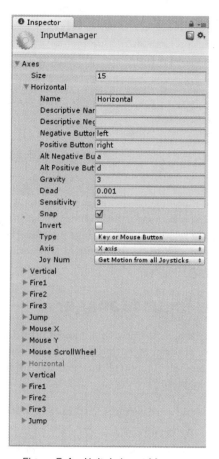

Figure 5.4   Unity's Input Manager

- **Alt Negative Button:** Alternative button for movement in a negative axial direction.

- **Alt Positive Button:** Alternative button for movement in a positive axial direction.

- **Gravity:** Speed (units per second) with which the output value falls toward neutral when the device is at rest.

- **Dead:** Size of the analog dead zone where input is considered neutral.

- **Sensitivity:** How fast (units per second) the input moves toward the target value for digital devices.

- **Snap:** If true, when input is received in the opposite direction to the current value, it will jump to a neutral value and then continue to the new value from there.

- **Invert:** Flips the positive and negative values.
- **Type:** Identifies the input as either a key/button (something you press on the keyboard or a peripheral device), mouse movement (meaning it is an axis controlled by the motions of a mouse), or joystick axis (meaning it is controlled by a stick or axis-based control on a peripheral device).
- **Joy Num:** The index of the joystick from which the input is derived.

It seems like a lot of information, but not all settings are used for all input types. Anything with a binary nature (such as a Jump button) isn't going to make use of the negative button settings, for example.

The default inputs provided by Unity account for many actions, but it's inevitable that you'll want to add your own or change the names of ones that already exist. Be aware that when changing a name, you're also invalidating any existing references to that input. In Chapter 12, "Organization and Optimization," we will discuss how to make such changes with minimal risk or issue.

> **Note**
>
> Multiple inputs can share the same name without issue. By default, a Unity Project has two versions of each of its inputs. No one input will supersede the others bearing its name. For example, naming one input "Jump" and assigning it to the spacebar does not preclude you from also making a second input named "Jump" and assigning it to a peripheral gamepad button. Both will be considered valid inputs during runtime.

Error Handling and Debugging

If you've been correctly entering the code to this point, you will not have encountered any errors while playing the game. Eventually, however, mistakes will be made, and you're going to need to know how to handle the resulting errors.

There are two kinds of common errors that you'll encounter as you work: errors in the code and unexpected behavior in the game. The former throws glaring errors, as something is structurally wrong within a script, while the latter can be a bit more insidious, as the code runs but the end results aren't what you expected. We're going to introduce and discuss ways to manage both types.

To that end, we'll discuss the tools available in the MonoDevelop-Unity IDE, and we'll introduce a bug or two into our code.

Handling Exceptions

Exceptions are the glaring errors thrown by problematic code. They show themselves in the Unity Console, which provides us with a snippet of information about the error and a link to the script line where it encountered the error.

Open the PlayerController script and scroll down to the following line:

```
float move = Input.GetAxis("Horizontal");
```

Remove a letter from the word "Horizontal". Any letter. Take your pick. We know that the line is no longer correct, but the script is still going to build because there are no syntax errors present. Save the script, return to Unity, and run the game. You'll find that the Console is immediately plagued with error messages like those seen in Figure 5.5.

Stop the game and double-click on one of those errors. MonoDevelop will pop up (or open itself if you closed it), open the script that contains the error, and highlight the line where it was encountered. The error itself states that an input by that name doesn't exist and suggests that we edit the input settings. In our case, we clearly made a mistake with the input name and need to fix it, but this error would also catch a new input that we called in the script and forgot to create in the input settings.

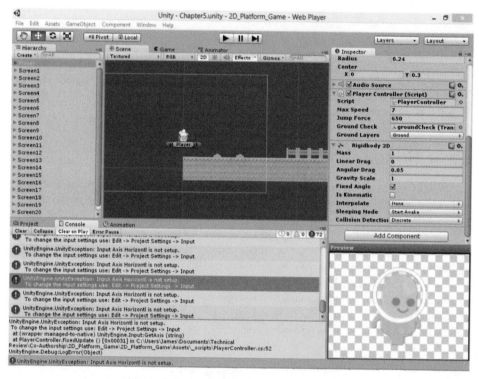

Figure 5.5   Exceptions in the Unity Console

Try-Catch-Finally—Gracefully Handling Exceptions

The kind of exception we just dealt with is known as an **unhandled exception**; we allowed the code to break and reacted by fixing it. What if we wanted to deal with potential exceptions proactively?

This is where the **Try–Catch–Finally** statement comes in. It permits us to gracefully handle the errors in our code which, in turn, prevents the Console from being flooded with messages and may even prevent your game from locking up or crashing during runtime.

Nesting your code in a Try block just tells it to expect either a Catch or a Finally block of code immediately after. In the event that the code in a Try block would throw an exception, it immediately executes those subsequent code blocks. This block must be followed by Catch and/or Finally, in that order.

The Catch block captures the exception as the specified type. You could use that data to print something to the Unity Console or to halt program execution, or you could do nothing with it at all and leave this block empty.

The Finally block tells the code what to do after it's done with the other two blocks. It's important to note that this block fires regardless of whether or not an error has been encountered, so anything you put in here will always happen. It has some uses in debugging, but in many cases you'll just want the Try and Catch blocks.

Leaving our broken script as is, make the adjustments given in Listing 5.6.

> **Tip**
>
> There may be times when you genuinely prefer a hard crash or Console error spam if the error is so grievous that you don't want to run the risk of missing it, in which case leaving it unhandled may be a consideration. This is something you should ever consider only during development, and be forewarned that it is typically dangerous. Do not, under any circumstances, release your code in this state. All errors should be handled in the code of a released project.

Listing 5.6   Adding Try-Catch-Finally to the `FixedUpdate()` Method

```
void FixedUpdate()
{
  isGrounded = Physics2D.OverlapCircle
    (groundCheck.position, groundCheckRadius, groundLayers);
  try
  {
    float move = Input.GetAxis("Horizontl");
    this.rigidbody2D.velocity =
      new Vector2(move * maxSpeed, rigidbody2D.velocity.y);
  }
  catch(UnityException error)
```

(continues)

```
{
  Debug.LogError(error.ToString());
}
finally
{
  Debug.LogWarning("Our input check failed!");
}
}
```

Save the script and run the game in Unity. Your Console is going to look a lot like Figure 5.6 now.

The amount of feedback being received may be a bit excessive right now. The Catch block is returning the same error we saw before, by capturing it as a UnityException and then outputting that information as a string via the `Debug.LogError()` function. Our Finally block is also throwing a custom warning. We know that the Finally block always runs its code, so what purpose does it serve? Its value is not immediately

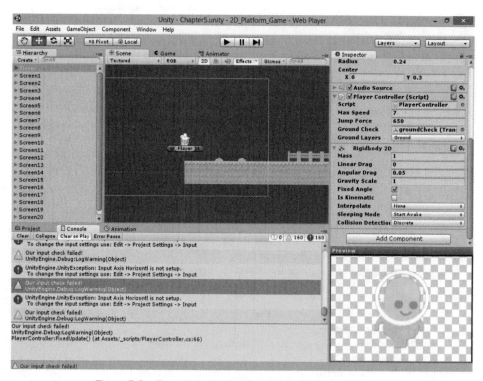

Figure 5.6   Exceptions and debug warnings in the Console

apparent as Finally will (almost always) run whether an exception is caught or not. The purpose of the Finally block is to give you a chance to perform resource management and cleaning in order to keep the code going. For what we've done here, however, our Finally block has served its purpose of showing when the function executes, so feel free to delete it.

If this had been code where an exception resulted in the halting of the game, our Try-Catch-Finally block would have allowed the script to continue beyond that point rather than hanging on the erroneous line.

Correct the typo we introduced into our "Horizontal" string , save the script, and run the game to make sure that the player is moving properly again.

> **Tip**
>
> You can filter the contents of the Console by clicking on any of the three icons in its upper right to show/hide those particular kinds of messages. From left to right, they are Logs, Warnings, and Errors/Exceptions.

Debug.Log() Is Your Friend

The Debug() function we used in our Try-Catch-Finally block has many uses for debugging. You can slip it into your code to test and examine values at runtime. For instance, let's say that we want to know whenever the player has pushed the Jump button but the character is already in the air. Debug.Log() gives us a quick and dirty way to get that information. Try adjusting the code in our PlayerController script as shown in Listing 5.7.

Listing 5.7   Adding **Debug.Log()** to the **Update()** Method

```
void Update()
{
  if(Input.GetButtonDown("Jump"))
  {
    if(isGrounded == true)
    {
      this.rigidbody2D.velocity = new Vector2(rigidbody2D.velocity.x,0);
      this.rigidbody2D.AddForce(new Vector2(0, jumpForce));
    }
    else
    {
      Debug.Log("Jump pressed while not grounded");
    }
  }
}
```

Save the script and run the game. Try jumping and then pressing the Jump button again while your character is already in the air and note that our `Debug.Log()` message appears in the Console.

There will be plenty of times when you'll want an indication that a specific bit of code has been executed or to get a variable's value without interrupting the game, and this can be an excellent way to do it. As you may have noticed earlier, though, using it within a frequently called method such as `FixedUpdate()` or `Update()` can result in the Console being spammed.

Using Breakpoints to Halt Code Execution

There are times when you're going to want to closely examine the code during runtime and `Debug()` won't cut it. In these situations, we can attach MonoDevelop directly to the Unity process and step through code execution by using breakpoints.

Breakpoints cause the code to halt when they're encountered. You can then use MonoDevelop to step through the code, one line at a time, to see where it goes and what it does. You can also monitor the values of variables while doing this, making it an excellent way to catch and resolve unexpected behaviors in your game.

We're going to introduce one such behavior into our game and then use the debugger to catch it. Start by altering the PlayerController script to match Listing 5.8.

Listing 5.8   **Creating an Unexpected Behavior Bug**

```
void FixedUpdate()
{
  isGrounded = Physics2D.OverlapCircle
    (groundCheck.position, groundCheckRadius, groundLayers);
  try
  {
    float move = Input.GetAxis("Horizontal");
    maxSpeed = 3.0f;
    this.rigidbody2D.velocity =
      new Vector2(move * maxSpeed, rigidbody2D.velocity.y);
  }
  catch(UnityException error)
  {
    Debug.LogError(error.ToString());
  }
}
```

Save the script and run the game. We've now introduced a bug that will cause the player's maximum speed to always be 3, which is far lower than the value we originally assigned. If you check the PlayerController Component on the Player GameObject during runtime, you'll see that the value of the "Max Speed" property is 3. If you check it again when the game isn't running, it will be 7.

This is an **unexpected behavior**, meaning that the script is throwing no exceptions but still isn't performing the way that we want it to. In order to find out exactly when that "Max Speed" property is being altered, we're going to connect the debugger and set up our breakpoint:

1. Open the PlayerController script in MonoDevelop-Unity.
2. Click the Run menu and select Attach to Process to open the window shown in Figure 5.7.
3. There should be only one Unity process running right now, so select that and click Attach.

The debugger is now attached to your Unity process, but without a breakpoint it's not going to do much for us. To add a breakpoint, simply click in the left-hand margin of the MonoDevelop-Unity main window next to the line on which you want code execution to halt. Add a breakpoint to the location shown in Figure 5.8.

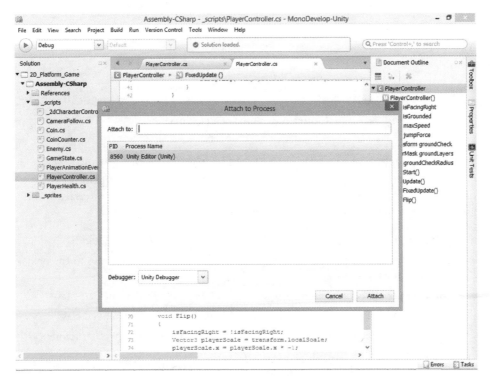

Figure 5.7   Attach to Process window

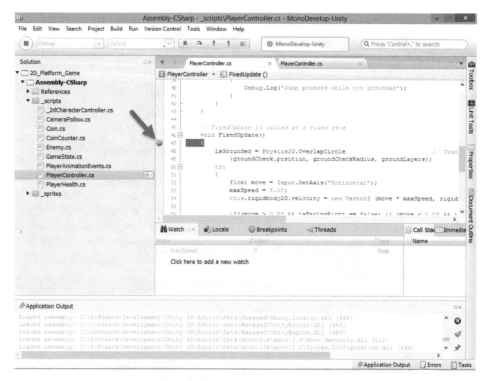

Figure 5.8   Breakpoint location

Return to Unity and start the game. As soon as the `FixedUpdate()` method of our PlayerController script is run, that breakpoint will trigger and the game's execution will halt. You'll notice some changes in the MonoDevelop-Unity interface at this point, such as a highlighted line of code and a new toolbar at the top.

- **Highlighted Code:** The next line that will execute in the code logic
- **Continue Execution:** Executes the highlighted line and continues to the next line in code logic
- **Step Over:** Executes the next line of executable code in that specific class
- **Step Into:** Executes the next line of executable code in a referenced class
- **Step Out:** Executes the next line of executable code in the class that references this class
- **Detach:** Detaches the debugger from the current Unity process

We know that the player's maximum speed is managed by the *maxSpeed* float, so we need to keep an eye on its value. To better accomplish that, we can add it to the Watch tab with the following steps:

1. If the Watch tab isn't already open, open it via View > Debug Windows > Watch.

2. Click the "Click here to add new" text.

3. Type the name of our *maxSpeed* variable to select it from the list.

4. Press Enter.

The variable is now being monitored by the Watch window. At this stage, the value should still be 7, meaning our bug hasn't yet affected the speed. Using the Step Over button, progress through the script, paying careful attention to the line of code being executed and the state of our *maxSpeed* variable. When the value changes to 3, look at the line of code that just executed. That is the source of our bug, so remove the offending line to resolve the issue.

Granted, the solution is obvious in this case because we introduced the error, but this method of halting code and stepping through it is something you will become intimately familiar with in your pursuit of deeper and nastier bugs.

Normally, you'd press the Continue Execution button to allow the code to continue running normally, but since our breakpoint is in the `FixedUpdate()` method, it would halt again immediately. You can either remove the breakpoint by left-clicking it, or you can select Enable/Disable Breakpoint from the right-click context menu. After doing either of those, you may press Continue Execution or simply press the Stop button at the upper left to end debugging entirely.

Summary

In this chapter we learned which scripting languages are used by Unity and discussed a bit about the principles of movement in 2D platformers. We took a look at how they applied to our game from a design standpoint and made some important decisions about how our player character would be controlled.

After this we had an overview of the MonoDevelop-Unity IDE and created our very first script, granting the player some basic movement in the form of running and jumping. We learned how to quickly flip our player's facing without having to mirror our sprites, and we also added a very basic camera setup that follows the player.

We delved into the Unity Input Manager and broke down the various properties that define an input's base behaviors.

Finally, we discussed the debugging tools and different error types. We reviewed ways to handle the errors gracefully as well as methods for tracking down unexpected behaviors during runtime.

In Chapter 6, "Adding Animations to Our Scene," we will start bringing our characters and Scene elements to life. We will learn how to add a series of complex behaviors and how we can make things move realistically in a short amount of time and with little effort. With that, let's get moving!

Exercises

The ability to receive information from our game as it runs is absolutely crucial, so let's spend a bit of time with the Debug.Log() function and have the game feed velocity information to the Console.

1. Open the PlayerController script.
2. Navigate to the FixedUpdate() function.
3. Locate the line where we get input from the "Horizontal" axis.
4. Use a Debug.Log() command to feed the value of the "move" to the Console. As it's not a string value, remember to use the ToString() function so that Debug.Log() can make use of it.
5. Start the game and experiment with your movement to see what sorts of values you get. Console information like this can be extremely useful when tracking down behavioral bugs.
6. Save the Scene and Project files.

On to the next chapter!

Adding Animations to Our Scene

In this chapter we will take a look at adding some life to our characters. We will take a look at 2D versus 3D animation and cover the key differences between transform and multi-sprite frame animations. We will also look at ways of using programming to create scripted animations that will save us time and help with continuously looping animations.

We will cover the Graph Editor and Dope Sheet tools and how best to utilize both of them for our animations. Last, we will take a look at how to set up an Animation State Machine to manage the various circumstances or "events" that might affect our player during the game, such as jumping onto a platform or taking damage from an enemy.

Some Rules for Animation

As we have been doing in previous chapters, let's go into a little more detail about the hows and whys of animating something. Creating a level for a game or a story for a character is important, but how you create animations and the "style" of the animation can be just as important. A simple change in the speed of a walk or the length of a jump can make all the difference.

Animation Principles

We won't go into a lot of detail about the rules of animations because there are many other detailed guides available on them. However, anyone creating animations should know at least the simple definitions of the principles of animating. These 12 rules have been the standard since the early days of animation, well before the first Mario was even an idea:

- **Anticipation:** The action before the main action; the windup before the pitch.
- **Appeal:** The natural connection to an audience through a believable story and character design. Though very different, both Snow White and the Evil Witch have their own appeal.

- **Arcs:** The natural direction and motion along an arced trajectory, such as the descent of an arrow as it moves toward its target.

- **Exaggeration:** The ability to add emphasis and to push the bounds of realism without breaking them. For example, imagine a character that is blasting off screen. In cartoons, the proportions of such characters are stretched to emphasize their acceleration.

- **Follow-through and overlapping action:** The continuation and "breaking" of parts to reinforce the laws of physics in the animation, such as a ripple in water as a wave moves through it.

- **Secondary action:** An action that gives emphasis or detail to the main action, such as the whip of a mouse's tail as it jumps.

- **Slow in and slow out:** The increase or decrease in an action as it transitions between movements. A rolling ball will gradually decrease in speed before finally coming to rest.

- **Solid drawing:** Maintaining consistent details of an object as it animates. A squishy ball will still maintain its volume, even as it compresses through a bounce.

- **Squash and stretch:** The deforming of an object to give it realism and flexibility. Superman will compress (squash) before extending (stretch) his body as he flies off.

- **Staging:** The deliberate attempt to direct an audience's attention to what is of greatest importance in a scene.

- **Straight-ahead action and pose to pose:** The methods of animating an action. You would either start from the beginning and go straight through, or create only the main storytelling poses or frames that define the overall action.

- **Timing:** The overall speed of an action to help establish certain characteristics or emotions.

2D versus 3D Animation

Another important discussion is about animating with a 2D approach versus a 3D one. While most of the rules and principles work in either case, it is good to discuss a few differences.

2D animation means using only two-dimensional depth. A scene is drawn as frames, one after another, on paper or in 2D software using only two axes (horizontal and vertical). In order to create the animation, you must draw each frame of the sequence, constantly paying attention to the previous and following frames. After a series of these are done, they can be recorded and played back in order to see the overall action. Most of our animation will be done with this method as we are dealing with 2D pixel art.

3D animation refers to a computer object or actor that is manipulated in the 3D environment. While 3D is still displayed in a 2D projection, the object has depth and volume which we can interpret through shape, lighting, and rendering. We will also use 3D when we have to manually animate a physical GameObject in our Scene, such as a moving platform.

Transform versus Frame Animation

Animation in Unity consists mostly of transform animations and frame (sprite) animations. These two styles basically boil down to 3D and 2D animation respectively, but let's get a better idea of when and why to use one or the other, or even possibly both.

Transform Animation

Transform animation refers to manipulating an object in 3D space over time. This means we either move, rotate, or scale the volume of the mesh to affect its position, orientation, or size. A good example is a bouncing ball animation in 3D. In order to make the ball (sphere) appear to bounce across a floor realistically, you have to affect the transform of the object.

All GameObjects in Unity have a Transform Component attached to them. By creating an Animation Component on the GameObject, you can then create an animation and affect it with the transform. We will cover the Animation Component and applying animations shortly.

> **Note**
>
> Although we are working from a fixed 2D view of our game, we are still in a 3D world space. This means that we still have to account for three axes of movement in which our GameObjects can move: left to right, up to down, and forward to back.

Frame Animation

Frame animation is simply that: a series of frames (images) that when played back one after another show a sequence that appears to be in motion. When using 2D sprites, the frames have to be laid out onto a sprite sheet and then arranged in an animation. Figure 6.1 shows the sprite sheet for our player character. Notice the simple but subtle changes in positions such as the feet. By playing back the different frames in a sequential order, we can create an animation, such as a walk sequence.

Applying Both

You may come across an instance where you need to use both transform and frame animations in order to get the effect you want. An example would be one of our enemy GameObjects: the bat. The frames of the bat will give an appearance of our bat character flapping its wings. However, this will not actually move the bat across the screen in 3D space. For this we will need to use a combination of the frames along with the transform.

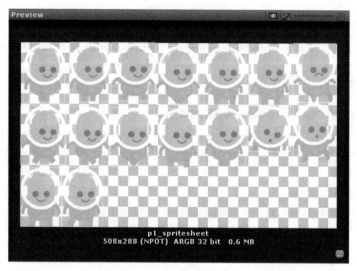

Figure 6.1   The player sprite sheet with all of the various frames
for the sprite's possible animations

> **Note**
>
> While a 2D sprite is simply a flat image, in order to be rendered in a game, it has to be placed
> onto an actual 3D polygon mesh (usually referred to as a card or plane). Since the sprite is
> assigned a transparent shader, we do not see the 3D mesh but only the 2D image with its
> transparency. To see the polygon mesh, in the Scene View toolbar, change the rendered mode
> from Textured to Wireframe. Now the sprites render the two triangulated polygons that make up
> the 3D card.

Scripted Animations

Another method for animating our sprites is through scripted or programmable animations. By writing a script that controls a set of movements or transforms, you can add
animations that can complement other elements. For example, we can script a platform
that moves back and forth for our character to jump to.

This method of animating has many uses, such as reusing the same script on other
GameObjects and editing values almost instantaneously. We will deal with scripting in
greater detail in the next chapter, but we will see this briefly used further along in this
chapter.

Imported Animations

We also have the ability to import an animation that we can apply to one of our
GameObjects. Using another application to create your animations may be more useful,

and it also allows others to help in your game pipeline. You can import the animation into Unity and apply it to your GameObject.

You may also find third-party animations to use for your Project. While this is mostly intended for 3D characters designed for locomotion, there is no reason you could not import a simple transform animation for your sprites.

Use the Assets > Import New Asset and browse to find the animation file you want to import. Unity works with FBX animations for 3D models and the .anim format for animations. Popular 3D packages can export both of these easily.

Creating Animations

Let's start building our animations for the player character. We will be creating the first few from scratch so that you can get a full understanding of how to create your own animations later on.

1. Find the Project files for Chapter 6 and load them in Unity.

2. In the _scenes folder, open the First_Animation Scene file to get started.

3. Select the Player GameObject from the Scene View or Hierarchy. Currently there are no animations assigned to it.

4. In the Inspector, click the Add Component button and select the Animation Component under the Miscellaneous section. Figure 6.2 shows the Animation Component with its default settings.

Figure 6.2   Our player character properties with the Animation Component added

Animation Component

The Animation Component plays back the animations for your character. You can assign multiple animations created within Unity to your GameObject with an Animation Component, which can then be played back through scripting. Let's look at the properties of the Animation Component:

- **Animation:** The default animation to be played.
- **Animations:** An array of animations that can be assigned to the GameObject and then played back.
- **Play Automatically:** If checked, this will play the default animation automatically.
- **Animate Physics:** If checked, the animations will interact with physics.
- **Culling Type:** Lets you determine when the animations will start and/or stop playing based on how they are currently being rendered.

Unity allows you to use only a single Animation Component, but it still allows you to assign multiple animations to it. Having multiple animations is great when you need a lot of variations or actions for your GameObject. A character is a great example because generally characters have a bunch of animations, such as an idle, a walk, a run, a jump, and anything else you may need the character to do. These are just examples, but you can see how you may want a lot of animations assigned to a single GameObject.

Animation Clip

We need to assign an Animation Clip to the Animation Component in order for it to animate our Player GameObject. But first we have to create that animation:

1. In the Project Browser under the _animations folder, right-click and choose Create > Animation.
2. Name the Animation Clip "Player_Idle."
3. In the Animation Component for our player, click the target next to the Animation reference. This will open the AnimationClip window.
4. Select the Player_Idle clip we just created. Tap the Enter (Return) key to assign the clip and close out of the AnimationClip window.

We have assigned the Animation Clip, but it currently does not contain animation frames. Let's take a look at the Animation window for editing our Animation Clips and adding these frames. Open the Animation window by going to the menu bar and selecting Window > Animation. Figure 6.3 shows the Animation window.

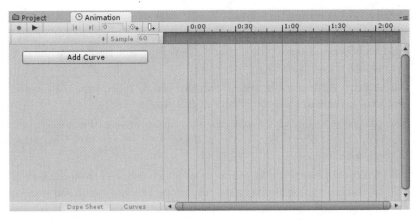

Figure 6.3   The Animation window docked with the Project Browser

Warning

There is a bug in the engine when creating 2D sprite animations. When creating the Animation Clip with the preceding steps, the animation type will be set to 2 (Generic Mecanim). This is viable for a 3D transform animation but will not work for our sprites. The method to fix this is to select the animation, and in the Inspector, set the mode to Debug (gear icon in the upper right). Then switch the animation type from 2 (Generic) to 1 (Legacy). Do not forget to set the mode back to Normal. To avoid this issue, try creating the Animation Clip by using the Clip drop-down and selecting New Clip in the Animation View.

Animation Window

When creating animations inside of Unity, you will always use the Animation window. The only exception would be when using scripted behaviors, but we will learn much more about those in the next chapter.

The Animation window by default looks empty, just as the Unity interface did when we first opened it back in Chapter 1, "Setting Up the Unity Development Environment." Don't let this fool you, however, as the window can become very chaotic and messy when dealing with a complex animation. Let's take a look at what all of the parts of the Animation window are before we dive in and start making our very own messy animations!

- **Record:** Lets you record changes to a GameObject by using its Transform Component or the axis handles in the Scene View to manipulate it and record the data. This can be handy for testing movements and positions in your levels.
- **Play:** Plays back an animation sequence from the timeline.
- **Previous/Next Keyframe:** Jumps to a previous keyframe or the next one in the sequence. Good for "flipping" your animations to see how they are working.

- **Frame:** The current frame. You can enter an absolute value or use the red tick marker to select a frame.

- **Add Keyframe Target:** Click to add a new keyframe to the timeline (based on the red tick marker's position).

- **Add Event:** Adds an Animation Event that can be called from the timeline. We will look at these in more detail later in this chapter.

- **Sample:** Sets the intended frame range for the animation. The default of 60 refers to 60 frames, or 1 second of animation. This value is typically independent of the game's frame rate.

- **Add Curve button:** Allows you to input which property from the GameObject will have an animation applied to it. Any property listed in the Animation View can be keyframed.

Note

A **keyframe** is a point in the animation that defines the starting and ending points of a transition. The transition can be accomplished smoothly, such as causing the sprite to slide up and down on screen, or it can be accomplished instantly, such as snapping a sprite immediately from one sprite image to another. The latter is what we will use for our Player GameObject's animations.

At the bottom of the Animation window are the Graph Editor and Dope Sheet buttons. Toggling these will set the Animation window to one of these layouts. Both of these are very different, but both are equally vital in creating smooth and convincing animations.

Graph Editor

The Graph Editor is the key to making strong and convincing animations for your characters and GameObjects. Through the use of defined curves you can control the movement from one pose to the next. When you set a keyframe at a position and time and then advance and set a second keyframe, the Graph Editor will determine or interpolate the values between the set keyframes.

Animating with the Graph Editor is for animations with Transform data such as a platform that moves and for skeletal characters that have rigged joints. These usually come from a 3D package where you can truly refine your animations and then bring them into Unity, but the Graph Editor is quite extensive in what it can do. Figure 6.4 shows the Graph Editor with an example animation and its curves.

Keyed Frames

The small diamonds represent keyframes that have been added or "keyed." They identify a value (to the left of the curves) that is placed at a point in time (values running along the top of the graph workspace).

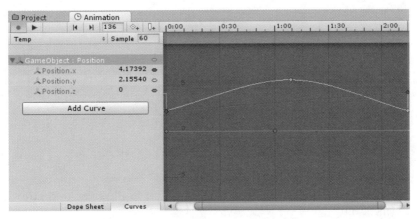

Figure 6.4   Graph Editor with example curves to show movement over time

In Figure 6.4, we can see that the topmost colored line represents the Y value of the Transform, simply by looking to the left where there is a corresponding colored oval for Position.y. We also can tell that the keyed value is 2.02088. By looking in the graph workspace, we get a rough estimate of the value, because it rests between 0 and 5 but not quite halfway (or roughly 2). Use the numerical input when you need exact values.

Tangents

In our example the curves flow in a smooth and wavelike form, but this may not be the action we intended. There may be an instance where you need your animation to move quickly and then stop suddenly (cartoon animations come to mind). We could use several keyframes, but less clutter would be better. **Tangents** are a means of effecting the easing of a keyed frame.

Each "keyed" frame has a direction the curve flows into and out of. Usually a straight path through a key is what you intend, but sometimes you may need to break the flow of an animation. The flow from both the input and output of a key is adjusted with the keyframe's tangent handles.

Right-click on one of the diamonds to bring up the Tangent Edit box (Figure 6.5). Here we can delete a keyframe or edit its tangents.

- **Delete Key:** Deletes the selected keyframe from the graph
- **Auto:** Automatically determines the tangent flow from the keyframe
- **Free Smooth:** Displays the tangent handles, allowing you to set the tangent direction
- **Flat:** Flattens the tangents to give a straight direction out of the key

Figure 6.5   The Tangent Edit box

- **Broken:** Breaks the left and right tangent handles to allow you to control them independently
- **Left Tangent:** Manually determines the flow of the left tangent only
- **Right Tangent:** Manually determines the flow of the right tangent only
- **Both Tangents:** Sets the flow of both tangent handles at once

Dope Sheet

The Dope Sheet (see Figure 6.6) has been used in animation for almost 100 years. It harks back to the days of traditional hand-drawn animating, when animators would block out the animation and then arrange each extreme pose to get the correct timing between keyframes. With complex animations, it can easily become troublesome to move keyframed attributes at once. Using the Dope Sheet, you simply select the attributes and then slide the corresponding keyframes in the timeline.

Just like the Graph Editor, the Dope Sheet uses colored diamonds. The key difference is that you cannot control the flow of the animation with curves. Instead, the

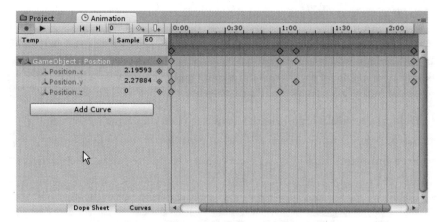

Figure 6.6   The Dope Sheet with an example animation

Dope Sheet allows you to easily select and drag symbols and rearrange them to change the timing and spacing of an animation. This can be quite handy when creating complex animations and you want to test the timing before going into the Graph Editor and adding extra detail.

The majority of the time we will be dealing with the Dope Sheet. The only reason for this is that our animations are mostly sprite-based and do not require any Transform movements. When the character walks or jumps, the actual movement is controlled through scripting.

Creating the Player's Idle and Walk Animations

In order to start creating the walk animation, take the following steps:

1. Select the Player GameObject. The Player Idle clip should be loaded into the Animation View.
2. Click the Add Curve button and, under Sprite Renderer, click the + sign next to Sprite.
3. Examine the timeline. It should now contain keyframes at the beginning and end of the animation based on the sample range, as shown in Figure 6.7.

We have our first keyframes laid down. As you may have noticed, these are sprite frames. Since we are dealing with a sprite GameObject, we will be animating the image rather than the GameObject properties.

If you hit Play now, nothing will really appear to be happening, simply because our sprite keyframes are of the same image. We need to add different frames between these, as well as adjust the frame range and speed of the animation.

Another reason we cannot view our animations in real time is a sprite-specific reason. An Animator Controller needs to be attached to the character as well. Take

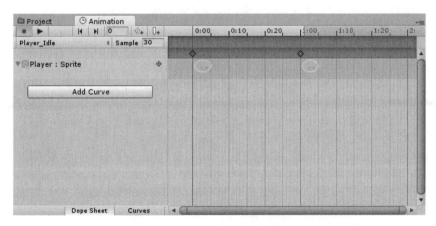

Figure 6.7   The keyframes recorded for the current animation

the following steps to create an Animator Controller and flesh out the Player_Idle animation:

1. In the Project Browser, choose Create > Animator Controller and name it "Player." We'll hook this into the Player GameObject later in this chapter.

2. Return to the Animation View and ensure that the Player_Idle animation is selected.

3. Set the Sample value to 30, which is roughly 30 frames per second. This will give us 2 seconds, or 60 frames, in which our animation will play.

4. In the Project Browser, use the Label searching and choose "character" to sort only the character sprites.

5. Select the p1_spritesheet_11 sprite, then left-click and drag it to the timeline.

6. Place it at the 1:00-second mark, halfway between the first and last frames of the animation.

7. Left-click the Play button to the left to view the animation on the character. This is our simple idle animation.

Now that we understand the process, let's create the main animation for our character: his walk cycle. This time we will create it slightly differently:

1. With the character still selected and the Animation window still open, click the drop-down next to Player_Idle and select [Create New Clip].

2. Name the new clip "Player_Walk" and hit Save.

3. Again, set the Sample value to 30.

4. Next click Add Curve. As we did on the Player_Idle clip, under Sprite Renderer, click the + sign next to Sprite.

5. Remove the sprite keyframes that are placed automatically.

6. Once again, from the Project Browser, use the Label searching and choose "character" to sort only the character sprites.

7. Select and drag the p1_spritesheet_9 sprite, and place it on frame 0.

8. Move ahead three frames, select and drag p1_spritesheet_8, and place this on frame 3.

9. Place the p1_spritesheet_7 on frame 6, p1_spritesheet_3 on frame 9, and p1_spritesheet_8 on frame 12.

10. Last, place the p1_spritesheet_7 on frame 15. Figure 6.8 shows our version with the keyframes placed.

11. Left-click the Play button to view the walk animation sequence. This is our simple walk animation!

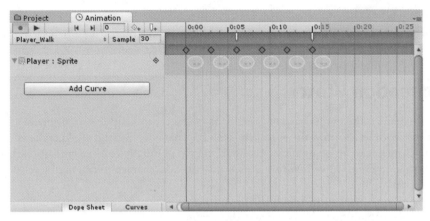

Figure 6.8   The Animation window with the final Player_Walk animation sequence

From here you can create more animations. Our character will need a jump animation and ultimately a damage animation. In Chapter 9, "Creating Hazards and Crafting Difficulty," we will see the enemies and damage take place, but we're going to add this animation now.

> **Note**
>
> Right now our animations are set up, but they aren't hooked in yet. For now, if you want to view the animations, you can do so in one of two ways. First, you can play the animation from the Animation window and view the output in the Scene or Game View. This will show the animation that is currently playing. A second way is through the Inspector. With the animation selected, look at the Preview window in the bottom of the Inspector. If your character is not visible, simply drag it from the Hierarchy into the window. You can now press Play to view the animation.

Animation Events

Another parameter we can assign to an animation is the **Animation Event**. This allows you to call a specific function or action from within the animation. For example, let's say you have a door with a light that activates when the door is shut and locked. You might have a script that makes the light active and plays an audio effect of locking. One method for calling the script could be to set it as an Animation Event in the door animation.

While we won't go into Animation Events in great detail here, creating them is simple enough. In the Animation window, right-click in the timeline and select Add Animation Event. You can also click the Add Event button that sits directly above the Sample value.

> **Tip**
>
> In order for an Animation Event to work, the GameObject must contain the animation with the event, as well as the script containing the function it should execute.

Animation States

In most games, the main character usually has some type of action or movement affecting it at all times. Simply, this is to help keep the character and the world realistic. Even if the character is not being interacted with, they will usually have an animation that plays to keep them "alive." We are doing this with our character with the Player_Idle animation.

But even with an animation made to cover every scenario (walk, run, jump, idle), being able to transition into and out of these requires a bit more detail. Unity helps with this by adding the Animation State Machine.

> **Note**
>
> **State machines** are a collection of discrete states, inputs, and connection paths. Based on the input received, the active state may switch to a different, connected state. As an example, a car's engine can go from an off state to an idle state and from an idle state to an accelerating state based on the input it receives from its driver.

The **Animation State Machine** allows you to connect a path or "flow," moving into and out of animations. Also named an "Animation Tree," it works like the branches of a tree where you can add and build onto existing animations and "trees." A good example would be the animations that play when a hero succeeds. You may just want a single "success" animation; however, if you wanted to have two or more, you could add them to the State Machine and then script for it to choose randomly between them.

Animator Controller

Our player character now has a couple of his animations ready to go! He has the ability to walk, jump, and stand idle. In time, he will also have the ability to take damage, collect health, and any number of other behaviors we might want to add. With the Animation Component, you can drive all of these, but a better solution is the Animator Controller.

The Animator Controller takes into account events and variables and helps control where and when blending occurs between these behaviors. Using a nodal workflow, it lets you see how each animation affects the next animation, and it lets you control how they blend and which animation takes precedence. On top of this, scripting is used to tell the controller when these new events should take place.

Tip

We added the Animator Controller for our character earlier when we created the Player_Idle animation. If you do not have the controller, you can add it from the Project Browser by right-clicking and choosing Create > Animator Controller.

Animator Component

Just as we added an Animation Component and were able to edit it from the Animation window, we need to be able to edit the Animator Controller as well. First we need to have the Animator Component attached to our GameObject, in this case our player character. With the Player GameObject selected, under Add Component, select Miscellaneous and then Animator (Figure 6.9). We can now assign the Animator Controller for our player.

The Animator Component links the Animator Controller to the character, meaning you could use the animations and behaviors on different types of characters. While most of this relates to 3D biped characters, we will use them to help drive and blend our character's animations. Let's go over what the Animator Component covers:

- **Controller:** The Animator Controller you assign to this character.
- **Avatar:** For 3D biped characters to define the type of 3D rig used. We will not cover 3D skeletal rigs in this book.
- **Apply Root Motion:** This again deals more with 3D bipedal characters, but it basically means whether a character will move in 3D space based on its animations or from a script.
- **Update Mode:** Allows you to set when the Animator updates per frame of the game. This is based on the frame rate at which your game runs. For this demo we can leave it set to Normal.
- **Culling Mode:** Controls whether or not animations occur when the object is not being rendered. This has strong optimization values as you may want your objects to continue moving in the background, for instance, but not want to spend any processing power animating that movement since the player can't see it. For the purposes of our game, we won't need to worry about this.

Figure 6.9   The Animator Component for our player character

Animator Window

We can edit the Animator Controller within the Animator. From the Window menu, select Animator. This will open the Animator window for editing our Controller. Figure 6.10 shows the Animator with the animations we have already created.

The Animator uses a nodal tree workflow. This means that a series of connections or nodes are strung together (transitions) to give us our final result. In our "Animation Tree" approach, the nodes are like the trunk, branches, and twigs of a tree, all connected in some manner to create a specific result.

Usually it starts with a base or "idle" animation to represent a state in which no input is being received. From here it branches out to other possible actions. The character might be able to jump, walk, or run. From the run he might be able to fire a weapon, engage in dialogue, or any number of other animations and actions. In essence, the flow of animations branches out like a tree.

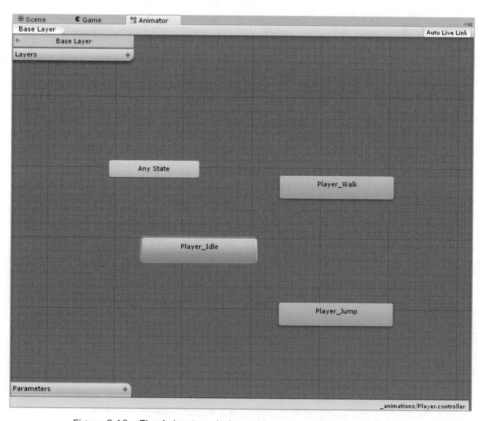

Figure 6.10   The Animator window with an example Animation Tree

Animation Layer

Animation Layer allows you to create a layering approach to your animations, with the top layer having precedence over the others. An example would be if you wanted to have a specific animation that when called would play over the top of the default animation—for example, a damage animation that plays when a character is trying to fire his weapon but is taking damage instead.

We will want to add a layer for our damage animation. Damage will be hooked up later in Chapter 9, "Creating Hazards and Crafting Difficulty," but we can add our layer now. The animation layers work the same as the Sorting Layers, from bottom to top. We want our damage animation to come ahead of our other animations. This way, when our player takes damage, it will have precedence over any other animation that might be playing. Let's set the layer up with the following steps:

1. Click the + symbol next to Layers to add a new Animation Layer.

2. Change the Layer name from "New Layer" to "Damage."

3. Leave the Blending mode set to Override.

State Machine

The middle section is the State Machine. This is the area in which you will add, edit, and transition between the different animations applied to your character. By transitioning between them and adjusting their blending, you in essence create a graph of the animations and how they work together. We will cover this in a lot more depth in just a second. First let's look at assigning some parameters.

Parameters

Here you can assign variables through scripts or other animations that will affect the State Machine when certain conditions are met. If we made a condition for our character's jump, we could set it to work only on certain collision types. So if our character is on water, we may not want to give him the ability to jump. By adding a trigger variable for our jump, we can tell our State Machine to play the jump animation only if triggered.

You can assign four types of variables to a parameter: a float, integer, bool, or trigger. We will look at a couple of these as we assign them. The first one we need to add is a float variable for our speed. We are basically saying that if a certain condition for speed is met, we want to transition into our walk. Let's set that up as follows:

1. In the Animator window, click the + sign next to the Parameter box.

2. Select Float for the first one. Change the name from "New Float" to "Speed."

3. Leave its initial value at 0.0. During runtime, the value will be modified by a script.

Go ahead and create the remaining parameters, and we will hook them up in the next section:

- Parameter called "Jump" as a trigger
- Parameter called "Ground" as a bool
- Parameter called "Damage" as a trigger

With these in place, let's look at setting up the transitions for the animations, and then tying in the parameters we just made.

Editing the Player Controller

Before we can view our animations working in the Game View, we need to update our PlayerController script from Chapter 5, "The Basics of Movement and Player Control." Everything needed to handle the movement of our player is in and working, but we need to hook the animations into these systems with a few lines of code.

Open the PlayerController from the _scripts folder by double-clicking on it. First let's add the variable for our script to recognize the Animator Component attached to our character. Just before the `void Start()` function, add the line shown in Listing 6.1.

Listing 6.1 **Accessing Our Animator Component**

```
Private Animator anim;
```

Next is the actual `Start()` function. Since we will not be using the `Start()` function for this script, we can remove it in favor of using the `Awake()` function. The contents of this function will be defined once the script is loaded into memory. That way this part of the script will be ready as soon as it is called. Remove the `Start()` function and enter the `Awake()` function code as shown in Listing 6.2.

Listing 6.2 **Awake() Function Added**

```
void Awake()
  {
  anim = this.GetComponent<Animator>();
  }
```

Next we will need to change the `Update()` function. There are a few additional lines of code we need to add. These will call the parameters for our jump as well as a bool to check if the character is on the ground or not. We will also need a flag to trigger the jump off and on again to perform our double jump mechanic.

Our `Update()` function should now look like Listing 6.3.

Listing 6.3   **Animator Parameters Callback**

```
void Update ()
{
  // Check for player input
  // Is the player pressing jump? Are they on the ground?
  if(Input.GetButtonDown("Jump"))
  {
    // Is the player on the ground?
    if(isGrounded == true)
    {
      // Zero out vertical velocity to prevent increased jump height
      // when going up an incline
      this.rigidbody2D.velocity = new Vector2(rigidbody2D.velocity.x,0);
      // Apply jump force value
      this.rigidbody2D.AddForce(new Vector2(0, jumpForce));
      this.anim.SetTrigger("Jump");
    }
    else if(isDoubleJumping == false)
    {
      // Mark player as double jumping so they can't jump again
      isDoubleJumping = true;
      // Zero out vertical velocity to prevent the previous jump's
      // velocity from influencing the new jump
      this.rigidbody2D.velocity = new Vector2(rigidbody2D.velocity.x,0);
      // Apply jump force value
      this.rigidbody2D.AddForce(new Vector2(0, jumpForce));
    }
  }
}
```

Last, we will need to set our Animation parameter for *Speed*. This will tell the code to play our walk animation when our *Speed* parameter is called. Update our `FixedUpdate()` function with the script shown in Listing 6.4.

Listing 6.4   **`FixedUpdate()` Function Changes**

```
void FixedUpdate()
{
  // Test if the player is touching ground
  isGrounded = Physics2D.OverlapCircle(groundCheck.position,
groundCheckRadius, groundLayers);
  // Get the material of the collider
  PhysicsMaterial2D material =
this.gameObject.GetComponent<CircleCollider2D>().sharedMaterial;
```

(continues)

```
// If the player is on the ground, clear the double jump flag
if(isGrounded == true)
{
  // Mark player as not double jumping
  isDoubleJumping = false;
}
// If the player is on the ground and still has the Jump Material active,
// remove it and reset the collider (workaround for Unity bug)
if(isGrounded == true && material == this.jumpMaterial)
{
  // Get the collider
  CircleCollider2D collision =
    this.gameObject.GetComponent<CircleCollider2D>();
  // Remove any assigned physics material from the player
  collision.sharedMaterial = null;

  // Disable the collider and immediately re-enable it to force reset
  collision.enabled = false;
  collision.enabled = true;
}
// If the player is in the air and doesn't have the Jump Material active,
// activate it and reset the collider (workaround for Unity bug)
else if(isGrounded == false &&
this.gameObject.GetComponent<CircleCollider2D>().sharedMaterial == null)
{
  // Get the collider
  CircleCollider2D collision =
    this.gameObject.GetComponent<CircleCollider2D>();
  // Assign the Jump Material
  collision.sharedMaterial = this.jumpMaterial;

  // Disable the collider and immediately re-enable to force reset
  collision.enabled = false;
  collision.enabled = true;
}

try
{
  float move = Input.GetAxis("Horizontal");
  this.rigidbody2D.velocity =
    new Vector2 (move * maxSpeed, rigidbody2D.velocity.y);
  this.anim.SetFloat("Speed", Mathf.Abs(move));

  if((move > 0.0f && isFacingRight == false) ||
    (move < 0.0f && isFacingRight == true))
  {
    Flip ();
  }
```

```
    }
    catch(UnityException error)
    {
        Debug.LogError(error.ToString());
    }
}
```

We now have all of the animations hooked into the scripts. Our character is now able to animate when walking or jumping; however, the speed and timing will be too fast. This is when transitions help to give our character a bit more life, and a bit less of that robotic feel.

Working with the State Machine

With our animations ready, we now need to link them all together. Using transitions and blending, we can affect how animations blend, as well as give them conditions for when they should play.

Transitions

Transitions are simply how an object switches from one animation into the next. Going from an idle position to a walk is an example of transitioning. The process is very simple, but the logic can be a little tricky. The best way to think about it is to ask yourself, "Which animation or 'state' am I able to go into and out of?" Starting with an idle animation, your character would be able to transition into a walk state, but also stop moving and go back to his idle state.

In the Animator window, with the Player_Idle clip highlighted, right-click and select Make Transition. Drag the arrow indicator to the Player_Walk clip and release. Once we set the parameters and add the last lines of code to our PlayerController script, we can see this transition in action.

Let's repeat the transition going back to the idle state. Select the Player_Walk clip, right-click, and once again select Make Transition. Attach this back to the Player_Idle animation. Our player can now transition between his idle state and his walk state.

Let's do this for the rest of our animation states. We will need to be able to go from a walk to a jump and back. We will also need to transition from idle to a jump. Figure 6.11 shows the animations with their transitions.

Any State

Any State allows us to set a condition where we force an animation to play overtop any other action going on. Basically, it will take any animation or "state" the player happens to be in and then interrupt it with a new action or animation.

A good case for this would be if you needed to play a looping animation, but if a condition was met, you could play an animation overtop of the looping one. Playing a damage animation would be a good example, but we will be adding this through code instead.

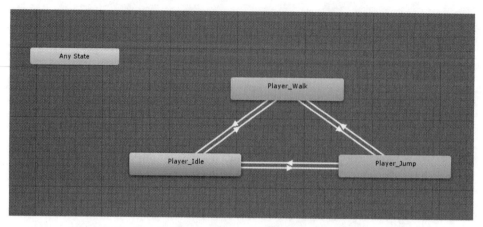

Figure 6.11   The Animator window with the animations for our player
and their transitions

Blend Trees

When using multiple animations, having a way to go into and out of them smoothly would be helpful. Having a great walk cycle and a great run cycle is good, but if they do not blend seamlessly, it will take away from the realism. This is when you want to add a Blend Tree.

Unlike an Animation Transition that blends between two animation states, a Blend Tree incorporates multiple animations that need to play at the same time, and all help to contribute to the final look.

Summary

In this chapter we have covered a lot of principles and best practices for adding animations and "states" for our character. We took a look at the rules of animation and how we can best add life and appeal to characters as we create them.

We looked at creating animations and adding them to our character. We looked at Unity's Graph Editor and Dope Sheet animation tools to better refine our animations.

Last, we looked at adding an Animator Controller and adding states and transitions to help link and blend our animations to make them as seamless and believable as 2D sprites can be.

In the next chapter we will look at adding the last few pieces to our character with some basic Rigidbody and collisions, as well as to the props and our 2D world.

We will add some physics and surface types to give our character and the world a bit more of an "organic" feel—some of that "bounce" that you find in a lot of platform games.

Exercises

We added our transitions, but we need to adjust the weighting as well as add the animation parameters to these transitions. This way the character will react correctly as it blends back into and out of an animation.

1. The jump states will need the *Jump* condition added to them. Add this coming from both the idle and walk state transitions.

2. The walk state will need a condition coming from the idle state. Add the *Speed* condition with a Greater than 0.1 value.

3. Add the same *Speed* condition when coming out of a jump state and into a walk state. Also add an *Exit Time* condition with a .98 value; this will let us transition out of the jump animation before going into the walk one.

4. Add another *Speed* condition going out of the walk and back into the idle state. This one will use a Less than 0.1 value as the player would no longer be moving.

5. Finally, add the same *Exit Time* condition, going back to the idle state, one for the walk state, and one for the jump state. These allow the animations to play and not abruptly halt back into the idle animation loop.

7

Setting Up Player Physics and Colliders

In this chapter we will take an in-depth look at Unity's physics tools and workflow. With the addition of the 2D game creation tools, Unity has also added their powerful physics engine to the two-dimensional side, allowing us to create unique behaviors and simulations, along with the occasional, unscripted, "happy" accident.

While the science of physics far exceeds the scope of this book (or most game design books for that matter), we will try to cover it to a small degree. Having a basic understanding of the laws of physics and how they work will help you in designing some realistic behaviors. Nothing screams "fake" or pulls you from an immersive game more than when something does not behave as it would in the real world. Even games that stretch the bounds of realism usually stay grounded within the laws of physics.

Understanding Physics

Just as the real world has physical behaviors and constraints, so must our game. In order to have something as simple as a character jumping, you must have some form of physics in place. With physics, we can give our world gravity and realistic forces, and our player their body mass and friction. They will be able interact and react with other enemies and the world around them. This will give them more realistic movement and real-world properties, which will help guide users to solve the puzzles and objectives they may face throughout the game.

Mass

The biggest contributor to realistic behaviors in our game is giving our objects mass. The mass of an object is determined by its resistance to force and its gravitational attraction. Put simply, it is the weight of an object and how it might affect other objects and the world around it.

An object's mass in Unity has an arbitrary unit of measure, meaning there is no real measurement of mass (kilograms) to specify how much something should weigh. The only rule Unity states is that the mass index of one element should not greatly exceed that of other elements. Try to keep them all relative in order to avoid weird results or issues.

Gravity

Gravity is another factor that helps to create believability. A game could be designed around the idea that gravity behaves exactly as it does in the real world, or you could take the exact opposite route and make a world with little to no gravity. The amount of gravity applied will affect how things move, how high our character can jump, and how an object reacts to a force against it. These are all things to consider when designing a game.

Force

Last, we need to consider the amount of force an object is able to exert and receive. Besides being affected by gravity and mass, our player will also interact with other elements in the game. While the enemies in our game do not exactly "attack," they will deal damage, which in turn will cause our character to react with a negative force. We will also have physics objects such as springs and platforms that our player will interact with. Their mass and physics properties will have an effect on how our player reacts when colliding with them. An example would be a sticky surface as opposed to a slick surface and how the player moves when walking across it.

As we move forward, we will go more into these rules of physics, but having this basic idea of mass, gravity, and force will help us in the creation of our GameObjects and how they behave. For now, let's look at a few other concepts we should understand before creating our physics Components.

2D versus 3D

Unity has a few subtle differences when working in a 2D workspace rather than in a 3D one. While they are only small differences, they are important and should be noted. We mentioned a few of these back in Chapter 3, "Creating 2D Sprites," but we will reiterate them here.

6DoF

In traditional 3D space, there is what is known as 6DoF, or six degrees of freedom. This refers to a Rigidbody's ability to move in three axes (up and down, left and right, or front and back), as well as three rotations (pitch, yaw, and roll), to give the object full freedom.

With 2D sprites, you lose the ability to translate with depth (front and back) as well as rotating with a pitch (forward and back) or yaw (rotating perpendicular to the horizontal axes, like a top). Since 2D is construed as "flat," you cannot truly go deeper into a Scene or rotate vertically around an object's pivot without faking it.

Z-Depth

Since we lose the ability to move in Z-depth (front to back), our 2D collision does not have depth either. This is good to remember. Even if the sprite's priority setting puts it in front of or behind an object, it will still behave as though they are on equal planes when it comes to collisions.

Rotations

Since a 2D sprite is a flat two-dimensional image, it really has the ability to rotate in only one axis: its directional axis. What this means is that if it can move down the Z-axis, rotating it will cause it to spin. Spinning in the Y will cause the sprite to flip, but as it does not have any depth, you would not see it as it flips. The last axis, the X, would act similarly to the Y, but top to bottom. Again, there is nothing to represent a 2D flat object graphically as it flips. We have set up a simple example (Figure 7.1) that may better explain this.

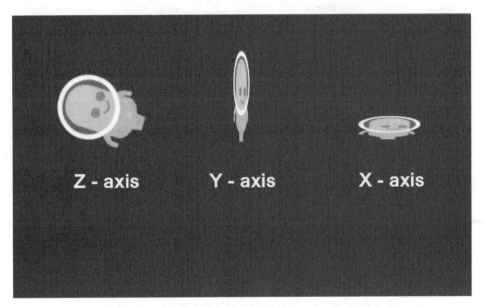

Figure 7.1   Examples of sprite rotation in the three axes

Physics 2D Settings

The Physics 2D Settings, shown in Figure 7.2, is where you will set all of the default behaviors for your physics objects. It also holds the Layer Collision Matrix. This allows you to determine whether or not the GameObjects on a chosen layer can interact and collide with GameObjects on another selected layer.

General Physics Settings

The following is an explanation of all the settings and options that are found in the Physics 2D Settings:

- **Gravity:** Amount of gravity applied to the Rigidbodies in your Project.
- **Default Material:** Default physics Material for any GameObject not assigned one.

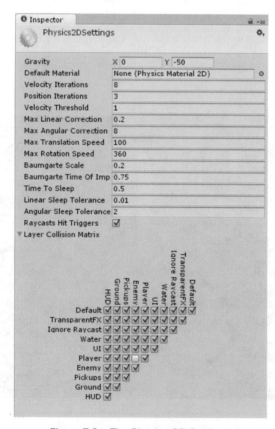

Figure 7.2   The Physics 2D Settings

- **Velocity Iterations:** Value that represents how often the physics engine iterates on velocity changes.
- **Position Iterations:** Value that represents how often the physics engine iterates for positional changes.
- **Velocity Threshold:** Determines the value at which two colliding objects will interact with one another. It is recommended not to lower this value below 1.
- **Max Linear Correction:** Used to correct positional overshoot from physics spikes.
- **Max Angular Correction:** Used to correct rotational overshoot from physics spikes.
- **Max Translation Speed:** Maximum amount of speed allowed by the physics engine. Use caution when increasing this value.
- **Max Rotational Speed:** Maximum amount of speed allowed by the physics engine. Use caution when increasing this value.
- **Baumgarte Scale:** Controls the scale amount of physics events as they compound on one another.
- **Baumgarte Time of Imp:** Controls the scale amount of physics impacts as they compound on one another.
- **Time To Sleep:** How long a Rigidbody must be at rest until the physics engine stops calculating on that GameObject.
- **Linear Sleep Tolerance:** Value at which the physics engine will continually check for positional changes.
- **Angular Sleep Tolerance:** Value at which the physics engine will continually check for rotational changes.
- **Raycasts Hit Triggers:** Returns a hit (interaction) if the object is raycasting and collides with another object.

Layer Collision Matrix

The Layer Collision Matrix allows you to control which GameObjects can collide and interact with others based on the layers to which they are assigned. This means you can have certain objects able to collide only with specific ones if desired. In Figure 7.2 you can see that we are allowing all objects the ability to interact with the exception of the player on himself. This is to avoid any anomalies with the physics of the player.

> **Note**
>
> If the dynamics of your GameObjects are unrealistic or not behaving as expected, you may need to adjust the GameObject's Rigidbody, or the Gravity or Drag values in the Physics 2D Settings. This is especially true with 2D sprites, as their weight may be affected differently. Also remember that everything is relative to the Scene, so use your best judgment when adding dynamics. Adjust in small increments and then test. Even slight changes can multiply the effects.

Rigidbodies

In order for our GameObjects to simulate realistic kinematic behaviors, we will need to attach a Rigidbody Component to them (Figure 7.3). Rigidbodies give the GameObjects attributes that mimic real-life properties, such as mass and drag. With a Rigidbody attached, GameObjects can act upon forces and torque applied to them, they are subject to the laws of gravity, and they can collide with other GameObjects. You can also script forces that will affect GameObjects with a Rigidbody Component attached to them.

- **Mass:** The mass of the GameObject to which the Rigidbody is attached
- **Linear Drag:** The drag or resistance on the object when translating
- **Angular Drag:** The drag or resistance on the object when rotating the object
- **Gravity Scale:** Amount an object is affected by gravity in the Scene
- **Fixed Angle:** Determines if an object can be rotated when affected by a force
- **Is Kinematic:** Allows gravity and other colliders to affect the object
- **Interpolate:** How the engine updates an object being affected by force in real time
- **Sleeping Mode:** Determines when the object is registered by physics; basically whether the object is "asleep" when not in use
- **Collision Detection:** How collisions are detected on the object at runtime

Tip

You can also have an object with a Rigidbody react to collisions but not gravity. On its Rigidbody Component, simply set the Gravity Scale to 0, and the GameObject will not be affected by the Gravity Settings.

An example of using a Rigidbody would be when you need an object to behave with force or gravity, such as a character falling. While this might be something that could be animated or scripted, the results are much better when they are dynamically

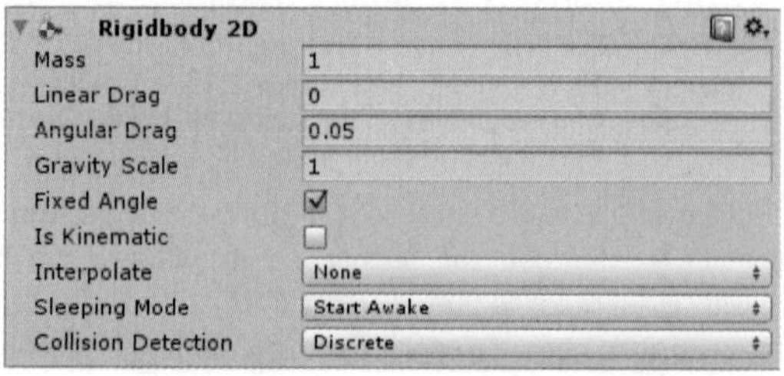

▼ ⚙ **Rigidbody 2D**		🔲 ✿.
Mass	1	
Linear Drag	0	
Angular Drag	0.05	
Gravity Scale	1	
Fixed Angle	☑	
Is Kinematic	☐	
Interpolate	None	‡
Sleeping Mode	Start Awake	‡
Collision Detection	Discrete	‡

Figure 7.3   The Rigidbody Component attached to our Player GameObject

built. Adding a Rigidbody gives the character mass and a resistance to gravity. As long as the gravity value outweighs the character's mass, when the character is no longer on solid ground, gravity takes over. Let's add a Rigidbody Component for our player:

1. From the Project Browser, Open the First_Level Scene from the Assets > _scenes folder.

2. In the Hierarchy or Scene View, select our Player GameObject by left-clicking on it.

3. In the Component menu, select Physics 2D > Rigidbody 2D to add this to our Player GameObject.

4. Make sure Fixed Angle is checked on and Is Kinematic is checked off.

Our object now has its Rigidbody applied. This means its actions are now influenced by the physics engine. But if you run the game, you will notice that the character just falls through the ground. This is because we have not given it any colliders to allow the player to interact with objects. Let's do this next.

> **Note**
>
> You can attach only a single Rigidbody to a GameObject. If your values do not seem to be affecting anything, or only adding subtle differences, just keep adding to the values. Make some tweaks and test. Dynamics can be challenging to get working but require even more iterations to get things to "feel right."

Colliders

Now that we have added a Rigidbody Component, our GameObject has mass, and it can interact with gravity and forces applied to it. But in order for this to happen, it needs to be able to understand when it comes in contact with these other elements. Our GameObject needs a collision type that will allow it to be affected by these forces and surfaces it comes in contact with. Let's look at the collision types available to us and then apply one to our Player GameObject.

Under the Component menu, find the drop-down for Physics 2D, which lists the four 2D collision types available to us. They are the Circle, Box, Edge, and Polygon Colliders.

Colliders all have unique attributes for their specific needs, but they do share two important ones:

- **Material:** This is where you can assign a certain physics Material to affect objects that collide with it.

- **Is Trigger:** With this checked, a GameObject can trigger an event when it collides with another GameObject. This is useful for setting up events you want to happen when your player comes in contact with them.

> **Note**
> We will go into greater detail on trigger events and scripting them in Chapter 8, "Creating and Applying Gameplay Systems."

Circle Collider

The Circle Collider adds a circular collision to a GameObject. It's a static collider, meaning the points of collision cannot be edited. You can adjust the radius and position of the Circle Collider.

Box Collider

Just like the Circle Collider, the Box Collider is not editable other than for size and position. You can vary the size in X and Y to create a rectangular collider if needed.

Edge Collider

The Edge Collider is slightly different from the Circle and Box Colliders. It uses two points to determine the length of the edge that can be edited individually to adjust the size in real time. Simply holding the Shift key while left-clicking a point will move that point in 2D space.

Polygon Collider

The Polygon Collider is a bit more involved but may be needed in certain situations for a GameObject that requires the collision to wrap it as close as possible. An example might be a large enemy boss with which the player can collide.

When a Polygon Collider is assigned to a GameObject, Unity will attempt to wrap the object with the fewest points possible. Usually this is sufficient; however, if needed, you can edit the points in the same manner as for the Edge Collider. While a Polygon Collider can represent a shape with excellent accuracy, it is also the most expensive collider to use in terms of draw calls (discussed in detail in Chapter 12, "Organization and Optimization") and should be used sparingly at best.

> **Tip**
> One slightly hidden gem is creating unique collisions based on the silhouette of a sprite. Simply left-click and drag a sprite onto a Polygon Collider and the collision will conform to that shape.

Let's create a Circle Collider for our Player GameObject:

1. Make sure our Player GameObject is still selected.
2. In the Inspector, select Add Component and then Physics 2D and select a Circle Collider.
3. Set the Radius to 0.24.

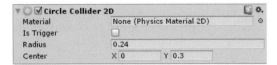

Figure 7.4   The Circle Collider assigned to our Player GameObject

4. Set the Center position to X: 0 and Y: 0.3. This will place the bottom of the circle flush with the bottom of our player sprite. Figure 7.4 shows the Circle Collider values for our player.

Take a look in the Scene View and you will now see the collider for our Player GameObject. All colliders are represented by a green outline. Figure 7.5 shows the player with the collision visible.

Note

Sometimes having the colliders be visible can be intrusive when viewing the objects in your Scene. You can hide them very easily, though. With the GameObject selected, simply click the arrow to condense the settings for the collider, showing only the name. In the Scene this particular GameObject will not show the collider attached to it.

Now that our player has collision, we will need to apply collisions to the GameObjects in our world. In order for our player to interact with enemies or collide with the ground and walls, every element will need its own collision surface.

Figure 7.5   Our Player GameObject with a Circle Collider attached

Adding collision to every GameObject would take a lot of time. Instead, we will add the collision to our Prefabs so that it can propagate throughout the pieces in the Scene:

1. From the Project Browser, go to the _prefabs folder and select the grassMid Prefab.

2. With this selected, from the Inspector select Add Component.

3. Assign a Physics 2D > Box Collider Component.

4. The Box Collider is created at the pivot point of the GameObject, which happens to sit at the bottom left. We will need to adjust its Center position. Change both the X and Y values for Center to 0.5.

5. Now in the Scene, all of the grassMid GameObjects will have been updated with a Box Collider attached to them.

Go ahead and add Box Colliders to all of the other Prefab GameObjects called grass. The grassLedgeLeft and grassLedgeRight Prefabs are the only ones that will not need a collider added to them. After this, run the game and you will be able to walk and jump across the Scene on all of the areas with the grass Prefabs. Our game is really starting to take shape!

Physics Materials

All physical objects have varying properties, which help make up their different surface types and how they interact with other objects. Imagine being hit in the head with a beach ball. Now imagine instead that it is a piece of wood. A beach ball's physical properties will behave (and feel) quite different from the wood's. This constitutes their physical properties.

Unity allows you to create physics Materials for both 3D and 2D colliders. Physics Materials affect only 3D colliders, while the Physics 2D are for 2D GameObjects. There are only two attributes for the Physics 2D Materials: Friction and Bounciness, as shown in Figure 7.6.

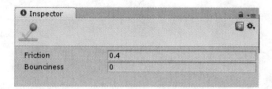

Figure 7.6   Example of a physics Material

Let's create a few physics Materials that we can then attach to some of our GameObjects to which we have assigned collision Components:

1. From the Project Browser, select the _PhysicsMaterials folder.
2. Right-click anywhere in the Project Browser and select Create > Physics 2D Material.
3. Rename this "Ground" and hit Enter on your keyboard to accept.
4. Change the Friction value to 0.01 and leave Bounciness at 0.
5. Select the grassMid Prefab from the _prefabs folder.
6. In the Inspector, select the target icon next to the Material slot of the Collider.
7. Left-click the Ground material to assign it.

Once again, you can go ahead and make these changes for all of the grass Prefabs in the Project. This way all of them will behave the same in our game.

> **Tip**
>
> Adding this physical Material with a low tolerance will have very little effect on our player or the game itself. We added this because we can always remove it later, or adjust it. This gives us a more modular approach when building the levels as the Prefabs have all of the elements we need, and we can adjust them at a much larger scale.

You can create a wide range of these physics Materials so that they behave similarly to real-world physical elements. Try varying the Friction and Bounciness values to come up with your own unique physical properties. Keep in mind your global gravity settings as well as your player's mass value.

Unity comes bundled with a Physics package that has preset values for a few different surface types, such as concrete, metal, rubber, and more. Use these as is or as a guide to building your own. The ones included are unfortunately all for 3D surface types, but keep them in mind going forward.

Constraints

The last part of simulating believable objects in the game world is adding constraints to our GameObjects. Constraints allow us to take objects with Rigidbody dynamics and add constraints (limitations) on how they are affected. A good example is a hinged object like a trapdoor. Adding a force against the trapdoor would allow it to drop, but the door would just fall with gravity (either indefinitely or until it hits another collidable object).

By adding a hinge constraint, we are able to tell the physics engine that this object has a point on it that will constrain it to its position but allow it to rotate with the force of gravity pulling on it. By constraining its position and allowing its rotation only in a single axis, we have in essence created a GameObject that can be released but will constrain its position: a trapdoor effect.

There are a few different constraint types you are able to add to a Rigidbody Component. Figure 7.7 shows them from the Components > Physics 2D menu.

- **Spring Joint 2D:** Creates a spring-type effect with two colliding GameObjects.
- **Distance Joint 2D:** Similar to Spring Joint 2D but adds a hard limit rather than a dampening, creating a hard impact when triggered.
- **Hinge Joint 2D:** Creates a point around which a GameObject can rotate. Can be triggered by a collision or powered like a gear to continually be active.
- **Slider Joint 2D:** Constrains a GameObject along a set path, like an elevator door. Can also be set to activate upon collision or continually.
- **Wheel Joint 2D:** Constrains an object to a position but allows it to rotate. This can also be passive or active in movement.

Constraints can be used for a multitude of different scenarios. Use them to create chains, doors, or lifts—anything you might need to allow the player to interact with and cause an event. But sometimes adding simple dynamics can help liven up the game and immerse the player that much more. Let's create a rope bridge effect for our level to give it some of that added dynamic:

1. From the Hierarchy, left-click the drop-down Screen14 group to expand its contents.
2. Left-click one of the bridge GameObjects to select it.
3. From the Game View window, hit the F key to focus on the GameObject you selected.
4. In case you selected a different bridge section, left-click on the leftmost bridge GameObject. See Figure 7.8 if you are unsure.
5. Let's rename this piece to make it easier to find later. From the Hierarchy panel, rename it "bridgeA."

Figure 7.7   The Physics 2D Constraints menu

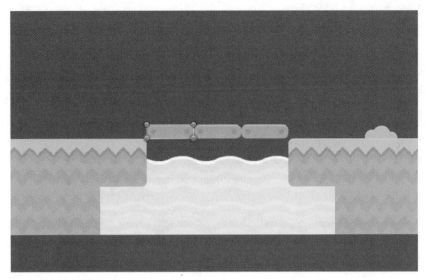

Figure 7.8   Our bridge GameObject with the Hinge Joint 2D attached

6. Assign a Hinge Joint 2D to this GameObject by going to Component > Physics 2D.

7. Select the middle bridge piece from the Scene View. Again, from the Hierarchy rename this "bridgeB."

8. Select the rightmost bridge piece. Once again, rename it "bridgeC."

9. Select and assign Hinge Joints to the bridgeB and bridgeC pieces.

Before we finalize our rope bridge simulation, let's look at the different attributes for the Hinge Joint 2D. The constraint types will have different attributes depending on their need, but the Hinge Joint 2D does share the majority of these attributes. Figure 7.9 shows the Hinge Joint 2D we added to the bridge GameObject.

- **Collide Connected:** Determines if any Rigidbody GameObjects can collide with this one.

- **Connected Rigid Body:** The Rigidbody tied to this object to create the hinge constraint.

- **Anchor:** The point around which the Rigidbody will anchor.

- **Connected Anchor:** The point from which the connected Rigidbody will anchor.

- **Use Motor:** When active, the Rigidbody will continually revolve.

- **Motor:** Motor speed and maximum force for the continual rotation.

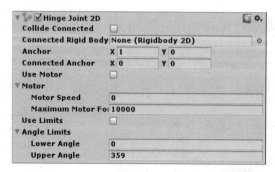

Figure 7.9   The Hinge Joint 2D for our rope bridge GameObject

- **Use Limits:** When active, sets limits for the maximum lower and higher angle values allowed.
- **Angle Limits:** Lower angle and upper angle values for the limits.

Now that we have applied constraints to all three of our rope bridge sections, let's set some of the attributes up to link all of them together. We will work from left to right to keep things simple and less confusing.

1. Select the bridgeA GameObject from the Hierarchy window.
2. Find the Hinge Joint 2D Component from the Inspector for our bridgeA GameObject. Again, if there isn't one, add it from the Component > Physics 2D menu.
3. Change the Anchor Y value to 0.14. This should place the anchor point to the top left of the bridge piece.
4. Change the Connected Anchor values to 130.9 for X and 1 for Y. The Connected Anchor point should sit on the slope of the adjacent terrain piece.

That's it for this piece of the rope bridge! Simple enough, right? Let's work on the middle one next:

1. Select the bridgeB GameObject. This time we will need to attach two Hinge Joint 2D Components to this bridge piece. This is because we will anchor this piece to the other two bridge elements. This will give it some movement when the player crosses it but will hold it to the other bridge elements.
2. From the Inspector, find the first Hinge Joint 2D, and left-click the target icon next to the Connected Rigid Body field.
3. Assign the bridgeA GameObject to this slot.
4. Back in the Inspector, locate the Anchor attribute. Set the Y value to 0.14.

5. For the Connected Anchor, set the X value to 1 and the Y value again to 0.14.

6. Find the second Hinge Joint Component. Once again, assign the Connected Rigid Body, but this time choose bridgeC.

7. Adjust the Anchor values to 1 for X and 0.14 for Y.

8. Adjust the value for the Connected Anchor to 0.14 for Y.

That's all we need to set up for the middle bridge span piece. Let's add the final values to the bridgeC piece:

1. Select the final bridge span (bridgeC) from either the Scene View or the Hierarchy.

2. In the Inspector, adjust the Anchor values for X to 1 and Y to 0.275.

3. For the Connected Anchor, set the X value to 134.1 and the Y value to 1.

With that, our rope bridge is set up! Figure 7.10 shows the rope bridge and where the anchor points are attached. If your physics are not behaving accurately, refer to the Chapter 7 example Scene to see how it was set up.

The final piece is setting the Layer mode of each of these three GameObjects. While our player can cross them, they will not be able to jump more than once. This is because we have not set the pieces with Ground properties. Doing so will allow the PlayerController script to treat the object as a Ground element. Switch this in the layer of the GameObject.

And with that, it is all done. Press Play and test it out!

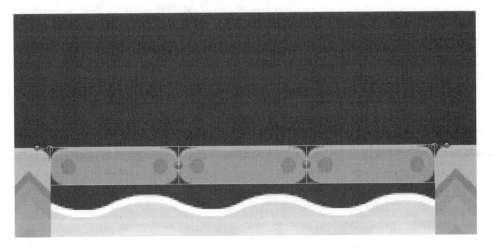

Figure 7.10   The final rope bridge with constraints

> **Note**
> You might have noticed that the two end pieces of the bridge had to have very high values
> for the Connected Anchor, while the middle did not. Since the middle piece is tied to actual
> Rigidbodies, the values were switched to local space. The end pieces do not have an object
> attached and therefore are in world space. Keep this in mind when using constraints.

Summary

In this chapter we took a look at physics and colliders and how they affect our
GameObjects. We went over Rigidbody dynamics and assigned one to our player.
We also went over the different collider surfaces and applied them to our Player
GameObject, along with setting up the physical Material types to simulate real-world
properties.

Last, we went over the 2D constraints available to us and what each of them can be
used for. Then, taking all three of these elements we just learned, we created a rope
bridge asset that behaves realistically with collision and dynamic reactions.

In the next chapter we will expand on some of the skills we learned here by adding
unique triggers for checkpoints and death planes. We will be adding a few enemy types
as well with their own dynamics and collisions.

On to the next!

Exercise

For this chapter exercise, re-create the bridge example for the other rope bridge elements of our Scene. There are two more places where the bridge should be identical to
the one we made here.

Just before the end of the level, we have placed one more rope bridge setup. This
one contains five rope bridge sections, but the same rules will apply. Remember to
move the anchor points and connect the Rigidbody GameObjects for the center pieces.

Good luck!

Creating and Applying Gameplay Systems

Now that we have a handle on the nature of Unity's physics and collider system, we can start adding gameplay elements to our Project. Our player can run and jump around, but we need to expand on what we have to create gameplay. We need collectibles to collect and coin boxes to hit. We also need to take into account that players can fall into the water or, eventually, get themselves knocked out by an enemy. Would we start them at the beginning of the level all over again? Of course not! We're going to create a checkpoint system to account for such circumstances. Welcome to the wonderful world of game systems.

In this chapter we will gain an understanding of Unity's trigger system and the functions it provides within the scripting language. We'll learn how to manipulate the player's location and use a bit of vector math to measure distance and angles between colliding objects. We'll also talk about enabling and disabling GameObjects and spawning new ones.

Trigger Volumes in Unity

A trigger is a piece of invisible collision geometry that defines a space within a game area. Unlike normal collisions, triggers do not throw standard collision events and do not block GameObjects from passing through them. Rather, as objects pass through a trigger, events are raised in a script that you can hook into. Triggers are an extremely useful way to react to events occurring in specific locations within a Unity Scene.

Trigger2D Functions

There are a handful of events that can be raised by any Collider 2D Component in Unity. The event functions, and the circumstances in which they are triggered, are as follows:

- **OnTriggerEnter2D():** Raised when an object first enters a trigger collider attached to this GameObject

- **OnTriggerExit2D():** Raised when an object exits a trigger collider attached to this GameObject
- **OnTriggerStay2D():** Raised each frame that an object is within a trigger collider attached to this GameObject

Put simply, a trigger knows whenever something enters, leaves, or stays within it. This has myriad uses in games, such as

- Opening an automatic door when the player approaches it
- Closing an automatic door when the player walks away
- Causing continuous damage to the player when they stand in fire

You can probably think of plenty more examples from games you've played!

Note

Not every trigger has to contain code for every event. If you're not making use of an event, feel free to leave it out of the code. It will help keep your scripts uncluttered and legible.

Adding Trigger Components to GameObjects

Adding a trigger Component to a GameObject is as easy as adding a Collider 2D Component. In fact, it's the same thing! Follow these steps to quickly create a trigger that we'll be putting to use shortly:

1. Open the First_Level Scene file.
2. Create an empty GameObject and name it "Checkpoint."
3. Click the Add Component button and select Physics 2D > Box Collider 2D.
4. Click the "Is Trigger" property to set it to true.

That's all it takes! Now, this collider will no longer act as physical collision. Instead, objects can pass through it and raise the appropriate events in any script Components that exist on the GameObject. Now that we can create triggers, it's time to make them do something useful for us.

Creating Checkpoints

Most games involve some sort of fail state for the player, be it taking too much damage, falling off a cliff, or missing a "press X not to die" moment. As designers, we need to consider how we will handle these fail states in the context of the kind of experience we want the player to have.

Let's look at the idea of falling off a cliff. Our map can have watery pits in it, and there's always a chance that the player will fall into one. How should we handle that? Is it the proverbial "Game Over," or are we going to treat it with more leniency?

For the purposes of this exercise, and in the interest of a more forgiving gameplay experience, we're going to take a respawn approach. Players who fall into a pit will be returned to the nearest checkpoint that they have successfully activated.

In Chapter 9, "Creating Hazards and Crafting Difficulty," we will also add a damage effect to this respawn in order to provide a penalty, adding an incentive for the player to better watch their step.

Scripting the Checkpoint Component

We've discussed how we want our checkpoint and respawn to work and have created a basic trigger as a starting point. Now we're going to create a Component to manage the trigger's events as they're raised:

1. Select the Checkpoint GameObject.
2. Click the Add Component button and choose New Script.
3. Name the script "CheckpointTrigger" and ensure that the language is set to CSharp.
4. In the Project Browser, select the newly created script and move it to the _scripts folder.
5. Double-click on the script to open it in the MonoDevelop-Unity IDE.

With the script in place, we can now tell the trigger how it should react to the player's action. While there are three functions available to us, we're only going to need to test whether or not the player has entered the trigger. Clear the default functions out of the script and replace them with the contents of Listing 8.1.

Listing 8.1   **The CheckpointTrigger Script**

```csharp
public class CheckpointTrigger : MonoBehaviour
{
  public bool isTriggered;

  void OnTriggerEnter2D(Collider2D collider)
  {
    if(collider.tag == "Player")
    {
      isTriggered = true;
    }
  }
}
```

It's a pretty simple script! Let's break it down. It has a single public bool variable—*isTriggered*—that we can use to see whether or not the checkpoint has been correctly activated. It also allows us to manually activate a checkpoint through the Inspector.

The event we're using registers when a Collider 2D enters the trigger. This means that objects without collision won't be recognized and won't raise the event. The script tests to see if the tag of the Collider 2D matches the player—we don't want enemies or collectibles activating checkpoints—and flags the checkpoint as active if it matches.

> **Tip**
>
> `collider.tag` returns the tag of the GameObject on which the collider exists. Alternatively, `collider.gameobject.tag` would return the same value.

> **Note**
>
> While we discussed error-handling techniques such as Try-Catch-Finally in Chapter 5, "The Basics of Movement and Player Control," you'll notice that it's not present in the scripts presented in this chapter. This is solely for the purpose of presenting the code in as legible and digestible a fashion as possible for this book. We always recommend the use of error handling in your own code.

Sizing and Placing Our Checkpoint Trigger

The size and placement of a trigger volume are extremely important. You want to be sure that the trigger is going to fulfill its purpose without interfering with other elements of your game. Given that this is a checkpoint and we don't want players to miss it, the size of the volume becomes increasingly important. We don't have to worry about players walking beside it in 2D, but we do have to worry about them finding a way to accidentally jump over it.

We created the basic Checkpoint trigger GameObject earlier, but it needs to be adjusted a bit in order to be useful to us:

1. Select the Checkpoint GameObject.
2. Drag it under the Scene1 GameObject in the Hierarchy.
3. Set the icon of the Checkpoint GameObject to something noticeable, such as a green circle.
4. Create a "Checkpoint" tag and assign it to the GameObject.
5. Set its Transform values to X: 1.5, Y: 1.5, Z: 0.
6. Set the Box Collider 2D's Size values to X: 1, Y: 13.
7. Set the Box Collider 2D's Center values to X: 0, Y: 6.

The trigger should now be centered on the grid, just as our tiles are. The small circle shows us where the trigger exists even when we don't have it selected, making it easier for us to select again in the future. It also indicates the specific point at which the player will eventually respawn, which is why we have it close to the ground. Last, the towering height of the trigger ensures that players will have no way to avoid it. Your Checkpoint GameObject should look similar to that shown in Figure 8.1.

With all of this done, drag the Checkpoint GameObject into the _prefabs folder for future use.

If you play the game now, you can see that the trigger's "Is Triggered" property is set to true when you walk into it. This is great, but what if something happens to the player before they even reach the first checkpoint? We can't assume that the player will walk directly ahead into it; they may turn and jump off the cliff instead. We could put the trigger where they spawn, as one option, but let's do something even safer:

1. Select the Checkpoint GameObject.
2. Click the "Is Triggered" property to set it to true.

Now there is one checkpoint active by default, so the player will never be without at least one respawn location.

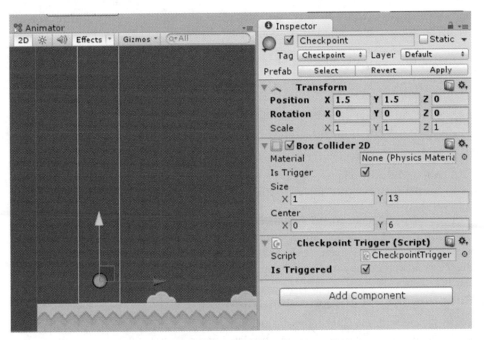

Figure 8.1   The finished Checkpoint GameObject

> **Tip**
>
> Always remember that how you *expect* the game to be played and how the game *will* be played are rarely the same thing. It's up to you to think of ways in which players may break your content or systems, accidentally or otherwise, and account for that.

> **Note**
>
> Content that the player is required to encounter in order to play a game through from start to finish is commonly referred to as the **critical path.** This is a term that comes up more often in games where the player has greater freedom of exploration, though we should consider our checkpoints to be critical path material at this time.

Using Checkpoints with Respawn

We can place checkpoints throughout our game level to remember places that the player has been. Let's make use of that information to create a respawn system that will place the player back at the nearest activated checkpoint after they fall into a pit.

Preparing the Pit Trigger Volume

We'll create our base pit trigger in much the same way that we created our base checkpoint trigger, albeit with a different script since we probably don't want to checkpoint the player as they plummet to their doom:

1. Create an empty GameObject and name it "Pit."
2. Select a recognizable icon, such as a red circle, to make it easier to find again in the future.
3. Click Add Component and choose Physics 2D > Box Collider 2D.
4. Click the "Is Trigger" property to set it to true.
5. Drag the Pit GameObject under a Scene containing a pit in the Hierarchy.
6. Adjust the size and position of the Box Collider 2D so that it's under the pit in a fashion similar to that shown in Figure 8.2.

The placement of our trigger volume is quite important here. We have to remember that the player can double jump, so a fall into a pit doesn't guarantee that they can't recover and jump out. By placing the volume a little way down into the pit, we are giving the player an opportunity to double jump to safety before we force them to respawn.

Scripting the Pit Trigger Component

Just as we did with the Checkpoint GameObject, we're going to create a Component that tells our trigger what to do when the player enters it:

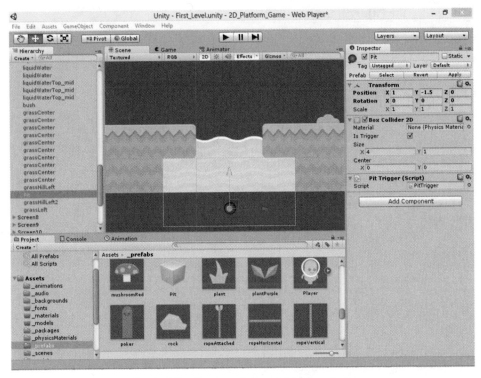

Figure 8.2   Placement of a pit trigger volume

1. Select the Pit GameObject.

2. Click the Add Component button and choose New Script.

3. Name the script "PitTrigger" and ensure that the language is set to CSharp.

4. In the Project Browser, select the newly created script and move it to the _scripts folder.

5. Double-click the script to open it in MonoDevelop-Unity.

The script will be relatively simple. We'll iterate through the level's checkpoints to find the nearest one that the player has activated and immediately return the player to its location. If anything other than the player contacts the trigger volume, we're going to destroy it to prevent it from falling forever.

Remove the default functions in the PitTrigger script and replace them with the code found in Listing 8.2.

Listing 8.2   **The PitTrigger Script**

```
public class PitTrigger : MonoBehaviour
{
  void OnTriggerEnter2D(Collider2D collider)
  {
    if(collider.tag == "Player")
    {
      GameObject trigger = GetNearestActiveCheckpoint();

      if(trigger != null)
      {
        collider.transform.position = trigger.transform.position;
      }
      else
      {
        Debug.LogError("No valid checkpoint was found!");
      }
    }
    else
    {
      Destroy(collider.gameObject);
    }
  }

  GameObject GetNearestActiveCheckpoint()
  {
    GameObject[] checkpoints =
      GameObject.FindGameObjectsWithTag("Checkpoint");
    GameObject nearestCheckpoint = null;
    float shortestDistance = Mathf.Infinity;

    foreach(GameObject checkpoint in checkpoints)
    {
      Vector3 checkpointPosition = checkpoint.transform.position;
      float distance =
        (checkpointPosition - transform.position).sqrMagnitude;


      CheckpointTrigger trigger =
        checkpoint.GetComponent<CheckpointTrigger>();

      if(distance < shortestDistance && trigger.isTriggered == true)
      {
        nearestCheckpoint = checkpoint;
        shortestDistance = distance;
      }
```

```
    }
    return nearestCheckpoint;
  }
}
```

This script is a fair bit more complicated than the previous one we wrote, so let's break it down.

We're using two functions this time: one for when the trigger is entered and a custom one that will find our nearest active checkpoint.

The `OnTriggerEnter2D()` Function

When an object enters the trigger, we first test to see if it's the player. If it is, we grab the nearest activated checkpoint and set the position of the player to match the position of that checkpoint; this is why it was important to have our Checkpoint GameObject close to the ground.

If no checkpoint can be found, we throw an error to the Unity Console. If the object entering the trigger is not the player, we tell it to destroy itself. This prevents coins or enemies from falling into the endless abyss and ultimately sucking up unnecessary resources.

> **Note**
>
> Since we manually flagged our first checkpoint as active, it's unlikely that we'll see the error log that we scripted, but it's there in case the script is used in future levels or something happens to the original checkpoint we placed.

The `GetNearestActiveCheckpoint()` Function

Now let's walk through our newly created function, step by step:

1. We create an array of GameObjects by finding everything with the "Checkpoint" tag.

2. We create a variable that will store the nearest checkpoint; this is ultimately the variable that the function returns.

3. We create a variable for storing distance to the nearest checkpoint; this is set to infinity by default so that any valid comparison will be shorter.

4. Iterate through the array (repeating steps 5 through 8 for each GameObject).

5. Get the position of the checkpoint.

6. Calculate the distance between the checkpoint and the pit trigger volume. This is done by converting the `Vector3` position values into a single float value using the `sqrMagnitude()` function.

7. Get the CheckpointTrigger Component off the Checkpoint GameObject so we can see if it's been activated.

8. If it's been activated and it's closer than the closest checkpoint we've tested thus far, we update our variables so that these values are what the next checkpoint will be tested against. If it isn't closer or isn't activated, we ignore it and move on.

9. With the iteration complete, the function sends back whichever GameObject was determined to be the closest activated checkpoint.

Note

We used a bit of vector math in this script, which can be daunting for the uninitiated. It's not as difficult as it may first seem. We highly recommend checking out some of the tutorials available on the Unity Web site, such as this primer video: http://unity3d.com/learn/tutorials/modules/ scripting/lessons/vector-maths-dot-cross-products

Save your script, load the game up, and jump into that pit. If everything is set up correctly, you'll immediately be snapped back to the closest active checkpoint, alive and well!

Drag the Pit GameObject from the Hierarchy into the _prefabs folder. You can now pepper your level with checkpoints and pit trigger volumes at will.

Tip

With modular Prefabs like our checkpoints or pits, you can quickly add a numeric identi-fier to the name as you place it so that it's easier to identify it later on (e.g., Checkpoint01, Pit03, etc.).

Creating Collectibles

Collectibles typically refers to items within the game world that the player can pick up as they play. Sometimes they're obvious, like coins, and other times they're hidden far from sight for explorers to find. Sometimes they add to the score or power up weapons. Other times they're purely for the bragging rights of being able to find them all. What-ever their purpose, it's hard to find a game that doesn't have them, so we'll be adding a few to our own game as well.

We're going to make a small variety of collectible coins according to the following specifications:

- **Floating coins**: These coins will hang suspended in the air and can be collected by jumping against them.

- **Coin boxes**: These boxes can be struck from below to cause a coin to pop out of them, which will then fall to the ground.

- **Three coin values**: We will have three values of coin: copper (value of 1), silver (value of 5), and gold (value of 10).

Some of these coins can be placed directly in the level during development, but the coins that come from the coin boxes are a bit different; these we'll be spawning at run-time via script.

Preparing the Floating Coin Prefabs for Collection

We're going to need a trigger in order to detect when the player comes into contact with the coin. Rather than make a trigger that's the size of the coin itself, we should consider making it a bit larger. From how far away do we want the player to be able to collect these coins? The wider the trigger, the easier it will be for them to do so, though it may look strange if we make it so large that the player collects the coin without appearing to touch it. Let's try the following for each of the coin Prefabs:

1. Select the coin Prefab.
2. Click the Add Component button and select Physics 2D > Circle Collider 2D.
3. Click the "Is Trigger" property to set it to true.
4. Set the "Radius" property to 0.3.

This gives us a trigger volume big enough for the player to collect at close range while still providing a bit of leeway. Once you've added the CoinPickup Component, feel free to play around with the radius value to see what feels best to you.

Scripting the CoinPickup Component

We're going to create a Component that we can attach to our coins so that the player can interact with them. With one of the coin Prefabs selected, create a new script and name it "CoinPickup." Enter the code shown in Listing 8.3.

Listing 8.3   **The CoinPickup Script**

```
public class CoinPickup : MonoBehaviour
{
  public int coinValue = 1;

  void OnTriggerEnter2D(Collider2D collider)
  {
    if(collider.tag == "Player")
    {
      Destroy(this.gameObject);
    }
  }
}
```

Our script will check to see when the player enters the trigger and will destroy the coin, giving the appearance that it has been "picked up." The public variable also allows us to set the value of the coin, which will come into play later in this chapter when we add stat tracking in preparation for our GUI.

For now, ensure that each of the coin Prefabs has the necessary Circle Collider 2D and CoinPickup Components on it. Set the values for the coins as follows:

- **coinBronze**: Set the "Coin Value" property to 1.
- **coinSilver**: Set the "Coin Value" property to 5.
- **coinGold**: Set the "Coin Value" property to 10.

Remember to click the Apply button on the Prefabs to save your changes to them. Your coins should now look similar to Figure 8.3.

> **Tip**
>
> You may have noticed that the scripts in this chapter frequently use the keyword `this`. It's a keyword that references the current object, and while it's not a necessity, it can help improve the readability of your code when dealing with some variables and properties. Both `this.gameObject` and `gameObject` are the same within our scripts, but we habitually use the former for clarity.

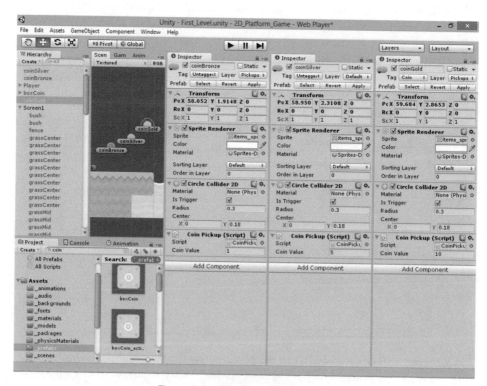

Figure 8.3   Finished coin Prefabs

Preparing the Popped Coin Prefabs for Collection

The player can run around and pick up our various floating coins now, but we're also going to have coins that pop out of boxes. We can easily leverage our existing coin Prefabs to make the new ones quickly. Start with the following steps:

1. Duplicate the coinBronze Prefab and name the new version "coinBronzePopped."

2. Duplicate the coinSilver Prefab and name the new version "coinSilverPopped."

3. Duplicate the coinGold Prefab and name the new version "coinGoldPopped."

At the moment, the new Prefabs are indistinguishable from the floating coins. They need to be influenced by gravity and responsive to the game's physics. To achieve that, take the following steps for each of the three new Prefabs:

1. Add a Circle Collider 2D to the coin.

2. Set the Circle Collider 2D's Radius property to 0.18.

3. Set the Circle Collider 2D's Center values to X: 0, Y: 0.18.

4. Click the Add Component button and select Physics 2D > Rigidbody 2D.

5. Apply the changes to save them to the Prefab.

Now our popped coins have all the same qualities as our floating coins. As a general rule, we wouldn't want there to be differences between how the two behave outside of the obvious; if the floating bronze coins look the same as the popped bronze coins, they should have the same coin value, for instance.

> **Tip**
>
> Consistent behavior is critical in games. It's important that whenever we use visual or audio cues to express something to the player, we're always expressing the same thing. If what you're expressing is intended to be random, ensure that it is consistently random; for example, if gold coins are worth a random value between 1 and 10, they should *always* be worth a random value of 1 through 10.

Preparing the Coin Box Prefabs

We need coin boxes that our coins can pop out of. These are going to be slightly more complicated Prefabs than we've done thus far, involving several nested GameObjects. After being struck, our coin boxes will visually change to inform the player that the box is now empty.

First, we'll create the active coin box Prefab by taking the following steps:

1. Create an empty GameObject and name it "boxCoin_active."

2. Add a Sprite Renderer Component to it and select tiles_spritesheet_122.

3. Add a Box Collider 2D Component to the GameObject.

4. Add a second Box Collider 2D Component and mark it as a trigger.

5. Use the Add Component button to create a new script named "CoinBox," then drag the script to our _scripts folder.

6. Drag the GameObject from the Hierarchy into the _prefabs folder to save it as a Prefab. You should now have a GameObject similar to that shown in Figure 8.4.

This Prefab represents the box before the player strikes it. The script Component we added is what will allow it to change to the disabled state Prefab, which we're going to create now.

Next, we'll create the disabled coin box Prefab by taking the following steps:

1. Create an empty GameObject and name it "boxCoin_disabled."

2. Add a Sprite Renderer Component to it and select "tiles_spritesheet_110."

3. Add a Box Collider 2D Component to the GameObject.

4. Use the Add Component button to create a new script named "CoinSpawner," then drag the script to our _scripts folder.

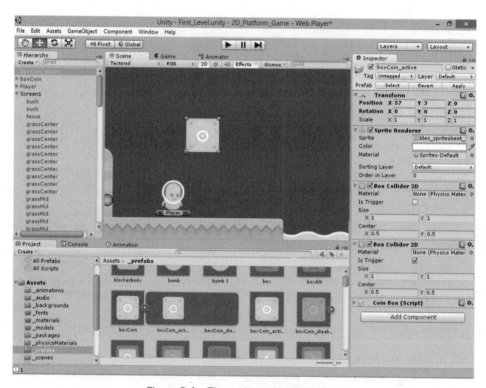

Figure 8.4   The active coin box Prefab

5. Create another empty GameObject and name it "boxCoin_spawnPoint."

6. Drag the boxCoin_spawnPoint GameObject and nest it under boxCoin_disabled in the Hierarchy.

7. Change the icon of boxCoin_spawnPoint to something visible, such as a yellow diamond, and position it at X: 0.5, Y: 1, Z: 0.

8. Drag the boxCoin_disabled GameObject from the Hierarchy into the _prefabs folder to save it as a Prefab. You should now have a GameObject similar to that shown in Figure 8.5.

The Prefab we just created has a second GameObject nested under it. We're going to use that as the location from which our coin spawns. By making it a GameObject, we can easily move it around to get a spawn point we like without having to change anything in our code.

We have one last thing to do before we're ready to start the scripting. Take the following steps to prepare the boxCoin Prefab:

1. Create an empty GameObject and name it "boxCoin."

2. Drag the boxCoin_active GameObject under it in the Hierarchy.

Figure 8.5   The disabled coin box Prefab

3. Reset its Transform to X: 0, Y: 0, Z: 0.

4. Drag the boxCoin_disabled GameObject under it in the Hierarchy.

5. Reset its Transform to X: 0, Y: 0, Z: 0.

6. Uncheck the box by the boxCoin_disabled GameObject's name to deactivate it.

7. Click Apply to save the changes to that Prefab.

8. Drag the boxCoin GameObject into the _prefabs folder to save it.

When we place coin boxes in the level, the boxCoin Prefab is the one that we'll actually use. It contains the active version of the coin box as well as the disabled version, which we've set to inactive by default (rendering it invisible and disabling its collision/scripts).

Scripting the Coin Box Component

The Component we're about to script will swap between the active and disabled versions of the coin box Prefabs when the player strikes the box from below. Open the CoinBox script and fill it out as shown in Listing 8.4.

Listing 8.4   **The CoinBox Script**

```
public class CoinBox : MonoBehaviour
{
  public GameObject poppedStatePrefab;

  void OnTriggerEnter2D(Collider2D collider)
  {
    Vector3 heading = this.transform.position -
collider.gameObject.transform.position;

    float distance = heading.magnitude;
    Vector3 direction = heading / distance;

    if((direction.x < 0.1 && direction.x > -1.1)
      && (direction.y < 1.1 && direction.y > 0.4)
      && collider.tag == "Player")
    {
      CoinPop();
    }
  }

  void CoinPop()
  {
    poppedStatePrefab.SetActive(true);
    this.gameObject.SetActive(false);
  }
}
```

The script employs some vector math, but it isn't as complicated as it may look. Let's break it down, one piece at a time.

The `OnTriggerEnter2D()` Function

- **`Vector3 heading`:** This `Vector3` represents the line drawn from the center of the trigger to the center of the colliding GameObject.

- **`float distance`:** This float is the magnitude, or length, of the `Vector3` that we grabbed above.

- **`Vector3 direction`:** This is the normalized distance of the line drawn between the two objects. Normalizing it reduces it to smaller values that we can work with for our test.

Using these values, the script tests to see whether the colliding object is the player and whether the heading is within a set of X and Y values that represent contact angles from below. If these all check out, the script calls the `CoinPop()` function that we created. If not, nothing happens.

> **Note**
>
> If you're wondering where the specific values for the contact test came from, they were actually the result of a series of tests. We placed a `Debug.Log()` command in the script to return the value whenever the player touched the box. We then tested the box from a variety of positions to get values that felt reasonable. Sometimes trial-and-error iteration is unavoidable. Experiment with it for yourself as well!

The `CoinPop()` Function

This function sets the boxCoin_disabled Prefab to an active state, causing it to show up in the game. Immediately after, it sets the boxCoin_active Prefab to a disabled state, shutting off its collision and scripts. This happens so quickly that it gives the appearance of a single object changing color.

We now need to fill in the "Popped State Prefab" property so that the script knows what object it's going to set to active. If there's nothing in that field, it will throw an error instead.

1. Select the boxCoin_active GameObject in the Hierarchy.

2. Drag the boxCoin_disabled GameObject from the Hierarchy onto the "Popped State Prefab" property of the Coin Box Component.

With that settled, we can move on to setting up the Component that will spawn our coin.

Scripting the CoinSpawner Component

Our spawning Component will create a randomly selected type of coin whenever the GameObject with this script becomes active. Create a new script named CoinSpawner and fill it out as shown in Listing 8.5.

Listing 8.5   **The CoinSpawner Script**

```
public class CoinSpawner : MonoBehaviour
{
  public GameObject coinSpawnPoint;
  public Object[] coinPrefabs;

  void Start()
  {
    this.SpawnCoin();
  }

  void SpawnCoin()
  {
    int random = Random.Range(0, coinPrefabs.Length);
    GameObject coin = Object.Instantiate
      (coinPrefabs[(Random.Range(0, coinPrefabs.Length))],
      coinSpawnPoint.transform.position,
      coinSpawnPoint.transform.rotation) as GameObject;

    coin.rigidbody2D.AddForce(new Vector2((Random.Range(-120, 120)), 700));
  }
}
```

Let's start by taking a look at our two public variables:

- **GameObject coinSpawnPoint:** This will contain a GameObject that we will use to determine our spawn location.

- **Object[] coinPrefabs:** This is an array (collection) of generic objects which we will populate with the coin Prefabs. [] designates any variable type as an array. The script will choose one of the entries in this array to spawn.

We also have two functions used in our script, one of which is a standard Unity function and one of which is custom.

The Start() Function

This function fires once, right before the first update event of a GameObject. In our case, it will fire the moment the GameObject becomes active. We're using this function to call our SpawnCoin() function and nothing else. While we could put the spawning code in here, having it somewhere separate means that we could potentially call it from elsewhere if we needed to.

The `SpawnCoin()` Function

This function will randomly grab one object from our array and instantiate it—meaning it creates a new instance of the object—at the location of our spawn point GameObject. Finally, we apply a little bit of physics force to the newly spawned coin so that it pops up into the air. The Y-axis force is a set value, while the X-axis value is randomized so that the coin angles a bit to the left or right.

> **Note**
>
> While arrays in Unity are zero based—meaning the first item in an array has an index of 0—it's interesting to note that the `Length` parameter we used in our random range will never return a value of 3, despite 3 being the length of our array. It will correctly return a range of 0 to 2.

Save and compile the script to test for errors, but don't run the game just yet.

Hooking It All Together

It's almost ready to work, but we still need to plug the appropriate objects into the public variable fields we've created for our CoinSpawner Component. We'll start by telling the Component where the spawn point is:

1. Select the boxCoin_disabled GameObject in the Hierarchy.
2. Drag the boxCoin_spawnPoint GameObject onto the "Coin Spawn Point" property of the Coin Spawner Component.

We still need to plug in the Prefabs for our coins, but these are a bit different. We won't be dragging them from the Hierarchy onto the property fields because we plan on instantiating them. This means that they don't already exist at runtime and will be created from a Prefab template instead. The following steps will finish setting up our coin spawning system:

1. Select the boxCoin_disabled Prefab.
2. Set the "Size" property of the Coin Spawner Component to 3.
3. Locate the Prefabs for the popped versions of our coins.
4. Drag coinBronzePopped from the Project window to Element 0 of the Coin Prefabs array.
5. Drag coinSilverPopped from the Project window to Element 1 of the Coin Prefabs array.
6. Drag coinGoldPopped from the Project window to Element 2 of the Coin Prefabs array.

That should do it! Save everything, run the game, and smack some coin boxes. Randomly chosen coins should pop out and fall to the ground. Running into them will cause them to disappear as though they're being "collected."

> **Note**
>
> By playing with the values of the array—the total number of entries and what is in those entries—you can change the odds of any given coin type being spawned. Just don't leave part of the array empty or you're going to see errors during runtime (unless you remembered to use a Try-Catch-Finally block to handle it!).

A Touch of Polish

Our coin boxes work, but they could be a bit more polished. We have obvious feedback that the player has successfully struck a box, with the color changing and the coin popping out, but how about adding a little "bump" animation as well so that it feels like we're really hitting it with some force? We'll do this by creating a small animation.

Creating a Bump Animation

Thankfully, our disabled coin box is under another GameObject so we can just use a Transform curve to make it bounce. Let's get it going with the following steps:

1. Select the boxCoin_disabled Prefab.
2. Click the Add Component button and select Miscellaneous > Animator.
3. Create a new Animator Controller named "Block" in the _animations folder of the Project window.
4. Select the boxCoin_disabled Prefab.
5. Drag the new Animator Controller from the Project window to the "Controller" property of the Animator Component.
6. With the coinBox_disabled Prefab still selected, open the Animation window.
7. Select Create New Clip from the drop-down menu in the Animation window and name it "Block_Bump."

We want to modify the position of the sprite we're using by just a small amount to make it appear as though the block has reacted to the player's contact. We can accomplish this by adding a curve that targets the coinBox_disabled Prefab's Transform position:

1. Click the Add Curve button and select Transform > Position.
2. Leave the default Sample value of 60.
3. Add keyframes for the Y-axis at 0:00, 0:05, and 0:10.
4. Select the keyframe at 0:05 and set the Position.y value to 0.35.

That's all it takes. If you scrub back and forth through the animation, you should see the box (if it's visible) bounce once. If it isn't visible, remember to make it active and then try again.

> **Tip**
>
> Our disabled coin box is moving 0.35 up the Y-axis locally because we have it nested under another GameObject. If we applied the same animation to a GameObject that is not nested under anything, it would move to 0, 0, 0 in world space, then animate up to 0, 0.35, 0 in that same space. All coin boxes would move to those coordinates when hit, so it's important to keep them nested under an empty object that we can use as an anchor point.

Adding the Animation to the Controller

We will need to add the animation to our controller, so locate the controller named "Block" in the _animations folder and double-click to open it.

You should be looking at a blank canvas. Take the following steps to set it all up:

1. Right-click on the canvas and select Create State > Empty.
2. Rename the new state "Spawn."
3. Assign Block_Bump to the "Motion" property.
4. Create a new state and name it "Idle."
5. Create a transition from Spawn to Idle.
6. Set the Conditions of the transition to an *Exit Time* value of 0.00.

The default animation—Spawn—will play when the GameObject activates, then will transition to its idle animation, which is no animation at all. There is no transition from the idle state to the spawn state because we don't want the Spawn animation to ever play again.

> **Tip**
>
> While we're spawning the coin as soon as the GameObject becomes active, we could just as easily call the `CoinSpawn()` function via an Animation Event in our Block_Bump animation. If the animation were a bit longer or more complex, this would be a great way to polish the timing with which the coin spawns.

Tracking the Player's Stats

We have the player collecting coins, but we're not actually storing that data anywhere at the moment. We're going to remedy that by creating a PlayerStats Component that will store information about the number of coins the player has collected and, eventually, will store the player's total health value as well. Nothing can damage the player at this point, but we'll be adding some hazards in the next chapter. In Chapter 10, "Creating the Menus and Interface Elements," we'll hook this information into the GUI so that the information is reflected on screen rather than only in the Inspector panel.

Create a new script named "PlayerStats" and add it to the Player GameObject in the usual fashion. Make sure the script is stored under the correct folder in the Project window and open it up in the MonoDevelop-Unity IDE. Fill it out as shown in Listing 8.6.

Listing 8.6   **The PlayerStats Script**

```
public class PlayerStats : MonoBehaviour
{
  public int health = 6;
  public int coinsCollected = 0;

  public void CollectCoin(int coinValue)
  {
    this.coinsCollected = this.coinsCollected + coinValue;
  }
}
```

The script is composed of two public variables—one representing health and one representing the sum value of coins collected—and a single function that we'll call when the player touches a coin.

The public nature of our variables means that we can see the values in the Inspector panel, allowing us to easily test and see if the number is correctly updating when the player collects a coin.

The CollectCoin() function takes an integer argument and increases the coinsCollected integer by that value. In this way, we can pass in the different values of the coins in our game and have the number increase accordingly.

By default, there's nothing calling the CollectCoin() function or passing it arguments. For that, we're going to have to revisit our CoinPickup script and update it slightly. See Listing 8.7.

Listing 8.7   **The Updated CoinPickup Script**

```
public class CoinPickup : MonoBehaviour
{
  public int coinValue = 1;

  void OnTriggerEnter2D(Collider2D collider)
  {
    if(collider.tag == "Player")
    {
      PlayerStats stats = collider.gameObject.GetComponent<PlayerStats>();
```

```
    stats.CollectCoin(this.coinValue);
    Destroy(this.gameObject);
  }
 }
}
```

In the updated script, we're getting the PlayerStats Component off of the colliding player and storing it in a variable. We then use that variable to call our public `CollectCoin()` function and pass it the value of the coin that's being picked up.

Save and compile the scripts, then run the game and test it out. Collect a few coins and then, using the Scene View, select the Player GameObject while the game is still running. The PlayerStats Component should reflect the value of all the coins you've picked up. Don't forget to apply the change to the Player Prefab to save it!

Note
The data we're storing on the Component is valid only in the active Scene. If the player moves to a new level, that Component's information will be lost. If you want to expand the game, persistence of data between Scenes and game sessions is covered on the Unity site here: http://unity3d.com/learn/tutorials/modules/beginner/live-training-archive/persistence-data-saving-loading

Tip
We've been leaving comments out of the scripts presented here to reduce clutter in the book's code, but you should always, always, *always* comment your work. Keep the comments brief, concise, and clear enough that you'll know what you were doing if you come back in six months' time.

Summary

In this chapter we learned about Unity's trigger system and how it allows us to react to the player's actions during runtime. We used the information to create pit trigger volumes to catch falling players and a system of checkpoints through which we can respawn them.

A number of Prefabs and scripts were created to support a collectible system for the game, and we briefly discussed some vector math for dealing with distance and contact angles. We also learned how to instantiate Prefabs so that we can spawn collectibles and other objects during runtime.

Last, we added a tracking script to the player so that we can see the value of all coins collected. This script will be hooked into the GUI in Chapter 10, "Creating the Menus and Interface Elements," so that the data can be reflected on screen.

In Chapter 9, "Creating Hazards and Crafting Difficulty," we'll expand the game with some much-needed obstacles and challenges in the form of enemies and moving platforms.

Exercises

We've created some valuable systems during this chapter. We should populate the game level accordingly!

1. Being mindful of how far the player can jump, add some pits to the level.
2. Place a Pit Prefab under each of the newly created holes.
3. Place a Checkpoint Prefab a short way before each jump (or each series of jumps if several are tightly spaced together).
4. Test each of your volumes and make sure the player respawns correctly.
5. Place some coin boxes throughout the level, paying attention to how high the player is able to jump in order to hit them. Be creative in your placement!
6. Play through what you've done and see how it feels. Does it feel comfortable to play? Can you effectively hit the coin boxes?
7. Save the Scene and Project files.

On to the next chapter!

Creating Hazards and Crafting Difficulty

We've been building this game one piece at a time, carefully fitting pieces together and building it up as we go. We understand how the player moves, and we've used Unity's trigger system to implement several backbone elements of the game. With this knowledge under our belt, we can now focus on expanding our game with some new elements in the form of hazards. We can then use these hazards as building blocks to craft challenging scenarios through which the player must navigate.

In this chapter we will create our first enemy and discuss a way in which to deal damage to the player. We'll create a system for placing moving platforms and then expand on that system to create a flying enemy type. Finally, we'll discuss the nature of difficulty in a game and some tips for managing your game's difficulty curve.

Creating Your First Enemy

The player can run and jump and fall down pits, but they're probably going to need more of a challenge—and more variety—than that. Let's add a Slime enemy to the world that the player must avoid. We'll give it a classic "shambler" Artificial Intelligence, or AI; it will walk in one direction until it encounters a wall, at which point it will turn around and head the other way. It will also change direction if it collides with another enemy of its kind.

Preparing the Slime Enemy GameObject

Our Slime enemy will be set up similarly to the way that we originally set up our player. Take the following steps to set up the basic GameObject:

1. Create an empty GameObject and name it "enemySlime."
2. Select a recognizable icon, such as a red rectangle, so that we can quickly see our enemy and its name in the Scene View.
3. Add a Sprite Renderer Component to the GameObject and point the "Sprite" property to enemies_spritesheet_16.

4. Add a Rigidbody 2D Component to the GameObject and check the Fixed Angle box so that our Slime can't get flipped over.

5. Add a Circle Collider 2D Component to the GameObject.

6. Set the Circle Collider 2D's Radius to 0.19. Set the Center values to X: −0.11, Y: 0.2.

7. Add a Box Collider 2D Component to the GameObject and check the "Is Trigger" box.

8. Set the Box Collider 2D's Size values to X: 0.1, Y: 0.2. Set the Center values to X: −0.36, Y: 0.18.

You should now have a GameObject similar to that shown in Figure 9.1. The trigger we created will be used to check for collisions with walls or other objects that would cause the Slime to turn around. The small size is important because we don't want it to accidentally contact something above or below it that would cause an undesired change in direction.

> **Tip**
>
> The circular collision we're using will allow the Slime to better adjust to minor hitches in the ground so that it doesn't get stuck if the collision isn't perfectly flat.

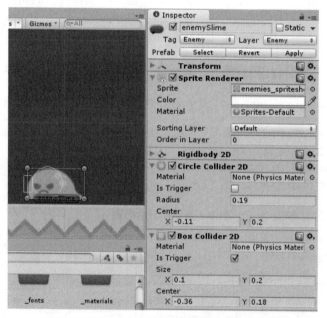

Figure 9.1   Initial setup of the enemySlime GameObject

> **Tip**
>
> If the sizing handles of a Sprite Renderer are ever getting in your way when you're trying to manipulate other elements (such as the vertices of a Polygon Collider 2D), you can hide them by collapsing the Sprite Renderer Component. Click the arrow to the left of the Component's name and those handles will no longer be shown. Just be aware that you can't move or scale sprites when you do that.

Inheritance and the EnemyController Component

Normally we'd create and add a controller script to our enemy at this time, but we're going to touch on class inheritance here as it applies to creature creation.

Enemies could easily share certain properties, such as having health, a score value, or specific flags. They may also use some of the same script functions. Rather than re-create these elements in every unique enemy controller script, we're going to create a core script from which they can be inherited:

1. Navigate to the _scripts directory in the Project View.
2. Right-click and select Create > C# Script.
3. Name the new script "EnemyController."

We're going to put very little into the script because the mechanics behind the game are simple, but this is an important lesson nonetheless. Open the newly created EnemyController script and enter the code in Listing 9.1.

Listing 9.1   The EnemyController Script

```
public class EnemyController : MonoBehaviour
{
  [HideInInspector]
  public bool isFacingRight = false;
  public float maxSpeed = 1.5f;

  public void Flip()
  {
    isFacingRight = !isFacingRight;
    Vector3 enemyScale = this.transform.localScale;
    enemyScale.x = enemyScale.x * -1;
    this.transform.localScale = enemyScale;
  }
}
```

The script contains a pair of variables that will be shared among enemy types, as well as a single—and familiar—function named Flip(). Since the enemies are likely to need to invert their facing in the same way that the player does, we've added the same function to the EnemyController script. See Table 9.1 for an explanation of the script's variables.

Table 9.1   **Enemy Controller Properties**

Variable	Type	Purpose
isFacingRight	Bool	Tracks whether or not the enemy is facing right
maxSpeed	Float	The movement speed of the enemy

Scripting the Enemy Slime Component

We've created our EnemyController script, but we won't be adding it directly to anything. Instead, we're going to create a script that will inherit from it as well as have its own code:

1. Select the enemySlime GameObject.

2. Click the Add Component button and choose New Script.

3. Name the script "EnemySlime" and ensure that the language is set to CSharp.

4. In the Project Browser, select the newly created script and move it to the _scripts folder.

5. Double-click the script to open it in MonoDevelop-Unity.

Clear the base `Start()` and `Update()` functions out of the script. For the moment, just adjust the script to match Listing 9.2.

Listing 9.2   **The EnemySlime Script Inheritance**

```
public class EnemySlime : EnemyController
{
}
```

Rather than inheriting from `MonoBehaviour`, we're inheriting from `EnemyController`. Return to Unity and select enemySlime. The public variable from our EnemyController script is now visible on the enemySlime Component, as shown in Figure 9.2.

Now we need to make our Slime do what we want: walk until it collides with a wall, then turn around and walk the other way. We'll put this directly within the EnemySlime script because not all creatures we make will act the same way. Let's set the Slime up to walk until it comes into contact with anything that has the tag "Wall." Fill the EnemySlime script out with the code shown in Listing 9.3.

> **Tip**
>
> An alternative way to set this up would be to create specific AI routine Components, such as a "shambler" Component that causes a creature to display the behavior we coded for our Slime. You could then attach this script to any enemy and have it act that way.

Figure 9.2   The enemySlime Component with inherited property

Listing 9.3   **The EnemySlime Script**

```
public class EnemySlime : EnemyController
{
  void FixedUpdate ()
  {
    if(this.isFacingRight == true)
    {
      this.rigidbody2D.velocity =
        new Vector2(maxSpeed, this.rigidbody2D.velocity.y);
    }
    else
    {
      this.rigidbody2D.velocity =
        new Vector2(maxSpeed * -1, this.rigidbody2D.velocity.y);
    }
  }

  void OnTriggerEnter2D(Collider2D collider)
  {
    if(collider.tag == "Wall")
    {
      Flip ();
    }
  }
}
```

The `FixedUpdate()` Function

The script uses `FixedUpdate()` to create movement in a fashion similar to what we did with the PlayerController script except no input is required here. The Slime is simply driven ever forward, based on its "Max Speed" property, in the direction that it is facing.

The `OnTriggerEnter2D()` Function

The trigger that travels in front of the Slime tests any colliding objects. If it encounters an object with the tag "Wall," it calls the `Flip()` function, changing the Slime's travel direction.

Save everything and run the game. The Slime should continuously try to move forward. Now it's time to prepare those walls so that the Slime can change direction!

Adding Walls to the Level

By now you should be very familiar with the process of creating a new GameObject and getting the basic elements set up. This is something that you'll do constantly when working in Unity, until you eventually have a full library of Prefabs from which to draw.

1. Create an empty GameObject and name it "Box."
2. Add a Sprite Renderer Component to it.
3. Set the Sprite Renderer's "Sprite" property to tiles_spritesheet_135.
4. Click the Add Component button and select Physics 2D > Box Collider 2D.
5. Set the GameObject's Layer to Ground, as this is something the player can stand on and, therefore, should refresh the player's flag for double jumping.

In order to make our walls work, we need a new tag and a wall Prefab so that we can quickly and easily place them into the level. We covered the creation and application of tags in Chapter 4, "Building the Game World," but here's a quick reminder in case you've forgotten:

1. Under the Edit menu, select Project Settings > Tags & Layers.
2. Expand the Tags section.
3. Create a new tag named "Wall."
4. Select the Box GameObject.
5. Set its Tag to "Wall."
6. Drag the Box GameObject from the Hierachy into the _prefabs folder.

Place a pair of boxes in your level, a few tiles apart, and place a Slime between them. Load the game up and watch how the enemy acts. When it encounters a box, it should turn around and head the other way.

Handling Collision with Other Slimes

The Slime changes direction if it encounters a wall, but it would be nice if it reacted to other Slimes as well, don't you think? There are a couple of ways we could approach this. We could set the Slimes on a layer that has no self-collision, so that they would pass through one another. In our case, however, we're going to have them change direction instead.

If we just adjust the OnTriggerEnter2D() function's IF statement to include the "Enemy" tag, there's no guarantee that both enemies will flip. In fact, there's a good chance that only one of them will. To prevent this, we're going to tell both of them to change direction at the same time. Update your EnemySlime script with the code in Listing 9.4.

Listing 9.4   Updating the EnemySlime Script's **OnTriggerEnter2D**

```
public class EnemySlime : EnemyController
{
  void OnTriggerEnter2D(Collider2D collider)
  {
    if(collider.tag == "Wall")
    {
      Flip ();
    }
    else if (collider.tag == "Enemy")
    {
      EnemyController controller =
        collider.gameObject.GetComponent<EnemyController>();
      controller.Flip();
      Flip ();
    }
  }
}
```

The change to our script allows it to grab the EnemyController Component of the enemy it collides with and order it to execute the Flip() function. With enemies doing this, we can create some interesting scenarios where the movement pattern of the enemies changes more often, such as is shown in Figure 9.3.

Tip

While there is no EnemyController Component specifically on our Slime, the EnemySlime Component that inherits from it is able to be captured at runtime and order the Flip().

Figure 9.3   Colliding Slimes in a moderately small space

Adding Animation to the Slime

We've created an enemy and told it how to react to various forms of collision. It looks pretty strange sliding along the ground, though. We learned about adding animations in Chapter 6, "Adding Animations to Our Scene," so let's go ahead and set one up:

1. Select the enemySlime GameObject.

2. Click the Add Component button and select Miscellaneous > Animator.

3. Navigate to the _animations folder in the Project window.

4. Right-click and select Create > Animator Controller.

5. Name the new controller "Slime" and open it.

6. Create an idle state.

7. With the enemySlime GameObject selected, open the Animation panel and create a new clip named "Slime_Move."

8. Set the Sample value to 30 and add a curve for the Sprite Renderer's "Sprite" property.

9. Assign the enemies_spritesheet_16 sprite to keyframes at 0:00 and 0:10.

10. Assign the enemies_spritesheet_17 sprite to a keyframe at 0:05. The end result is shown in Figure 9.4.

11. In the Slime Animation Controller, ensure that the Slime_Move animation is assigned to the idle state.

12. Select the enemySlime GameObject and ensure that the Animator's "Controller" property points to the Slime Animation Controller.

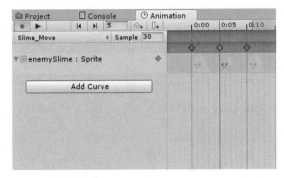

Figure 9.4   Keyframes in the Slime_Move animation

If you run the game now, the Slime enemy should play a two-sprite bobbing animation as it oozes along the ground, which looks far more acceptable than the gliding it used to do. If you haven't already turned the Slime into a Prefab, be sure to do that now. If you've already done so, hit Apply to save the changes you've made to it. Next, we'll work on some scripts that will allow us to deal damage to the player's health.

Dealing Damage

The Slime behaves the way that we'd like, but it's still not a "hazard" that warrants player caution. It needs to be able to deal damage to the player's health. This is going to be broken down into two parts: a Component that tells the player they *should* take damage, and some adjustments to the PlayerStats Component so that it knows *how* to take damage.

Once the Slime can successfully deal damage to the player, we'll update our pit trigger volumes to include damage. We'll also grant the player temporary immunity after they take a hit so that they aren't spammed with damage when struck by multiple enemies at once.

Scripting Damage into the PlayerStats Component

How do we tell the player that they've been injured? We could do it from the script that deals damage, but there could be many such scripts created as the game grows, leading to a lot of unnecessarily duplicated code that you'd have to maintain. Instead, we will add a `TakeDamage()` function to the PlayerStats script. We will call this function whenever the player is hurt, and it will handle the necessary math and effects from one centralized location.

Update your PlayerStats script to match Listing 9.5 now.

Listing 9.5   **Updating the PlayerStats Script**

```
public class PlayerStats : MonoBehaviour
{
  public int health = 6;
  public int coinsCollected = 0;

  public void CollectCoin(int coinValue)
  {
    this.coinsCollected = this.coinsCollected + coinValue;
  }

  public void TakeDamage(int damage, bool playHitReaction)
  {
    this.health = this.health - damage;
    Debug.Log("Player Health:" + this.health.ToString());

    if(playHitReaction == true)
    {
      Debug.Log("Hit reaction called");
    }
  }
}
```

The `TakeDamage()` Function

We've added a new function that takes two arguments: an integer and a bool. The integer reflects how much the player's health will be reduced, and the bool is used to determine if the player should play any sort of hit reaction. In this wây, we can use the same function for damage taken in situations where a hit reaction would look odd (e.g., falling into a pit).

Two messages are potentially thrown to the Console. The first tells us how much health the player has remaining, and the second shows only if a hit reaction should have played.

> **Tip**
>
> If you wanted to add healing items to the game at some point, you could use the same func-tion and pass it a negative number rather than a positive for damage, causing it to increase the player's health value instead. Re-appropriating a system for a new use is a fairly common practice, though it can get quite messy.

Creating the Damage Trigger

We're going to create a trigger for the express purpose of dealing damage to the player when they come into contact with it so that our Slime can injure them as it oozes its way through the game world. While we could leverage part of the Slime that we already have here, it would actually become a problem later on when we make some layer adjustments so that the player and enemies don't physically collide. We're simply going to nest a second GameObject under the enemySlime GameObject. Set one up as follows:

1. With the Slime selected, create an empty child GameObject and name it "triggerDamage."
2. Add a Circle Collider 2D Component and check the "Is Trigger" box.
3. Set the Circle Collider 2D's radius to 0.22. Set the Center values to X: −0.11, Y: 0.15.

This should give us a circle that, while larger than the collision we provided the Slime with, should cleanly encompass the bulk of the sprite's visual footprint. We could use a Polygon Collider 2D Component to more accurately match the Slime's shape, but this way will make allowances for players touching the outer edge of the enemy without harm. It will feel a bit more forgiving. Conversely, making the collision a box would likely feel unfairly punishing. What we have created is a good compromise between accuracy and efficiency that errs on the side of favoring the player.

On to the scripting! Take the following steps (this routine is likely becoming second nature to you by now):

1. Select the triggerDamage GameObject.
2. Click the Add Component button and choose New Script.
3. Name the script "ContactDamage" and ensure that the language is set to CSharp.
4. In the Project Browser, select the newly created script and move it to the _scripts folder.
5. Double-click the script to open it in MonoDevelop–Unity and fill the script out as shown in Listing 9.6.

Listing 9.6   **The ContactDamage Script**

```csharp
public class ContactDamage : MonoBehaviour
{
  public int damage = 1;
  public bool playHitReaction = false;

  void OnTriggerEnter2D(Collider2D collider)
  {
    if(collider.tag == "Player")
    {
      PlayerStats stats = collider.gameObject.GetComponent<PlayerStats>();
      stats.TakeDamage(this.damage, this.playHitReaction);
    }
  }
}
```

Table 9.2   **Contact Damage Properties**

Variable	Type	Purpose
damage	Integer	The amount of health that the player will lose
playHitReaction	Bool	Tracks whether or not the player should play the hit reaction found in `PlayerStats.TakeDamage()`

The two public variables—described in Table 9.2—control the amount of damage sustained and whether or not a hit reaction should be played. This way, we can quickly adjust how much damage is dealt on a case-by-case basis (e.g., an enemy may deal less damage than falling into a pit), or set it not to fire a hit reaction in the case of pits or other, similar hazards.

We could even use a negative damage number to act as healing, though our script currently doesn't account for the player having more than 6 health.

The `OnTriggerEnter2D()` Function

The trigger simply checks whether or not it has contacted anything with the "Player" tag, and if it has, it calls the `PlayerStats.TakeDamage()` function we just created. The *damage* and *playHitReaction* values are passed to that function as arguments; they aren't actually used within this script.

Save the script and return to Unity. Select the Slime's triggerDamage GameObject and check the Play Hit Reaction box, as we want the player to eventually react to being struck by an enemy. If the player touches the Slime, you should see messages in the Console informing you of the player's remaining health and stating that a hit reaction was called. Make sure you apply changes to the enemySlime Prefab to save it. Your triggerDamage GameObject should now look similar to that shown in Figure 9.5.

Passing through the Player's Space

When testing the damage script, you probably noticed that the player and the Slime can push one another around. This is because both GameObjects have Rigidbody 2D Components and exist on the same layer. Naturally, they are colliding with one another and applying force. Amusing as it can be to push the enemies around, it doesn't quite feel right for this game.

We're going to make some simple changes to the enemySlime GameObject so that it passes through space occupied by the player but still collides with everything else in the world:

1. Open the Edit menu and select Project Settings > Tags & Layers. If it doesn't already exist, create a layer named "Enemy."

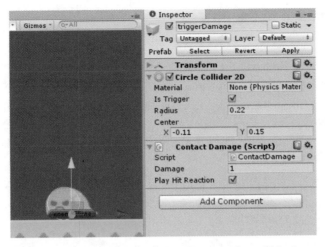

Figure 9.5   The finished triggerDamage GameObject

2. Open the Edit menu and select Project Settings > Physics 2D.

3. In the Layer Collision Matrix box, locate the box for Player/Enemy. Uncheck this box so that the two layers no longer collide.

4. Select the enemySlime GameObject and assign it to the Enemy Layer. When the Change Layer prompt appears, select "No, this object only."

5. Select the triggerDamage GameObject and assign it to the Default Layer if it isn't already.

What we've just done is tell the game that our Slime enemy should never collide with the player. It will walk right through them as though they aren't even there. However, the trigger we use to deal damage exists in a layer that the player collides with so it will still harm them. This is why we put our damage trigger on a nested GameObject, rather than adding a trigger to the enemy itself.

Start the game up and give it a try. You should see the usual Console messages for damage when the Slime passes through the player!

> **Note**
> The Trigger2D events in a script can't naturally identify what trigger called them, so having multiple triggers on one GameObject that are all meant to do something different can become tricky to manage. We recommend against putting yourself in that position. A nested GameObject with its own trigger makes for a much cleaner solution.

Adding Damage to the Pits

This is a short and sweet affair that makes our pits into proper hazards:

1. Select the Pit Prefab in the Project View.
2. Click the Add Component button and select Scripts > ContactDamage.
3. Set the "Damage" property to a value of 2. We're going to make falling into a pit really hurt.
4. Check the Play Hit Reaction box. Your Pit Prefab should now look similar to that shown in Figure 9.6.

That's it! Load the game up and have the player jump into a pit trigger. In addition to being respawned, you'll see damage messages in the Console. Now they're a proper threat to the player's survival.

Adding Temporary Immunity Post-Damage

You may have noticed that your player's health plummets quite quickly if they get caught by a couple of Slimes, as they deal damage with each contact of the trigger. This seems horribly unfair to the player as we're punishing them repeatedly for one mistake. To remedy this, we should add a brief period in which the player cannot be harmed after taking a hit.

To accomplish this, we're going to introduce time measurement into our PlayerStats script. For a brief period, we'll prevent the player from being harmed if they contact another damage trigger.

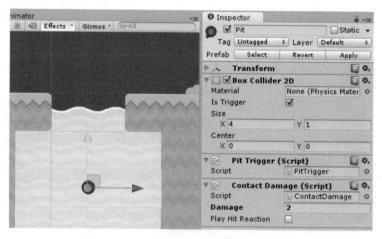

Figure 9.6   An updated instance of the Pit Prefab

We're going to assume that, in this game, the immunity is a triggered response to a hit reaction, so no hit reaction means no immunity will be granted. We could always split the immunity and hit reaction into separate functions if that were not the case. Refer to Listing 9.7 for new variables and a new function.

Listing 9.7   **Expanding the PlayerStats Script**

```
public bool isImmune = false;
public float immunityDuration = 1.5f;
private float immunityTime = 0f;

void Update()
{
  if(this.isImmune == true)
  {
    immunityTime = immunityTime + Time.deltaTime;
    if(immunityTime >= immunityDuration)
    {
      this.isImmune = false;
      Debug.Log("Immunity has ended");
    }
  }
}

public void TakeDamage(int damage, bool playHitReaction)
{
  if(this.isImmune == false)
  {
    this.health = this.health - damage;
    Debug.Log("Player Health:" + this.health.ToString());

    if(playHitReaction == true)
    {
      Debug.Log("Immunity has started");
      PlayHitReaction();
    }
  }
}

void PlayHitReaction()
{
  this.isImmune = true;
  this.immunityTime = 0f;
  this.gameObject.GetComponent<Animator>().SetTrigger("Damage");
}
```

Table 9.3   **New PlayerStats Properties**

Variable	Type	Purpose
isImmune	Bool	Tracks whether or not the player is currently considered to be immune to damage
immunityDuration	Float	The total time (in seconds) during which the player is immune to further damage
immunityTime	Float	The elapsed time (in seconds) during which the player has had immunity thus far

We've added several new variables—two public, one only for internal use—to the script. We've also updated the `Update()` and `TakeDamage()` functions as well as added a `PlayHitReaction()` function. Let's look it over, one piece at a time. Table 9.3 describes each of the new variables.

Updates to the `TakeDamage()` Function

`TakeDamage()` now includes a check against the *isImmune* bool; nothing will be done if the player is told to take damage while that flag is true. The Console message has been updated to state that the immunity duration has started and the `PlayHitReaction()` function is then called.

> **Tip**
>
> Try to think ahead as you write your scripts. In the preceding example, we're preventing anything from happening if the player is currently immune. It makes sense, doesn't it? However, if we were later to add healing by throwing negative values at the `TakeDamage()` function, the player wouldn't be able to heal while immune. We could easily fix that, here, by expanding the conditional statement, but it's something to keep in mind while you work regardless. What you write a system to *do,* and how you *use* it, can wind up quite different!

The `PlayHitReaction()` Function

There is very little to this function. It sets *isImmune* to true, marking the player as temporarily immune, and sets the *immunityTime* counter to 0. This counter will be used to track the duration in which the player has been immune so that we can tell when to remove it. The `Update()` function will be updated with the code necessary to track this. Last, we're throwing an animation trigger call to the Player GameObject's Animator Component. This will cause it to play the damage animation that was prepared in Chapter 6, "Adding Animations to Our Scene."

The `Updated Update()` Function

The `Update()` function now increments the immunityTime value by using `Time.DeltaTime`, which tracks how much time has passed since the previous frame. This is extremely useful for anything that you want to happen over a set period of time.

If the elapsed time equals or exceeds the duration we set for immunity, the immunity flag is revoked and a message is thrown to the Console.

Return to Unity and run the game. Run around with a Slime or two and see what happens. You should no longer see additional damage messages in the Console until the message stating that immunity has ended is shown.

> **Note**
>
> Timed work like this can also be accomplished using coroutines, but those are a little outside the scope of what we're addressing here. Please refer to the excellent tutorials on the Unity site when you want to expand your knowledge beyond what we discuss: http://unity3d.com/learn/tutorials/modules/intermediate/scripting/coroutines

Visually Representing Immunity, the Classical Way

Console messages are well and good for us, as developers, testing and monitoring our systems, but they do nothing for players. We need something to visually represent the temporary immunity for all to see.

In classic sprite-based games, such conditions are often conveyed by causing the sprite to flicker for a few moments. As this is such a recognizable visual cue, let's do the same. We'll be making some further changes to the PlayerStats script, as seen in Listing 9.8.

Listing 9.8   **Further Expanding the PlayerStats Script**

```
private float flickerDuration = 0.1f;
private float flickerTime = 0f;
private SpriteRenderer spriteRenderer;

void Start()
{
  spriteRenderer = this.gameObject.GetComponent<SpriteRenderer>();
}

void Update()
{
  if(this.isImmune == true)
  {
    SpriteFlicker();
    immunityTime = immunityTime + Time.deltaTime;

    if(immunityTime >= immunityDuration)
    {
      this.isImmune = false;
      this.spriteRenderer.enabled = true;
```

(continues)

```
    }
  }
}

void SpriteFlicker()
{
  if(this.flickerTime < this.flickerDuration)
  {
    this.flickerTime = this.flickerTime + Time.deltaTime;
  }
  else if (this.flickerTime >= this.flickerDuration)
  {
    spriteRenderer.enabled = !(spriteRenderer.enabled);
    this.flickerTime = 0;
  }
}
```

We've added a few new variable declarations—described in Table 9.4—to the top of the script. We've also updated the Update() function and added both Start() and SpriteFlicker() functions.

The Start() Function

This is a default function that all Unity GameObjects can have. We're going to use it simply to grab the Sprite Renderer Component off the Player GameObject. Alternatively, we could make it a public variable and plug the Sprite Renderer Component directly into it, but as we have only one such Component here, we'll do it this way instead. This prevents errors in case we forgot to plug in the Sprite Renderer.

The SpriteFlicker() Function

This is a new function that will handle our flickering effect. It measures the amount of time elapsed—again using Time.DeltaTime—against the *flickerDuration* value. Whenever that value is reached or exceeded, the state of the Sprite Renderer's "enabled"

Table 9.4   (More) New PlayerStats Properties

Variable	Type	Purpose
flickerDuration	Float	The length of time (in seconds) that the sprite is rendered or not. This determines how frequently the sprite flickers.
flickerTime	Float	The elapsed time (in seconds) that the current flicker state of the sprite has lasted.
spriteRenderer	SpriteRenderer	The Sprite Renderer Component that we will be enabling/disabling to create the flicker effect.

property is inverted. If it's on, we turn it off, and vice versa. The *flickerTime* variable is reset to a value of 0 when we do so.

(Another) Update to the `Update()` Function

The Console messages were removed as they're no longer necessary. If the player is currently immune, we call the `SpriteFlicker()` function. When we remove immunity, we forcibly set the Sprite Renderer Component's "enabled" property to true. This ensures that the player doesn't accidentally wind up invisible due to a quirk of timing!

Save everything and run the game. When you touch a Slime, your character should now flicker! Feel free to play with the *flickerDuration* variable in PlayerStats to get a flicker frequency that feels good to you.

Handling Player Death

Now that we can deal damage, it's entirely possible that the player will run out of health and perish. We'll hook this into a proper Game Over screen in Chapter 13, "Bringing It All Together," but for now, let's do something quick and easy to represent the loss.

Let's make the changes to our PlayerStats script shown in Listing 9.9.

Listing 9.9   **Handling Death in the PlayerStats Script**

```
private bool isDead = false;

public void TakeDamage(int damage, bool playHitReaction)
{
  if(this.isImmune == false && isDead == false)
  {
    this.health = this.health - damage;
    Debug.Log("Player Health: " + this.health.ToString());

    if(this.health <= 0)
    {
      PlayerIsDead();
    }
    else if(playHitReaction == true)
    {
      PlayHitReaction();
    }
  }
}

void PlayerIsDead()
```

(continues)

```
{
  this.isDead = true;
  this.gameObject.GetComponent<Animator>().SetTrigger("Damage");
  PlayerController controller =
this.gameObject.GetComponent<PlayerController>();
  controller.enabled = false;
  this.rigidbody2D.velocity = new Vector2(0,0);
  if(controller.isFacingRight == true)
  {
    this.rigidbody2D.AddForce(new Vector2(-400,400));
  }
  else
  {
    this.rigidbody2D.AddForce(new Vector2(400,400));
  }
}
```

We've added a new private bool named *isDead,* made changes to the `TakeDamage()` function, and added the new `PlayerIsDead()` function.

The `TakeDamage()` Function

In addition to testing whether or not the player is immune before calling the `TakeDamage()` function, we now test whether or not the player is dead. If they're dead, they can't take any further damage, right? If the player's health reaches 0 or lower, we call the `PlayerIsDead()` function. Otherwise, we call the `PlayHitReaction()` function as usual.

The `PlayerIsDead()` Function

This function sets the *isDead* flag to true, preventing the player from reacting to any further hits, and throws a trigger to the Animator, telling it to play the damage animation. It then disables the PlayerController so that the player can't input any further movement commands and sets the player's velocity to 0, 0 in preparation for the force we're about to apply. Based on the player's facing, we apply force to knock them backward.

At the moment, the player will just remain unmoving until the game is ended, but we'll tie this into a proper Game Over screen in Chapter 13, "Bringing It All Together."

Expanding on Platforming

This game is a 2D platformer, but it could use a little more "platforming," so to speak. Let's try adding another staple of the genre: floating platforms. Platforming is all about working your way through a series of challenges based on timing and precision, and nothing embodies those qualities quite like having to leap for ground that won't be there a second later.

Preparing the Moving Platform Prefab

The moving platform is going to involve some nested GameObjects once again. We'll construct it in such a way that we can move the whole platform—waypoints and all—by dragging a single root object. Let's start with the basic setup:

1. Create an empty GameObject and name it "platformMoving."
2. Create an empty child GameObject under platformMoving and name it "platform."
3. Create an empty child GameObject under platform and name it "bridgeLogs."
4. Add a Sprite Renderer Component to the bridgeLogs GameObject and set the "Sprite" property to point to tiles_spritesheet_134.
5. Add a BoxCollider 2D Component to the bridgeLogs GameObject. The default settings should match the sprite accurately.
6. Duplicate the bridgeLogs GameObject and move the new one to X: −1, Y: 0, Z: 0.

This gives us the basic, visible Component of the platform, but we're going to need something to act as waypoints so that the script we write knows where the platform is heading:

1. Create an empty child GameObject under platformMoving and name it "waypointA."
2. Set the waypointA GameObject's icon to a blue diamond to make it clearly visible. It won't have any other visible characteristics.
3. Duplicate waypointA and name the new GameObject "waypointB."
4. Use Ctrl-drag to move waypointB up two grid spaces, keeping it in line with waypointA.
5. Drag the platformMoving GameObject from the Hierarchy to the _prefabs folder.

You should now have a nested setup that looks similar to Figure 9.7.

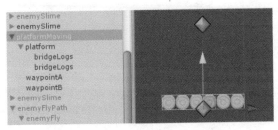

Figure 9.7   Nested GameObjects in the platformMoving Prefab

> **Tip**
>
> Be careful when nesting your waypoint GameObjects or you may send the platform chasing after a waypoint that moves whenever the platform does!

Scripting the Flight Points Component

This script will cause the platform to move between two points in space at a set speed. When it reaches a waypoint, it will begin to travel back toward the previous waypoint.

In keeping with our building block nature, it's a simple setup that could easily be expanded later to include more points on a flight path or scripted to pause for a duration at the ends before resuming movement.

1. Select the platform GameObject (not platformMoving).
2. Click the Add Component button and choose New Script.
3. Name the script "FlightPoints" and ensure that the language is set to CSharp.
4. In the Project Browser, select the newly created script and move it to the _scripts folder.
5. Double-click the script to open it in MonoDevelop-Unity and fill it out as shown in Listing 9.10.

Listing 9.10   **The FlightPoints Script**

```
public class FlightPoints : MonoBehaviour
{
  public GameObject waypointA;
  public GameObject waypointB;
  public float speed = 1;
  private bool directionAB = true;

  void FixedUpdate()
  {
    if(this.transform.position == waypointA.transform.position
      && directionAB == false || this.transform.position ==
      waypointB.transform.position && directionAB == true)
    {
      directionAB = !directionAB;
    }

    if(directionAB == true)
    {
      this.transform.position =
        Vector3.MoveTowards(this.transform.position,
        waypointB.transform.position, speed * Time.fixedDeltaTime );
```

```
    }
    else
    {
      this.transform.position =
        Vector3.MoveTowards(this.transform.position,
        waypointA.transform.position, speed * Time.fixedDeltaTime );
    }
  }
}
```

There are some long lines in this one, but it's not that scary, honest! Let's take a look at the properties of this script in Table 9.5 first.

The `FixedUpdate()` Function

We use only one function for this script, and in spite of how it looks, it's actually fairly simple. `FixedUpdate()` was chosen, rather than `Update()`, in an effort to keep the movement of the platform smooth. Step by step, it does the following:

1. The script checks whether or not the platform has reached its destination. If it has, it inverts the *directionAB* bool value so that the script knows it should head in the opposite direction now.

2. Is the script heading from waypoint A to waypoint B? If so, tell it to move toward waypoint B by an amount based on the speed and time passed since the last `FixedUpdate()` frame.

3. If not moving toward waypoint B, the platform must be moving toward waypoint A, so move it in that direction based on the speed and time passed since the last `FixedUpdate()` frame.

Table 9.5   **Properties of the FlightPoints Script**

Variable	Type	Purpose
waypointA	GameObject	One of two GameObjects whose position will be traveled to by the platform
waypointB	GameObject	One of two GameObjects whose position will be traveled to by the platform
speed	Float	The speed at which the platform will travel between waypointA and waypointB
directionAB	Bool	Tracks whether the player is heading from waypointA to waypointB or vice versa

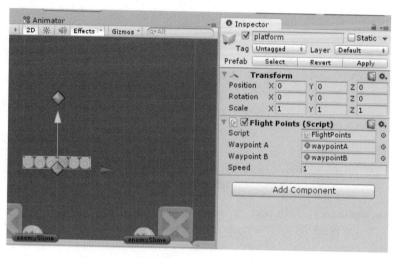

Figure 9.8   Completed moving platform Prefab

Save the script and return to Unity. The platform is ready, but we need to plug in the appropriate parts:

1. Drag the waypointA GameObject to the "Waypoint A" property.
2. Drag the waypointB GameObject to the "Waypoint B" property.
3. Click the Apply button to save the changes to the Prefab.

If you run the game now, the platform will move from point A to point B and vice versa! See Figure 9.8.

There is a lot we can do with a simple system like this. We could create walls that move up and down, platforms that slide from side to side, or coins that move through the air. We can stick this Component on anything that we want.

> **Tip**
>
> Remember that our moving platforms are based on speed, not time. If you keep them on the grid, it will be a bit easier to arrange your patterns so that platforms are consistently in the same locations relative to one another.

Creating Your Second Enemy

We did say that we could put that FlightPoints script on *anything* we want, right? Well, we've actually made for ourselves a relatively easy way to add a flying enemy type that moves on a two-point patrol, so let's go ahead and do that too!

We'll create a Fly that moves between two points and deals damage to the player if it comes into contact with them. We'll also make some minor adjustments to the Flight-Points script so that our Fly faces the correct way while it travels.

Preparing the Fly Enemy GameObject

While we're creating another enemy, the nested nature of GameObjects on this one will bear more similarity to the moving platform than to the Slime we created earlier. We'll start by setting it up the same way:

1. Create an empty GameObject and name it "enemyFlyPath." Give it the same icon as you gave the Slime and place it in the Enemy Layer.

2. Create an empty child GameObject under enemyFlyPath and name it "enemyFly."

3. With enemyFly selected, click the Add Component button and select Rendering > Sprite Renderer. Set the "Sprite" property to enemies_spritesheet_0.

4. Create an empty child GameObject under enemyFly and name it "triggerDamage."

5. Add a Circle Collider 2D Component to the triggerDamage GameObject. Set its Radius to 0.22 and its Center to X: −0.06, Y: 0.22.

6. Check the Circle Collider 2D's "Is Trigger" box.

7. Add a ContactDamage script Component and check the Play Hit Reaction box.

You'll notice that there is neither a Rigidbody 2D Component nor any Collider Components on our Fly. In this case, the Fly's movement is completely controlled by the two waypoints that we'll assign to it. We don't want it to be affected by gravity, and it can't directly collide with anything, so it doesn't need either Component.

That completes the "enemy" portion of the Fly. Now we need to blend in some of the moving platform bits and pieces, as follows:

1. Create an empty child GameObject under enemyFlyPath and name it "waypointA."

2. Set the waypointA GameObject's icon to a red diamond to make it clearly visible, yet distinguishable from the waypoints we use for non-hazard moving platforms.

3. Duplicate waypointA and name the new GameObject "waypointB."

4. Use Ctrl-drag to move waypointB up two grid spaces, keeping it in line with waypointA.

5. Add the FlightPoints script to the enemyFly GameObject.

6. Plug waypointA into the "Waypoint A" property and waypointB into the "Waypoint B" property.

7. Drag the enemyFlyPath GameObject from the Hierarchy to the _prefabs folder.

Now we have a GameObject that is part enemy, part moving platform! Start the game up and the Fly will ping-pong between waypoints A and B, just as the moving platform did. It still lacks animation, however, so let's take care of that now.

Adding Animation to the Fly

Similarly to our Slime, we'll add a short animation that uses two sprites to give the illusion of movement, in this case, the flapping of wings:

1. Select the enemyFly GameObject.
2. Click the Add Component button and select Miscellaneous > Animator.
3. Navigate to the _animations folder in the Project window.
4. Right-click and select Create > Animator Controller.
5. Name the new controller "Fly" and open it.
6. Create an idle state.
7. With the enemySlime GameObject selected, open the Animation panel and create a new clip named "Fly_Move."
8. Set the Sample value to 30 and add a curve for the Sprite Renderer's "Sprite" property.
9. Assign the enemies_spritesheet_0 sprite to keyframes at 0:00 and 0:10.
10. Assign the enemies_spritesheet_6 sprite to a keyframe at 0:05. Your animation should look similar to that shown in Figure 9.9.
11. In the Fly Animation Controller, ensure that the Fly_Move animation is assigned to the idle state.
12. Select the enemyFly GameObject and ensure that the Animator's "Controller" property points to the Fly Animation Controller.

If you run the game now, the Fly enemy should play a two-sprite bobbing animation as it glides through the air. Hit Apply to save the changes you've made to it.

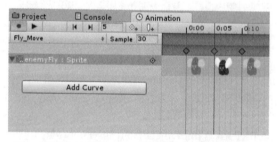

Figure 9.9   Keyframes in the Fly_Move animation

This all works great if the Fly is just flying up and down, but what if it's traveling side to side? There's nothing to tell it to change the direction it's facing. In the interests of making this system a bit more useful, let's take care of that.

Scripting the FlyController Component

Before we can make the necessary changes to our FlightPoints script in order to allow an enemy to change its facing direction, we need to first create the FlyController script, as shown in Listing 9.11.

Listing 9.11 **The FlyController Script**

```
public class FlyController : EnemyController
{
}
```

That's it. No, really, that's all there is to this script. All we need to do is point it to the EnemyController so that our Fly inherits the `Flip()` function. We also inherit the "Max Speed" property, but that won't affect our Fly, as its speed is derived from the FlightPoints Component instead.

> **Tip**
>
> It may seem pointless to create a script like this, but if we ever wanted to provide unique functionality to this particular enemy, we'd need this script anyway. It's best to be prepared, and this keeps our enemy script design consistent.

Adjusting the FlightPoints Script

We have a few small changes to make to the FlightPoints script in order to tell it how to handle an enemy. Specifically, we need to tell it how and when to tell the enemy sprite to change its facing. The new code is introduced in Listing 9.12.

Listing 9.12 **The Revised FlightPoints Script**

```
public class FlightPoints : MonoBehaviour
{
    public GameObject waypointA;
    public GameObject waypointB;
    public float speed = 1;
    public bool shouldChangeFacing = false;
    private bool directionAB = true;

    void FixedUpdate()
    {
```

(continues)

```
if(this.transform.position == waypointA.transform.position
    && directionAB == false || this.transform.position ==
    waypointB.transform.position && directionAB == true)
{
    directionAB = !directionAB;
    if(this.shouldChangeFacing == true)
    {
        this.gameObject.GetComponent<EnemyController>().Flip();
    }
}

if(directionAB == true)
{
    this.transform.position =
        Vector3.MoveTowards(this.transform.position,
        waypointB.transform.position, speed * Time.fixedDeltaTime );
}
else
{
    this.transform.position =
        Vector3.MoveTowards(this.transform.position,
        waypointA.transform.position, speed * Time.fixedDeltaTime );
}
}
}
```

We've added a new public variable known as *shouldChangeFacing*. This tells the script that whatever it's attached to is actually an enemy or something where the directional facing is important.

Changes to the `FixedUpdate()` Function

We added a small conditional to the `FixedUpdate()` function. Whenever the moving object reaches waypoint A or B, it checks to see if *shouldChangeFacing* is true. If so, it grabs the EnemyController Component on the object and invokes the `Flip()` function to change its facing.

It's time to test it out!

1. Rearrange the Fly's waypoints to create a horizontal path rather than a vertical one.

2. Select the enemyFly GameObject.

3. Check the FlightPoints Component's Should Change Facing box.

Save everything and run the game. The Fly should now change direction whenever it hits the end of the path. Be aware that it's traveling "left" by default, due to the sprite's facing, so be careful how you arrange your waypoints or it will look like the Fly is always flying backward.

> **Tip**
>
> You can create separate horizontal and vertical Prefabs for the Fly enemy or platforms to make placing them a more efficient affair.

Maintaining Your Enemy Arrangements

While we can make lots of interesting arrangements of enemies for the player to encounter, you may find that arrangements involving the Slimes have fallen apart by the time you arrive. As an example, let's create an arrangement of Slimes that work their way down some "stairs" toward the player. Create a scenario in your level that matches Figure 9.10.

If you run the game, you'll get to see the Slimes advancing down the steps toward the player. It's neat to watch, and you can see the hazard coming. Eventually they'll all fall into the pit and be destroyed.

There's one tiny catch, however. If you start the player farther back, the Slimes will have destroyed themselves long before the player gets there. What a waste! To alleviate this tragedy of timing, we'll implement a small "spawning" system.

The goal of the system is simply to make enemies active at the correct times. We could instantiate Prefabs of them during runtime, but it will be faster and cheaper to place them during development and mark them as inactive. We'll use our spawn triggers to activate them as the player approaches. This system will apply equally to enemies and level geometry alike.

Figure 9.10   Slimes and steps arrangement

> **Note**
>
> From a programming perspective, "spawning" is the act of instantiating objects at runtime, which is not what we're actually doing here. Rather, we're using it from a design perspective, where "spawning" is the act of introducing something into the game world through either activation or instantiation. The term *spawn* is frequently used in reference to the introduction of enemies or other non-player characters (NPCs) into the player's game space.

Preparing the Spawn Trigger

Similarly to the creation of our checkpoint and pit trigger volumes, we'll be creating a Slime-activating trigger volume:

1. Create an empty GameObject and name it "triggerSpawn."
2. Select the yellow circle icon so that it stands out from our checkpoint and pit trigger volumes.
3. Click Add Component and choose Physics 2D > Box Collider 2D.
4. Click the "Is Trigger" property to set it to true.
5. Place the triggerSpawn GameObject far enough back that the player will hit it shortly before they would see the stairs on screen.
6. Adjust the size and position of the Box Collider 2D so that it's tall enough to be unavoidable, as we did with our checkpoint triggers. See Figure 9.11 for an example.

We want our trigger to be just far enough away that the Slimes will appear off screen so that they seem to have been there the whole time. Seeing something pop into existence without an appropriate spawn visual effect tends to look terrible and buggy.

Figure 9.11   Placement of the spawn trigger

Scripting the Spawn Trigger Component

We'll make a short script that takes an array of GameObjects and flips them all to an active state when the player enters the trigger:

1. Select the spawnTrigger GameObject.
2. Click the Add Component button and choose New Script.
3. Name the script "SpawnTrigger" and ensure that the language is set to CSharp.
4. In the Project Browser, select the newly created script and move it to the _scripts folder.
5. Double-click the script to open it in MonoDevelop-Unity.

With the script open, enter the code found in Listing 9.13.

Listing 9.13 **The SpawnTrigger Script**

```
public class SpawnTrigger : MonoBehaviour
{
  public GameObject[] gameObjects;
  public bool isTriggered = false;

  void OnTriggerEnter2D(Collider2D collider)
  {
    if(collider.tag == "Player" && this.isTriggered == false)
    {
      this.isTriggered = true;
      foreach(GameObject gameObject in gameObjects)
      {

        gameObject.SetActive(true);
      }
    }
  }
}
```

We've created a pair of public variables in the script, the functions of which are described in Table 9.6.

Table 9.6 **Spawn Trigger Properties**

Variable	Type	Purpose
gameObjects	GameObject array	An array of all GameObjects that the script will attempt to set to active
isTriggered	Bool	Tracks whether or not the script has fired, as we want that happening only once

The `OnTriggerEnter2D()` Function

As usual, our `OnTriggerEnter2D()` function first checks to see if the colliding GameObject has the tag of "Player." It also checks to see if the trigger itself has already been fired. If not, it iterates through the array of GameObjects and tells each of them to become active. If any of them are already active for some reason, nothing untoward will happen.

Return to Unity and take the following steps to complete our setup:

1. Select the triggerSpawn GameObject.
2. Expand the "GameObjects" property of the SpawnTrigger Component.
3. Set the "Size" sub-property to 4.
4. Drag one of the Slime GameObjects from the Hierarchy into each of the open slots in the "GameObjects" property.
5. Uncheck the box by the name of each Slime GameObject to set it to an inactive state.

Save the game and experiment with your spawn trigger. When the player touches it, the Slimes should immediately pop into existence and begin moving forward. Move the trigger closer if you want to see it happen, then place it somewhere more appropriate for actual gameplay when you're done testing.

A Few Words on Challenge

We've covered a lot of ground in this chapter. The game still needs polish, but we now have enemies and platforms with which to populate our level. As you develop your game, remember to test and iterate *constantly,* especially with the fiddly bits that some of these elements have (e.g., waypoint positions, speed, damage).

Keep in mind the difficulty of the level in the context of the overall game and build toward that. Is this an early level in a hard-core platformer or a late level in a moderately challenging one? Levels should become increasingly challenging as they progress, but you have to remember how difficult the overall game is meant to be. A late level in an introductory platformer is still likely to be easier than the first level of a hard-core one, for example. Sure, you could make a level full of nothing but moving platforms or weave flight paths for the Flies into a terrifying net, but remember to ask yourself if these things *fit.*

Always consider the amount of control the player has over their character and create situations that they'll have the ability to react to. How precise do you want them to be? Moderate? Set your pit width accordingly, perhaps making it slightly more than a standard jump so that a double jump can easily clear it. Do you want them to be incredibly precise? Make the jumps the max distance of a double jump, or double jump across a pit to a single tile's width of land. Another easy way to increase difficulty is with movement, as more moving parts tend to equate to greater complexity in timing and precision.

How difficult the game becomes is up to you, but try to keep the difficulty curve consistent. Introduce an enemy or situation and then build on it. Put it into the level again later, but in a slightly more complicated way. Add it a third time and make it even more complex. By that time, players recognize the individual elements that make up the challenge so they can handle more. A good way to experiment is to create a level that's just a collection of interesting puzzle bits. You can see how they feel individually before assembling everything into a coherent level.

Summary

In this chapter we instituted a classic shambler AI in the form of our Slime enemy. We created contact damage scripts, prepared a quick and dirty version of player death, and incorporated player immunity to improve the player experience. A system for moving platforms between two points was added and then repurposed so that we could have a flying type of enemy for variety.

We wrote a Component that would allow us to activate inactive enemies, and finally, we discussed a few thoughts on the subject of platformer challenges.

In Chapter 10, "Creating the Menus and Interface Elements," we'll create the basic menus for getting into and out of our game, as well as add the interface elements that make up the game's GUI.

Exercises

We've just added a lot of new functionality that provides us with some great options for creating properly challenging levels. Rather than jumping straight to using it in a level, however, let's try experimenting with it a bit. It's important to test new features so that we have a better understanding of how they can be used to influence the player's experience.

1. Create and open a new Scene named "Test_Bed."

2. Experiment with the Slime enemy. Try making an interesting scenario related to Slimes walking down steps toward the player.

3. Experiment with the moving platforms. Try creating an arrangement of moving platforms over a large chasm. Pay close attention to keeping them in sync with one another.

4. Experiment with the Fly enemy. Try adding some to the previous moving platform experiment and see how drastically they can change the experience.

5. Return to the First_Level Scene and try incorporating what you've learned from your experiments.

6. Save the Scene and Project files.

On to the next chapter!

Creating the Menus and Interface Elements

We have come a long way toward having a fully playable game. Our game has a main character with animations and mechanics. We have a fully designed level complete with GameObjects, physics, and even coin boxes that spit out collectible coins. What would really help to tie everything together is wrapping the game with a title screen, adding a few menu options, and adding an interface to tell us the player's health and other important information.

In this chapter we will look at adding these menus and interface elements. We will go through the process of creating screens, hooking them up, and allowing you to start the game from the very beginning, all the way into the gameplay.

We will also look at in-game elements to help the player. Heads-up display (HUD for short) means the on-screen elements that are used to feed the player information, such as health, ammo, and so on. We will look at a couple of different scenarios for adding these, also hooking them up so they work in real time with what is going on in the game.

So let's get into it and give our game some menus and interface treatment!

UI Design

Before diving into creating our UI, let's get an idea of design and how it is a factor in our game and the impact it has on the experience. The way information is delivered to the player through the game interface can make or break a good immersive game. While our platform game will use a simple UI to deliver information, it's good to understand each of the UI design styles and how they might contribute to sharing vital information.

The four types of interfaces are diegetic, non-diegetic, meta, and spatial. Each type has its own purpose, but the types can be intermixed to create some interesting interfaces. Ours is going to use the simple non-diegetic approach—something very simple, but it shows all of the information the player needs. So let's explain what these mean, shall we?

Diegetic

A **diegetic** interface is one that uses elements of the game itself to give the player information or statistics. Because the elements are actual game elements, they do not pull the player from the experience and do not interfere with the action. A good example would be the dashboard in a racing game, using the gauges and readouts to give the player accurate information. This is still part of the game world, but it's not an overlay and it still helps the player with vital information.

Non-diegetic

Non-diegetic UIs are usually 2D elements laid over the screen. These are found in most simple games, such as the one we are building now. A lot of inventory-type games consist of simple sprites and text that are not part of the actual game world but are simply overlaid on the camera to share the necessary information.

Meta

Meta refers to elements in the interface that are not part of the game world per se but that give the player information in the form of actual gameplay elements. A meta interface is more interactive than a non-diegetic interface but does not use actual objects in the game world. Rain falling on the screen and the splatter of blood as if the player was hurt would be good examples.

Spatial

Last is a **spatial** user interface. This refers to the use of elements in the game world that are only intended for the player to see but are not real-life objects or meant for the AI to see. Back to our example of the driving game: a trail to guide the player in the direction they were to travel would be an example of a spatial UI. While it is in the game, it serves no purpose other than to guide the player.

All of these can be used separately or even together to make a unique experience for the end user. Remember that the information should be easily accessible and not confusing, and it should help or guide the player without interfering with their progress.

Our game will use a non-diegetic interface to keep things simple. But think of ways you could incorporate the other styles going forward. In the end, the goal is to deliver all of the information the player will need to help them progress through the game.

Unity Native GUI

The Unity native GUI is an older method that has been with Unity since the beginning. While it has been used in countless games and Projects, its methods are archaic in nature and are not the most optimal when it comes to performance and a game's frame rate. It doesn't optimize assets very well and is really only functional with a bunch of scripting to get the desired effects.

But we are not giving it enough credit! It does have its fans in the community, and it has worked for four-plus versions now, so who are we to be the critics? Let's look at the different elements of this approach, so you have an understanding of it and what it entails to create your own GUI with it.

GUI Style

The native GUI uses a CSS (Cascading Style Sheet) approach that is familiar to those in the Web development field. A GUI Style holds a series of GUI Controls for all of the different elements you might use in your interface. Anytime you create a button, label, text field, or other element, it uses the GUI Style you have defined. This is handy if you want all of your GUI elements to follow the same rules, allowing you to control them from a single script.

Note

Unity comes with its own internal GUI Style. You can create your own, but if you choose not to, when you call the `OnGUI()` function, the internal Unity one will be used.

GUI Skin

A GUI Skin is a collection of GUI Styles that can be easily controlled through a single asset. The benefit of this is that it allows you to use different Styles that can be easily altered in a single place rather than through a bunch of GUI Style scripts separating them all. Figure 10.1 shows the default GUI Skin.

As you can see, there are a lot of elements that make up a GUI Skin. Each section expands to show the different states for each of these when affected by the player, each with its own settings.

GUI Controls

As seen in Figure 10.1, the GUI Skin holds all of the GUI Controls that you can adjust and tweak to fit your needs. There are quite a few Controls that you might want to use for your interfaces:

- **Label:** Just like it sounds, a label is used to display textual information. It cannot be clicked and used. For this you would need a Button Control.
- **Button:** For clicking to cause an event or action to happen. Buttons are used extensively within the menus, for moving in and out of them.
- **Repeat Button:** Like the Button Control, but continuously performs a function as long as the button is pressed, whereas the button will execute only on a single press.
- **Text Field:** Creates a text entry to allow you to type in information that can then be used. An example would be a name entry field, possibly for a character name.

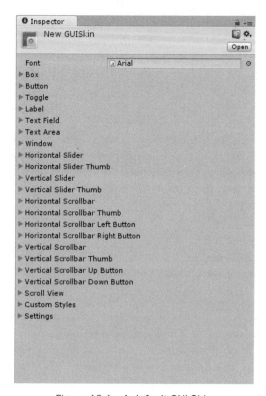

Figure 10.1   A default GUI Skin

- **Toggle Control:** A checkbox or entry that you click to make it active or true. If you needed to have a way of choosing a specific item, you might use a Toggle Control to make it active.

- **Toolbar:** A Toolbar Control is a row of buttons, but it allows only one of them to be clicked and active at a time.

- **Selection Grid:** Like a Toolbar Control, but uses both columns and rows of buttons.

- **Horizontal Slider:** A sliding knob Control that can be dragged left to right. A good example for use would be to change the color of a specific object.

- **Vertical Slider:** Just like the Horizontal Slider, but instead slides up and down.

- **Horizontal Scroll Bar:** A wider version of the Horizontal Slider that resembles more of a Web page scroll bar. Also used for the Scroll View to drag through the entire window.

- **Vertical Scroll Bar:** Like the Horizontal Scroll bar, only it works up and down.

- **Scroll View:** Creates a window with horizontal and/or vertical sliders to show all the information present in a small space. An inventory with a lot of items might need to use a Scroll View so the user can view all of the information.
- **Window:** A Window is a Control that can be moved around on screen. This is useful for allowing users to reorganize their interface. The Window Control requires it to use an ID value to determine to which window focus needs to be dragged.

Compound Controls

Unity also has a few options for using Compound Controls. These are combined Control types, such as a Label used with a Slider. Simply enough, this would be a LabelSlider Control. This approach lets you focus on editing a single element and use slightly less code for it.

GUI Class

A GUI Class is the grouping of variables, functions, and methods making up the GUI elements. Basically a GUI Skin is a GUI Class that stores all of the Controls and parameters for the specific Style. GUI Classes have additional Control types you might need to use. A good GUI Control not previously mentioned would be a background element.

GUI Layouts

We now understand what a GUI Style is, how a GUI Skin allows you to use a collection of Styles, and the different types of GUI Controls we can use and their purpose. Next is laying them out on screen in the correct position and spacing we call for.

The OnGUI() function allows two types of layout styles: the Automatic Layout and the Fixed Layout.

Automatic Layout

The **Automatic Layout** does not use positioning to place the elements of your GUI. This is useful if you are not certain of the look you are trying to create or you do not know the exact number of elements that you will need in your GUI. An example of this type of use might be if your game lets you pick up an infinite number of items, and you wish to show them in the GUI. Since you would need to keep adding on-screen Window and possibly Label Controls, it would be hard to know exactly how to lay all of them out.

Fixed Layout

The **Fixed Layout** approach uses the Rect Class to define the Control on screen. Using 2D screen values, you set values for the X and Y positions or use min and max values for its distance from the edges of the screen.

Keep in mind that you are not limited to using just one layout style for your GUIs. Since both methods fall under the OnGUI() function, you can mix and match them as you see fit. Imagine that you needed a list of character names, but the number of names could change. You could create a Fixed Layout for the interface overlay, but then have an Automatic Layout for the actual names that get populated.

GUI Text

GUI Text is basically just like a GUI Label. You use it to create a textual element to show on screen. There are two big differences, however, in that you create a GUI Text as a GameObject and place it/position it, all in 3D space. Second, you can interact with the GUI Text, use it in your Scene, and add functionality to use it as a clickable object, such as a button.

GUI Texture

GUI Texture allows you to use a single Texture as an element for the interface; usually this is a Button Control. GUI Textures display an image using a simple X/Y plane with simple parameters to control its position, scale, and rotation. Like the GUI Text, it is set up as a GameObject, allowing you to control it independently of the conventional 2D GUI, using it in the actual 3D Scene of your game.

Now that we have covered GUI Styles and Layouts, we can use this information to create the screens and menus we will need for our playable game. Let's start from the beginning by creating a simple splash screen and title screen that the end user will see when first loading the game.

Creating a Splash Screen

The first thing we can add is a splash screen. This is an image or background that is displayed (splashed) on screen before the title or menu screen is shown. Its purpose is to show publisher or developer logos or any acknowledgments you might want to include. The awesome 2D artist who provided us with all of the assets we are using has also provided us with a sponsor image. Since he has so graciously let us use a lot of his work, the least we can do is let others know, right?

> **Note**
>
> We are using a Scene to create a splash screen in our game, but this is not the same as the Splash Image setting in the Player Settings, which we will discuss in Chapter 13, "Bringing It All Together."

We have provided you with the image we will use for this. To begin with, let's create a new Scene:

1. Create a new Scene by using the keyboard shortcut Ctrl + N keys.

2. Create an empty GameObject by using the shortcut Ctrl + Shift + N.

3. From the Inspector, rename this empty GameObject "splashScreen" and make sure its Transform values are all set to 0.

4. From the Project Browser, open the _backgrounds folder and select the MWK_background image. Drag it into the Hierarchy.

5. Move both the Main Camera and background under the splashScreen GameObject. This is just for organizational purposes.

That is all there is to it for the graphics. But we have to write the code to make it functional. There are a couple of things we want to happen for this screen. We want it to show some information, but only briefly so the player can move on. Therefore, we will add a delay for it to stay on screen and the option to bypass it with a click. Create a new script under the _gui folder and name it "SplashScreenDelayed." Open the script and adjust it so it looks like the contents of Listing 10.1.

Listing 10.1   **The SplashScreenDelayed Script**

```
public class SplashScreenDelayed : MonoBehaviour
{
  public float delayTime = 5f;

  void Start()
  {
    StartCoroutine("Delay");
  }

  IEnumerator Delay()
  {
    yield return new WaitForSeconds(delayTime);
    Application.LoadLevel(Constants.SCENE_LEVEL_1);
    Debug.Log("Time's Up!");
  }

  void Update()
  {
    if (Input.anyKeyDown)
    {
      Application.LoadLevel(0);
      Debug.Log("A key or mouse click has been detected");
    }
  }
}
```

Save your script and attach it to the splashScreen GameObject. That's it! Save the Scene with the name "Splash_Screen." We will hook this up in Chapter 13, "Bringing It All Together." Let's move on to our title screen.

> **Note**
>
> The script in Listing 10.1 contains a `Coroutine()` function. In essence, **coroutines** are functions that can pause their own execution, return control to Unity, and pick up again where they left off on the next frame that calls them. They can be extremely useful for timed events or for spreading an event out so that it doesn't occur in every single frame, which can become computationally expensive.

Title Screen

The title screen is for the name of our game and some representation of what's to come, like the cover of a book that shows off the main character in some sort of action element of the story. For our title screen we will need a simple background with a text element with the text "Press Any Button to Begin." We will want the player to sit here until they have pressed the button to indicate they are ready to start the game.

1. Start by creating a new Scene again, using the keyboard shortcut Ctrl + N.

2. From the Project Browser, open the _backgrounds folder and select the titleScreen_background image. Drag this into the Hierarchy. Make certain its Transform values are all reset to 0, 0, 0.

3. Move the titleScreen_background image under the Main Camera as we did with the splash screen example.

4. From the _scripts folder, create a new script called "TitleScreenScript" and attach it to the Main Camera in the Hierarchy.

5. Double-click to open the script in MonoDevelop-Unity and adjust its contents to match what is shown in Listing 10.2.

6. Save your Scene with the name "Title_Screen."

Listing 10.2 **The TitleScreenScript Script**

```
public class TitleScreenScript : MonoBehaviour
{
  public GUISkin Skin;

  void Update()
  {
    if (Input.anyKeyDown)
```

```
    {
        Application.LoadLevel(0);
    }
}

void OnGUI()
{
    // Set the skin to use
    GUI.skin = Skin;

    GUILayout.BeginArea(new Rect (300, 480, Screen.width, Screen.height));
    GUILayout.BeginVertical();
    GUILayout.Label("Press Any Key To Begin", GUILayout.ExpandWidth(true));
    GUILayout.EndVertical();
    GUILayout.EndArea ();
    }
}
```

Game Over Screen

We will create the Game Over screen slightly differently from the last two we made. Now we need to incorporate a few buttons so that the user can navigate selections and levels of the game. Buttons still fall under the OnGUI() method and can use the GUI Skin we created, so the only real concern we have is with the layout. Once again, start by creating a new Scene file:

1. Create a Scene by using the keyboard shortcut Ctrl + N keys.
2. Find the gameOver_background under the _backgrounds folder in the Project Browser and drag it into the Scene. Once again, make sure its Transform values are all set to 0, 0, 0 for the translates.
3. Create a new script in the _scripts folder. Call this one "GameOverScript."
4. Double-click to open the script, and adjust its contents to match Listing 10.3.
5. Save the Scene with the name "Game_Over."

Listing 10.3 **The GameOverScript Script**

```
public class GameOverScript : MonoBehaviour
{

    public GUISkin Skin;
    public float gapSize = 20f;
```

(continues)

```
void OnGUI()
{
  // Set the skin to use
  GUI.skin = Skin;

  //Create a GUI Area to draw the Controls
  GUILayout.BeginArea (new Rect ((Screen.height / 2)
    - Screen.height / 4,(Screen.width / 2) - Screen.width / 4,
    Screen.height, Screen.width));
  GUILayout.BeginVertical();
  GUILayout.Label( "Game Over" );
  GUILayout.Space( gapSize );

  // Make the first button. If it is pressed, reload current level
  if(GUILayout.Button ("Retry!"))
  {
    // This is where code for reloading level goes in Chapter 13
  }

  GUILayout.Space( gapSize );

  // Make the second button. If it is pressed, restart the game
  if(GUILayout.Button("Restart!"))
  {
    // Code for restarting the game goes here in Chapter 13
  }

  GUILayout.Space( gapSize );

  // Make the third button. If pressed, game will exit
  if(GUILayout.Button("Quit!"))
  {
    // This is where code to exit the game goes in Chapter 13
  }

  GUILayout.EndVertical();
  GUILayout.EndArea ();
  }
}
```

Game Win Screen

The last one we will need is the Game Win screen for when you finish the game. This one is very similar to the Game Over screen, with a replay from the Start button and then the Quit button.

1. Create a new Scene again with the shortcut command.

2. Find the gameWin_background under the _backgrounds folder in the Project Browser and drag it into the Scene. Once again, make sure its Transform values are all set to 0, 0, 0 for the translates.

3. Create a new script in the _scripts folder. Call this one "GameWinScript."

4. Double-click to open the script, and adjust its contents to match Listing 10.4.

5. Save the Scene with the name "Game_Win."

Listing 10.4   The GameWinScript Script

```
public class GameWinScript : MonoBehaviour
{

  public GUISkin Skin;
  public float gapSize = 20f;

  void OnGUI()
  {

    // Set the skin to use
    GUI.skin = Skin;

    //Create a GUI Area to draw the Controls
    GUILayout.BeginArea (new Rect ((Screen.height / 2)
      - Screen.height / 4,(Screen.width / 2) - Screen.width / 4,
      Screen.height, Screen.width));
    GUILayout.BeginVertical();
    GUILayout.Label( "You Won!" );
    GUILayout.Space( gapSize );

    // Make the first button. If it is pressed, restart the game
    if(GUILayout.Button("Restart!"))
    {
      // Code for restarting the game goes here in Chapter 13
    }

    GUILayout.Space( gapSize );

    // Make the second button. If pressed, game will exit
    if(GUILayout.Button("Quit!"))
    {
      // This is where code to exit the game goes in Chapter 13
    }

    GUILayout.EndVertical();
    GUILayout.EndArea ();
  }}
```

HUD

Now that we have the menu stuff behind us, let's look at adding the elements for our HUD. HUD stands for heads-up display, referring to the elements on screen that display the information that needs to be shared with the player.

Creating the Visuals

For our game example, the only elements we will be using are a health display and a coin display. The health display will show the health of our player as they take damage in the world and how much they have left before going "kaput." The coin display will show the current number of coins and will change as the player collects more and more of them.

But the first thing we need is an empty GameObject where we can store all of our HUD GameObjects and scripts. HUD elements are on-screen elements that sit in front of the player view and do not interact with the game world. As such, we should treat them as their own unique element within the Scene.

1. Open the Chapter 10 Scene.

2. Create a new empty GameObject and rename it "HUD."

3. Set its Transform to X: 0, Y: 25, Z: 0. This will reposition it straight above our level.

4. Create a new camera by going to Create > GameObject > Camera.

5. Rename this "HUD_Camera." Drag it and place it under the HUD GameObject.

6. Set the Transform values for the camera to X: 8, Y: 5, and Z: −10.

7. Next, under the Camera Component, change the Clear Flags to Depth Only and set the Culling Mask to UI.

> **Note**
>
> You might not have a layer for UI at this point. If not, you will need to add one. For clarification, see Chapter 2, "Understanding Asset Creation."

> **Tip**
>
> You might be asking yourself why we created a second camera. Unity allows the use of more than one camera, and you can specify what is being rendered to each of them independently. Using a second camera has no real performance hit, and it can help you manage your Scene a little more efficiently. Any visual output you have will require a camera in order to be displayed, so multiple outputs may require multiple cameras.

Let's add our GameObjects for our HUD display for health and coins. The Prefab elements have already been created, so it's just a matter of finding and placing them:

1. From the Project Browser > _prefabs folder, find the hud_coin GameObject and drag it into your Scene or Hierarchy.

2. Drag the hud_coin Prefab into the Hierarchy, and place it under the HUD group.

3. Set its Transform positions to X: 14.4, Y: 9.5.

4. Do the same for the hud_sprite Prefab. Drag it into the Scene.

5. Drag this GameObject under the HUD group as well as into the Hierarchy.

6. Set its values to X: 14.9 and Y: 9.5. This will place the hud_sprite just to the right of the hud_coin one we added.

Next, we need to represent the player's health. For this we will use a heart icon, which we will script to change when health is lost. Let's add and place these hearts for our HUD:

1. From the _prefabs folder in the Project Browser, find the hud_heart_full Prefab and drag it into the Scene.

2. Place it under the HUD group from the Hierarchy.

3. Set its Transform values to X: 0.5 and Y: 0.5.

4. Repeat steps 1 through 3 twice more for our three-hearts display. You will need to adjust the position of each heart to the right, by 0.55 units. The first will sit at X = 0.5, the second at X = 1.05 and the third at X = 1.6. Their values for Y direction will all stay the same.

That is it for the visual part of the process. Figure 10.2 shows what our final HUD layout should look like. Again, we won't see any of the game level, as the camera sits a lot higher in world space and away from the action.

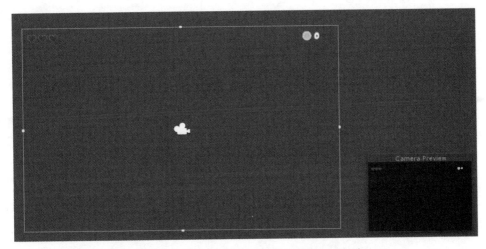

Figure 10.2   Final HUD layout for our game design

Creating the Scripts

Next, we will need to create a few scripts to hook the player up to the HUD elements, so when we take damage or collect coins in the level, they will update accordingly.

Let's first add a script to the hud_sprite display so that we can add to the total when we collect coins. This will be slightly different from anything we have learned yet, as we are counting up but displaying the results using sprites.

1. Create a new script and call it "CoinCounter." Place it inside the GUI folder of our _scripts folder, just for organizational reasons.

2. With the script selected, drag it and attach it to the hud_sprite element in the Scene or Hierarchy.

3. Double-click to open it and adjust the contents to match Listing 10.5.

Listing 10.5 **CoinCounter Script**

```
void Update ()
  {
  // If the value has changed, we need to re-render our sprites
  if (displayValue != value)
  {
    // Turn our value into a string: 956 becomes "956"
    string digits = value.ToString();
    // Get any SpriteRenderer children
    SpriteRenderer[] renderers = GetComponentsInChildren<SpriteRenderer>();
    // Count how many we have
    int numRenderers = renderers.Length;

    // If we don't have enough SpriteRenderers (one for each "place"
    // of our value), add them
    if(numRenderers < digits.Length)
    {
      // Keep adding until we have enough
      while(numRenderers < digits.Length)
      {
        // Create a new empty GameObject
        GameObject spr = new GameObject();
        // Add a SpriteRenderer Component
        spr.AddComponent<SpriteRenderer>();
        // Set this new GameObject to be a child of our current object
        spr.transform.parent = transform;
        // Set its position so we can line up the
        // 1s next to the 10s next to the 100s, etc.
        spr.transform.localPosition = new Vector3
          (numRenderers * spacing, 0.0f, 0.0f);
```

```
        // Add the new GameObject to the UI layer
        spr.layer = 5;
        // Increment how many renderers we have so the
        // loop doesn't execute forever
        numRenderers = numRenderers + 1;
      }


    // Refresh our list of renderers
    renderers = GetComponentsInChildren<SpriteRenderer>();
    }
// If we have too many renderers (e.g. 4 when we only have a
// 3-digit number) hide them
else if(numRenderers > digits.Length)
{
    // While we have too many renderers
    while(numRenderers > digits.Length)
    {
      // Clear their sprites
      renderers[numRenderers-1].sprite = null;
      // Decrement how many renderers we have so the
      // loop doesn't execute forever
      // Note: this doesn't actually remove the renderer
      numRenderers = numRenderers -1;
    }
}
// Set the sprite for each renderer based on our value
int rendererIndex = 0;
foreach(char digit in digits)
  {
      // Convert the char digit into an int which will be the index
      int spriteIndex = int.Parse(digit.ToString());
      // Update the proper renderer (starting at 0 which is the far left)
      // Set its sprite to be the proper sprite from our spriteDigits array
      // Because index 0 of spriteDigits is the sprite
      // "0" and 1 is "1", this works
      renderers[rendererIndex].sprite = spriteDigits[spriteIndex];

      // Increment the rendererIndex so the next digit
      // in our number displays on the proper renderer
      rendererIndex = rendererIndex +1;
  }
  displayValue = value;
}
}
```

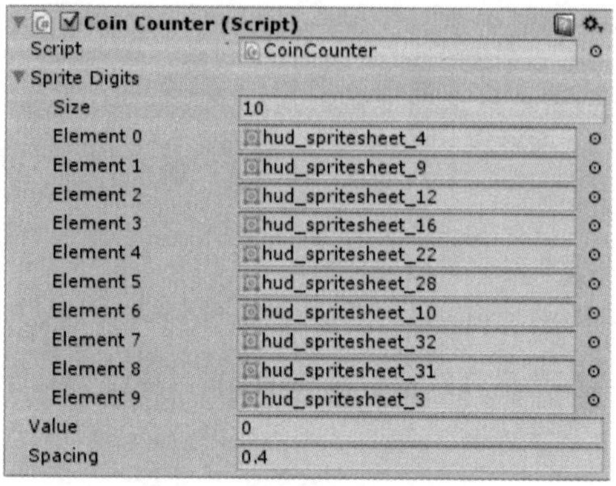

Figure 10.3   CoinCounter script with its array filled in with the hud_spritesheet assets

Once again, select the hud_sprite GameObject in the Scene or Hierarchy, and look at the CoinCounter script we attached to it. It has a sprite digit array where we can set a quantity value that we can then populate. We will be using this to track the value of all coins collected. We will want to add ten of these sprite parameters to represent the numbers 0 through 9.

For the Value, we will leave it at 0 as the first number we want to show is 0 (the player hasn't collected any coins yet, so the value would start at 0). For the Spacing, we chose 0.4 to give each number a small amount of padding from the next.

Next, we need to fill the array with sprite assets for each of these numbers. Open the _sprite > HUD folder, and then click the arrow to expand the hud_spritesheet atlas. Inside this will be the sprite digit assets we will want to use. Since we set up the sprite atlas for this, the numbers will all fall under the same draw call.

When all is said and done, your script Component for the hud_sprite GameObject should look something like Figure 10.3.

That is all we need for the CoinCounter for now. Next, let's tie in the health logic, so our heart health will update in real time:

1. Create a new script and call it "GUIGame." Make sure to place it in the GUI _scripts folder.

2. From the Hierarchy, select the HUD_Camera and attach the new GUIGame script to it, by dragging it onto the Camera GameObject.

3. Open the GUIGame script by double-clicking on it.

4. Adjust it so its contents match Listing 10.6.

5. Save your script and close it.

Listing 10.6   **GUIGame Script**

```
public class GUIGame : MonoBehaviour
{
  public GameObject heart1;
  public GameObject heart2;
  public GameObject heart3;
  public Sprite heartFull;
  public Sprite heartHalf;
  public Sprite heartEmpty;

  public void UpdateHealth(int health)
  {
    switch(health)
    {
      case 0:
        heart1.GetComponent<SpriteRenderer>().sprite = this.heartEmpty;
        heart2.GetComponent<SpriteRenderer>().sprite = this.heartEmpty;
        heart3.GetComponent<SpriteRenderer>().sprite = this.heartEmpty;
        break;
      case 1:
        heart1.GetComponent<SpriteRenderer>().sprite = this.heartHalf;
        heart2.GetComponent<SpriteRenderer>().sprite = this.heartEmpty;
        heart3.GetComponent<SpriteRenderer>().sprite = this.heartEmpty;
        break;
      case 2:
        heart1.GetComponent<SpriteRenderer>().sprite = this.heartFull;
        heart2.GetComponent<SpriteRenderer>().sprite = this.heartEmpty;
        heart3.GetComponent<SpriteRenderer>().sprite = this.heartEmpty;
        break;
      case 3:
        heart1.GetComponent<SpriteRenderer>().sprite = this.heartFull;
        heart2.GetComponent<SpriteRenderer>().sprite = this.heartHalf;
        heart3.GetComponent<SpriteRenderer>().sprite = this.heartEmpty;
        break;
      case 4:
        heart1.GetComponent<SpriteRenderer>().sprite = this.heartFull;
        heart2.GetComponent<SpriteRenderer>().sprite = this.heartFull;
        heart3.GetComponent<SpriteRenderer>().sprite = this.heartEmpty;
        break;
      case 5:
        heart1.GetComponent<SpriteRenderer>().sprite = this.heartFull;
        heart2.GetComponent<SpriteRenderer>().sprite = this.heartFull;
        heart3.GetComponent<SpriteRenderer>().sprite = this.heartHalf;
        break;
```

(continues)

```
    case 6:
      heart1.GetComponent<SpriteRenderer>().sprite = this.heartFull;
      heart2.GetComponent<SpriteRenderer>().sprite = this.heartFull;
      heart3.GetComponent<SpriteRenderer>().sprite = this.heartFull;
      break;
  }
 }
}
```

Now that we have the script set up, we will need to add the variable contents in the Inspector. Select the HUD camera again and notice we are missing the heart GameObjects as well as the heart sprites for when we show Full, Half, and Empty. Let's add these now:

1. Make sure we have the HUD_Camera selected and that the contents of the GUIGame script are visible in the Inspector.

2. From the Hierarchy, select the hud_heart from the HUD group, making sure it is the leftmost one. Drag and drop it on the Heart 1 slot in the GUIGame Component.

3. Do the same for the Heart 2 slot by grabbing the middle hud_heart GameObject and placing this one in its slot.

4. Repeat this for the Heart 3 slot and the rightmost hud_heart GameObject.

For the Heart Full, Heart Half, and Heart Empty slots, we will pull the sprite assets. These will update the sprites used in the Heart 1 slots instead of assigning new GameObjects:

1. You should still have the HUD_Camera selected and the GUIGame script visible in the Inspector.

2. Under the _sprites folder, find the HUD sprites folder and the HUD_spritesheet atlas. If this is not opened out to show the contents, do this now so we can see all of the sprites.

3. Find the hud_heart_full and drag and drop it into the Inspector for the Heart Full slot.

4. Find the Hud_heart_half and drag it into the slot for Heart Half.

5. Last, do the same for the Heart Empty by dropping the hud_heart_empty into it.

And that's it for the Heart GUI setup. If everything was added correctly, your GUIGame Component should look like Figure 10.4.

The last piece for making all this work is hooking it up to our Player GameObject so it will update whenever the player picks up coins or takes damage. Luckily all of these

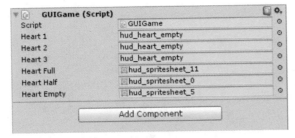

Figure 10.4   GUIGame script with all of the GameObjects and sprites assigned correctly

changes just need to be reflected in the PlayerStats script. Find it in the _scripts > Player folder and double-click to open it in MonoDevelop-Unity. Update it so it matches Listing 10.7.

Listing 10.7   **PlayerStats Script Changes**

```
public class PlayerStats : MonoBehaviour
{

    private GameObject HUDCamera;
    private GameObject HUDSprite;

    void Start()
    {
      spriteRenderer = this.gameObject.GetComponent<SpriteRenderer>();
      HUDCamera = GameObject.FindGameObjectWithTag("HUDCamera");
      HUDSprite = GameObject.FindGameObjectWithTag("HUDSprite");
    }

    public void CollectCoin(int coinValue)
    {
      this.coinsCollected = this.coinsCollected + coinValue;
      this.HUDSprite.GetComponent<CoinCounter>().value = this.coinsCollected;
    }

    public void TakeDamage(int damage, bool playHitReaction)
    {
      if(this.isImmune == false && isDead == false)
      {
        this.health = this.health - damage;
        Debug.Log("Player Health: " + this.health.ToString());
        this.HUDCamera.GetComponent<GUIGame>().UpdateHealth(this.health);
```
(continues)

```
    if(this.health <= 0)
    {
      PlayerIsDead(playHitReaction);
    }
    else if(playHitReaction == true)
    {
      PlayHitReaction();
    }
  }
}}
```

And that is it! We now have a fully functioning HUD display that will sit on top of our game camera. The hearts function and update as the player takes damage, and the coin counter will update as the player collects coins. Figure 10.5 shows an in-game shot with these active.

Summary

In this chapter we covered a great deal about GUIs and menus and some of the script logic for making your own native GUI layout. We looked at creating splash and title screens for our game when it loads. We also created our Game Over and Game Win screens, complete with buttons that link the player back to retry the level, restart the whole game, or quit out of it completely.

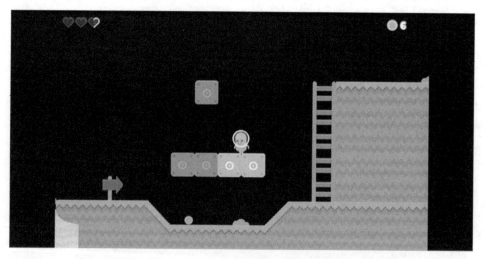

Figure 10.5   In-game shot with our HUD display visible and active

Last, we looked at creating the HUD for our game, with a coin counter display and a three-heart system for the player's health. We added our scripts and updated a few for the player. In the end, we have a menu flow system that works, and we have a HUD display that functions as you play the game.

In the next chapter we will add the final elements before getting into building and deploying the game and all of the last-minute organization and optimization techniques we could mess with. Chapter 11, "Applying Effects to the GameObjects," looks to bring some exciting last-minute effects for animation, particles, and dynamics to our game.

Exercise

We have all of our menus in place and our HUD display up and working. Some possible trials or additional enhancements you could make might be to try adding animations to the HUD elements, or possibly updating the art and positions for the menu pieces. Remember to keep things within your abilities, but also try to challenge yourself. Good luck!

11

Applying Effects to the GameObjects

In this chapter we'll be looking at ways to polish the game in a variety of ways. First, we'll explore the Shuriken Particle System and discuss how it works. We'll put the system to use, creating some particle effects—visual effects that are often composed of several 2D sprites and/or 3D objects—to play at a couple of key moments during gameplay.

After that, we'll go over Unity's audio system and the various Components that create a functional audio experience. We'll use the system to provide audio feedback for several important player events, such as movement and damage.

Finally, we'll spend a little time applying a bit of bonus polish to some of our systems, such as our camera, to make the overall experience feel a little bit smoother and cleaner.

Introducing the Shuriken Particle System

Unity's particle system is known as the Shuriken Particle System. The Shuriken Particle System is extremely deep and rather complicated, but it's also a ton of fun to play with, and you can see immediate results. There's a great deal to learn here and the system has incredible depth. We're only going to scratch the surface, but even that will give us plenty to work with.

Terms to Know

These are the parts that make up the Shuriken Particle System:

- **Particle:** A piece of geometry, such as a sprite or mesh, whose movement and appearance are managed by a particle system, for example, a single ember from a torch.
- **Particle system:** The Component that controls how a specific set of particles act and spawn, for example, the smoke from a torch. These are sometimes also referred to as "particle emitters."

- **Particle effect:** A collection of particle systems working together; for example, a torch particle effect could contain particle systems for fire, smoke, and embers.

The Shuriken Particle System also has an editor window that can be used instead of the Inspector panel, as shown in Figure 11.1.

Creating a Particle System

Take the following steps to create your first particle system:

1. Click the GameObject menu and select Create Other > Particle System to create a GameObject with a Particle System Component attached.

2. Select a recognizable icon, such as the diamond icon, so that we can quickly see our particle system in the Scene View.

This creates an empty GameObject with a Particle System Component attached to it. You can see the white particles, similar to snow, being thrown out by the particle system as demonstrated in Figure 11.2.

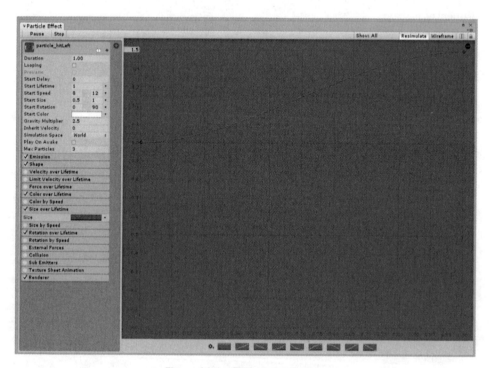

Figure 11.1   The particle editor

Figure 11.2   Basic particle system in action

> **Tip**
>
> Whenever you have an active GameObject that has a Particle System Component selected, that system will animate in the Scene View. This provides an excellent way to test, tweak, and iterate on your effect without having to constantly restart the game.

Modules and Properties of a Particle System

This is an extremely complicated system with a lot of knobs and dials, so let's try to step through it slowly. Every particle system has a set of basic properties that influence it. Beyond the basic properties, you can activate additional sets of properties known as Modules. These contain controls that pertain to very specific manipulations of the particle system.

Let's demystify some of those properties now, shall we?

Base Particle System Properties

These are the core properties used by the particle system to control its most basic behaviors:

- **Duration:** How long (in seconds) the particle system emits its particles. If set to Looping, this is how long a single cycle lasts before looping.
- **Looping:** If set to true, will cause this particle system to play continuously.
- **Prewarm:** If set to true, the particle system will appear to have already emitted one loop of particles thus far when activated. This can be used only if Looping is true.

- **Start Delay:** How long (in seconds) before the system will begin to emit particles after becoming active.
- **Start Lifetime:** Duration (in seconds) that a particle will last after its creation. At the end of this duration, the particle will vanish.
- **Start Speed:** The initial velocity of a particle in the direction it's created.
- **Start Size:** The initial scale of the particle at creation.
- **Start Rotation:** The initial rotation of the particle in degrees.
- **Start Color:** The initial color of the particle.
- **Gravity Multiplier:** How much the gravity defined in the Physics Manager influences the particles emitted. This is a scale value, with 1 being equal to 100%.
- **Inherit Velocity:** How much of the current directional velocity is applied to newly created particles. This has effect only if the Simulation Space is set to World.
- **Simulation Space:** The space in which the particles will be simulated. Local simulation will move all particles relative to the GameObject's Transform.
- **Play On Awake:** If set to true, the particle system will start playing automatically if the GameObject is active.
- **Max Particles:** The maximum number of particles that can be active as part of this particle system at one time. If this number is reached, no additional particles will be created until an existing one has expired.

Other Particle System Modules

Each Module contains a series of properties dedicated to a specific purpose:

- **Emission:** Controls the rate or timing with which particles are emitted.
- **Shape:** Determines the shape of particles and the direction in which they are emitted.
- **Velocity over Lifetime:** Affects the velocity of the particles along each axis, in local or world space.
- **Limit Velocity over Lifetime:** Controls the maximum velocity of particles emitted, as well the degree to which velocity exceeding that value is dampened.
- **Force over Lifetime:** Controls the amount of force that is applied to emitted particles.
- **Color over Lifetime:** Adjusts the color of individual particles using gradients and/or random values.
- **Color by Speed:** Adjusts the color of a particle based on a range of speed values.
- **Size over Lifetime:** Alters the scale of a particle over the course of its lifetime.
- **Size by Speed:** Alters the scale of a particle based on a range of speed values.

- **Rotation over Lifetime:** Controls the angular velocity of emitted particles over their lifetime.

- **Rotation by Speed:** Controls the angular velocity of emitted particles based on a range of speed values.

- **External Forces:** Influences how strongly particles emitted respond to wind zones (another Unity Component).

- **Collision:** Controls if/how the emitted particles can collide and bounce off elements of the game world. Note that, at the time of this writing, this Module does not cause particles to collide with 2D colliders.

- **Sub Emitters:** Allows this particle system to trigger other particle systems via specific events.

- **Texture Sheet Animation:** Allows you to use a texture sheet as a particle. It can be animated or randomized per particle.

- **Renderer:** Controls how the particles are rendered, such as whether or not they cast/receive shadows, how large the particles are, and so on.

Particle System Curves

While most properties of a particle system use numbers, some use curves instead. The Particle System Curves window, shown in Figure 11.3, appears below the Inspector whenever a GameObject with a Particle System Component is selected.

In the event that the Particle System Editor is open, the window appears as a large part of the editor instead of appearing below the Inspector.

- You can change the maximum value of the X-axis by clicking on the number in the upper left and entering a new value.

- The Y-axis values are static, typically being derived from the life span of the particle.

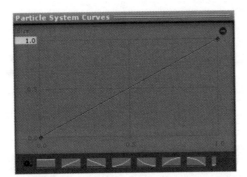

Figure 11.3   The Particle System Curves window

- New keys can be added by double-clicking at a point on the curve.
- An arrangement of preset curves can be selected from the bottom of the Particle System Curves window.

Now that we understand a bit about the Shuriken Particle System, let's get our hands dirty!

Adding Particle Effects to the Game

A well-placed particle effect can add a surprising amount of feedback value and visual impact to a game event, so let's examine some ways in which our game could benefit from a little added flair.

Creating a Particle Effect for Coin Boxes

The best way to understand a system is to put it to use, so let's create a particle effect to play when the player strikes a coin box. We'll make it something simple, using the most basic elements of the particle system. Take the following steps to get things started:

1. Use GameObject > Create Other > Particle System to create a GameObject with a Particle System Component.
2. Select a recognizable icon, such as a purple diamond, so that we can quickly see our particle system in the Scene View.
3. Name the GameObject "particle_coinBox."

We now have a standard particle system that we can work from. We'll look at the settings, one at a time, to create an appropriate visual effect for when the player picks up a coin. Let's start with adjusting the properties under the Particle System section:

- **Duration:** Set to 1. It could be shorter, but this gives a reasonable repeat rate if you want to review the effect in action.
- **Looping:** Turn this on while testing, but turn it off when you're done. The effect should play only once.
- **Start Lifetime:** Set to 0.25. We want these particles to last only for a brief moment.
- **Start Speed:** Set to 5. The particles will be seen briefly but at fairly high speed.
- **Start Size:** Set to 0.4. This size will work much better with the scale of our sprites.
- **Start Color:** You can set this to whatever you want, but given that we're working with coins and yellow coin boxes, let's make it yellow.
- **Gravity Multiplier:** Set to 1. A little gravity will give a nice arc to the particles, which will look smoother than if they were shot straight out.

- **Simulation Space:** Set to World. We want the particles to behave independently of anything they're parented to.
- **Play On Awake:** Set to true. We'll have this effect fire when the deactivated coin box is swapped for the active version.
- **Max Particles:** Set to 10. We don't need very many.

The particle looks a little bit weird right now, but we're only just getting started. Activate the Modules and adjust their settings as detailed in the following subsections.

Emission

We need to control the rate at which the particles are emitted. Rather than the constant spray we have right now, we need a single burst.

- **Rate:** Set to 0. The particles won't be emitted in a standard fashion. They'll be controlled purely by the Bursts property.
- **Bursts:** Create a single burst at a time of 0.00 with a particle count of 10.

Shape

We need our burst to be directional, as we don't want our stars to spray downward through the box or straight off to the side. The following settings will give us an appropriate shape to work with:

- **Shape:** Set to HemiSphere. This will give a nice burst effect that looks more organic than the default cone.
- **Radius:** Set to 0.5. This gives us a great approximation of the size of the coin box.

Size over Lifetime

Create a curve that runs from 1.0 size at 0.0 time to 0.0 size at 1.0 time. Over the course of their lifetime, the particles will shrink and effectively "disappear." The curve should look similar to Figure 11.4.

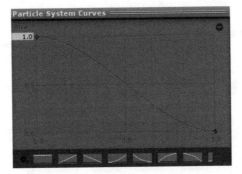

Figure 11.4   Size over Lifetime curve

Renderer

This Module should be active by default. We need to make only two minor adjustments:

- **Cast Shadows:** Set to false. We don't need the extra processing overhead of something like this.
- **Receive Shadows:** Set to false. As before, this is an unnecessary additional cost.

We now have the bulk of our particle effect prepared. It works but it doesn't quite feel like it fits the rest of the game art. We're going to assign it a sprite texture to use instead of the standard spherical geometry that it's using right now. Take the following steps:

1. Navigate to the _sprites > Items folder in the Project window.
2. Select the star sprite (if you haven't already sliced it from the items_sprites sprite sheet, you may have to do that now).
3. Set the star's "Texture Type" property to Texture. The particle system won't accept Sprite Texture Types.
4. Drag the star sprite from the Project window onto the particle_coinBox GameObject.

Just like that, our particle system should now spray tiny stars! Don't forget to uncheck the "Looping" property of the particle system and set the coinBox_disabled GameObject back to an inactive state. Save all changes to the Prefab. Start the game up and try hitting your coin boxes. As the disabled coin box GameObjects activate, the particle effect should fire off. See Figure 11.5 for an example of how it should look.

> **Note**
>
> You can also drag a sprite directly onto a GameObject with a Particle System Component, or you can drag it onto the Component itself.

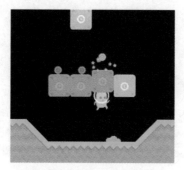

Figure 11.5   Coin box particles

Hooking Up the Coin Box Particle Effect

The particle system works, but we need to tie it into the game now. Fortunately, given the nature of this particular effect, we can do that very easily with the following steps:

1. Drag the particle_coinBox GameObject under a boxCoin_disabled GameObject in the Project window.

2. Set the particle_coinBox GameObject's Transform position to X: 0.5, Y: 1.1. This puts it near the spawn point for coins but keeps it accessible.

3. Double-check the rotation of the particle_coinBox. Make sure that the hemisphere is still pointing up.

4. Apply the changes to the Prefab and save it.

No code is required to make this particle system play when we want it to. After the coin box has been struck, causing the disabled version to appear, our particle_coinBox GameObject will appear with it. Our particle system is set to play on awake so the effect will fire at that time.

Run the game and hit some coin boxes to see the new particle system in action!

Creating a Particle Effect for Damage

Now that we know how to create particle effects, we should try hooking one up to the player's hit reaction. This will require us to create a new particle system, attach it to the player, and call it from code.

Let's get started by crafting the effect itself. We'll make use of the star texture again, albeit in a slightly different way. When the player's hit reaction is called, we'll throw a small spray of spinning stars up and out behind the player. Just for fun, we'll have them increase in size and shift in color as they go.

1. Use GameObject > Create Other > Particle System to create a GameObject with a Particle System Component.

2. Select a recognizable icon, such as a purple diamond, so that we can quickly see our particle system in the Scene View.

3. Name the GameObject "particle_hitLeft."

4. Drag the particle_hitLeft GameObject under the Player GameObject in the Hierarchy view so that it's nested. We're going to want this effect to travel with the player.

5. Name the GameObject "particle_hitLeft."

6. Set the Transform Position to X: 0, Y: 0.4, Z: 0.

7. Set the Transform Rotation to X: −65, Y: −90, Z: 0.

8. Drag the star texture onto the particle system.

This gives us the basic setup and positioning we need for our particle system, so let's get to tailoring the fine points so that it acts the way we prefer. Adjust the basic properties under the Particle System section to match the following:

- **Duration:** Set to 1.00. The particle doesn't need much of a duration.
- **Looping:** Set to false. We want the stars to fire off only once, when called.
- **Start Lifetime:** Set to 1. The particles will last long enough to fall off screen and disappear.
- **Start Speed:** Select Random Between Two Constants and set to a range of 8 to 12. This will create a little variety in the star spray pattern.
- **Start Size:** Select Random Between Two Constants and set to a range of 0.5 to 1. This will provide some visual variety.
- **Start Rotation:** Select Random Between Two Constants and set to a range of 0 to 90. This will provide additional visual variety.
- **Gravity Multiplier:** Set to 2.5. Gravity will cause the stars to fall steeply after they spray.
- **Simulation Space:** Set to World. If we leave it on Local, the stars will move with the player and it will look buggy.
- **Play On Awake:** Set to false. Our effect will always be awake. We'll be firing it via code.
- **Max Particles:** Set to 3.

With the basic properties handled, we can move on to activating and adjusting the necessary Modules to tighten up this particle system.

Emission

We'll use a burst pattern similar to what we did for the coin boxes.

- **Rate:** Set to 0. We'll only be using Bursts.
- **Bursts:** Set Time to 0.00. Set Particles to 3.

Shape

We'll use a cone with a tight angle and radius to project the stars in the desired direction.

- **Shape:** Set to Cone, if it isn't already.
- **Angle:** Set to 15.
- **Radius:** Set to 0.1. This, coupled with the angle, gives us a tight cone.

Color over Lifetime

Let's set the stars up so that they shift hues from their default yellow to a deep red over their life span. Set the starting value of the gradient to white—which won't affect the star's color at all—and the end value of the gradient to red.

Size over Lifetime

Unlike the stars from the coin boxes we'll have these stars get a bit larger as they go. Set the curve to increase from size 1.0 at time 0.0 to size 1.5 at time 1.0, as shown in Figure 11.4. Remember that you can change the maximum value of an axis by clicking on the number.

Rotation over Lifetime

We want the stars to spin in the same direction they're traveling. They're firing back from the player (left by default), so we'll have them rotate to the left as well. The stars aren't visible for long, so we want to give them enough rotation for it to be noticeable. Try setting the curve to values of −360 at 0.00 and −720 at 1.0, as shown in Figure 11.6.

Renderer

We don't want these effects to cast any shadows as they would likely go unnoticed.

- **Cast Shadows:** Set to false.
- **Receive Shadows:** Set to false.

Unfortunately, the particle system is set up such that it will always fire to the left. Take the following steps to prepare one that can fire in the other direction as well:

1. Duplicate the particle_hitLeft GameObject.
2. Rename the duplicate "particle_hitRight."
3. Adjust the particle_hitRight GameObject's Transform Rotation to X: 295, Y: 90, Z: 0.
4. Apply the changes to the Prefab and save it.

Calling the Damage Particle System from Code

Now that we have our spray of stars looking right, we need to hook it into the code so that it fires when the player takes damage. We'll add some code to our PlayerStats script to take care of that now.

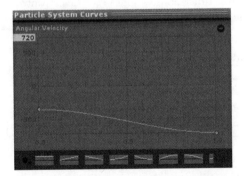

Figure 11.6   Rotation over Lifetime curve

Add the variables shown in Listing 11.1 and update the `PlayHitReaction()` function as shown.

Listing 11.1 **Changes to the PlayerStats Script**

```
public ParticleSystem particleHitLeft;
public ParticleSystem particleHitRight;

void PlayHitReaction()
{
  this.isImmune = true;
  this.immunityTime = 0f;

  PlayerController playerController =
this.gameObject.GetComponent<PlayerController>();

  if(playerController.isFacingRight == true)
  {
    this.particleHitLeft.Play();
  }
  else
  {
    this.particleHitRight.Play();
  }
}
```

The script contains two variables—described in Table 11.1—that will allow us to plug our hit reaction particle systems into the script.

As only one particle system can exist on a GameObject, you can simply drag the GameObjects from the Hierarchy view to the newly created properties on the PlayerStats Component. It will automatically insert their Particle System Component into the field.

Changes to the `PlayHitReaction()` Function

The `PlayHitReaction()` function now grabs the PlayerController Component so that we can make use of the *isFacingRight* bool. We check that bool when this function is

Table 11.1 **New PlayerStats Properties**

Variable	Type	Purpose
particleHitLeft	Particle system	The particle system that will fire stars to the left
particleHitRight	Particle system	The particle system that will fire stars to the right

called, and, based on the player's facing direction, we tell the appropriate particle system to play.

Save the changes to the script and test it in-game. When the player is facing right, stars should shoot out to the left, and when facing left, stars should shoot out to the right!

Having a Little Particle Fun

The Shuriken Particle System has a great deal to offer, and we've barely scratched the surface. The particle systems we're using will help to spice the game's visuals up a bit, but there's plenty more that you could add. You could easily create end-of-level fireworks, for instance, by using sub-emitters that activate on the death of a parent emitter. A little randomness in the direction the initial particle is thrown can create a randomized arrangement of particle explosions in the sky.

Now that we have some visual effects out of the way, we can look at polishing our material with a little bit of audio panache!

> **Tip**
>
> While it can be fun to go nuts with particle effects, remain aware of the effect they can have on your game's performance. Large numbers of particles can quickly bring a game's frame rate grinding to a halt if you aren't careful. As a general rule of thumb, try to make your effects look as good as they can with the fewest number of particles necessary.

Unity's Audio System

Unity employs a fairly powerful and flexible audio system that can be used to add music and sound effects to your game. The basics of the system are simple: audio is produced by an **Audio Source** and is heard by an **Audio Listener.** The position of the listener relative to the source can be used to adjust volume or simulate real audio effects such as the Doppler Effect.

Unity's audio system can also simulate the bouncing of sound through the use of **Audio Reverb Zones.** While Unity won't literally calculate the bouncing of sound off actual game geometry, these filters can provide the game with information about how it should adjust any audio heard in that space. You could apply a filter to make it sound like the audio is being heard in a cave, for example!

Unity supports the following audio file formats:

- AIFF
- MP3
- Ogg
- WAV

Unity also supports tracker modules for music. These modules can be imported from the following file formats:

- it
- mod
- s3m
- xm

As an added bonus, Unity can even access a computer's microphone via script and create audio clips, though this isn't something that we'll be addressing in this book.

> **Note**
>
> Interested in recording audio at runtime? Check out the Microphone API on Unity's site for details. You can find information here: http://docs.unity3d.com/ScriptReference/Microphone.html

Sounds in a game are more than just a simulation of reality. They're also a form of aural feedback for events in the game world. The right sound can add weight to an animation, warn the player of danger, or let the player know they've found a secret. Audio is a critical—and often overlooked—component of game design that should be considered from the beginning of a Project's development.

Right now, we have none of that critical feedback in our game. We're going to remedy that by adding audio to a few key places:

- The player's walk cycle
- The player's jump
- The player's damage event
- Striking a coin box
- Collecting a coin

Before we do that, however, let's take a look at the properties found in the major Components of Unity's audio system.

The Audio Source Component

All audio generated in a Unity Scene comes from an Audio Source Component. This Component also has a number of properties that control how the audio clip is played in both 2D and 3D space.

Basic Properties

These are the standard properties of the Audio Source Component that are generally applicable to all sound effects:

- **Audio Clip:** The sound file that will be played when the Audio Source is called.
- **Mute:** When true, mutes the sound from this Audio Source.
- **Bypass Effects:** Ignores any effects that are applied to this Audio Source.
- **Bypass Listener Effects:** Ignores any effects that are applied from the Audio Listener.
- **Bypass Reverb Zones:** Ignores the effects of any Audio Reverb Zone Components.
- **Play On Awake:** When true, plays the sound as soon as the GameObject with this Audio Source Component becomes active.
- **Loop:** When true, causes the audio clip to play repeatedly.
- **Priority:** Defines the priority of this sound being played compared to others. The highest priority is 0 and the lowest is 255.
- **Volume:** How loudly the sound plays. A value of 1 is equal to the imported audio's base volume.
- **Pitch:** Shifts the pitch of a sound up or down. A value of 1 is equal to the audio's original pitch, and it accepts a range of −3 to 3.

3D Sound Settings Properties

These properties are applied if the audio clip is a 3D sound:

- **Doppler Level:** Controls how much Doppler Effect is applied to the sound, with a value of 1 being standard and 0 being no effect.
- **Volume Rolloff:** Determines the rate at which sound fades over distance. Higher values mean that the Audio Listener must be closer before hearing the sound.
- **Min Distance:** The distance within which the sound will play at its loudest volume. Higher values result in sounds that can be heard at maximum volume from farther away.
- **Pan Level:** Determines how much influence the 3D engine has over this Audio Source. A value of 0 means that the 3D engine has no effect on this sound (and it is treated as a 2D sound), while a value of 1 means that the sound is handled entirely in 3D space.
- **Spread:** Determines the spread of a 3D sound in speaker space. A value of 0 means that all sound channels are located at the same speaker location, and a value of 360 means that all channels are located opposite to the speaker location they would normally use.
- **Max Distance:** The farthest distance at which attenuation of volume occurs. Beyond this value, the audio remains at whatever volume it would have been at this value (meaning it gets no quieter).

These properties also include a graph for visually representing the Volume Rolloff, as seen in Figure 11.7.

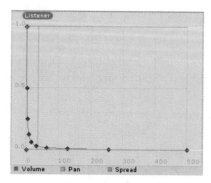

Figure 11.7   Volume Rolloff graph

2D Sound Settings Properties

This property is applied if the audio clip is a 2D sound:

- **Pan 2D:** Determines which speaker channels handle the audio. A value of −1.0 is full left, while a value of 1.0 is full right. A value of 0 is centered between both speakers. Only sounds that are mono or stereo in nature can be panned.

The Audio Listener Component

This Component determines where the player's virtual "ears" are located within the Scene. All Audio Sources are compared against this location to determine noise and apply appropriate filters, if any. Only one Audio Listener can be used in a Scene. By default, any newly created Camera GameObject contains this Component.

The Audio Reverb Zone Component

This Component provides a filter to sound generated on this area. It simulates the reverberation and dampening effect of sounds so that the audio sounds like it's in a cave, under water, in a carpeted hallway, and so on. Unity comes with many useful presets for this Component. We won't be making use of it here, but it's still a good feature to know about.

Basic Properties

While there are many properties on the Audio Reverb Zone Component, the following three are the ones that you'll most commonly find yourself dealing with:

- **Min Distance:** Inner radius of the reverb zone, where the effect is strongest
- **Max Distance:** Outer radius of the reverb zone, where the reverb effect begins to be applied
- **Reverb Preset:** Assigns values to all other properties based on a predesigned effect

> **Note**
>
> For details on the properties that are handled by the preset selections, we recommend delving into the Unity site. You can get a general idea of what each property does here: http://docs.unity3d.com/ScriptReference/AudioReverbZone.html. Fortunately, you can accomplish a great deal with the presets and some minor tweaking.

Adding Sound to the Player

There are a number of ways that we can play sounds off of the player. We can tie them into Animation Events or call them via script when certain input is received from the player. We're going to do a mix of both to provide all of the necessary sound events.

Adding Footsteps to the Walk Cycle

For the walk cycle, we'll use Animation Events to call a function that will randomly select from a small arrangement of footstep noises.

First, we'll need to set the Player GameObject up with an Audio Source Component as follows:

1. Select the Player GameObject.
2. Click the Add Component button and select Audio > Audio Source. Leave the Audio Clip field blank.
3. Apply the changes to the Prefab and save.
4. Open the PlayerController script and add the code shown in Listing 11.2 to it.

Listing 11.2 **Changes to the PlayerController Script**

```
public AudioClip footstepSounds;
private AudioSource audioSource;

void Awake()
{
  anim = this.GetComponent<Animator>();
  audioSource = this.GetComponent<AudioSource>();
}

void PlayFootstepAudio()
{
  this.audioSource.clip = footstepSounds;
  this.audioSource.Play();
}
```

We've added two new variables—one public and one private—to the PlayerController script, as detailed in Table 11.2.

Table 11.2 **New PlayerController Properties**

Variable	Type	Purpose
footstepSounds	Audio clip	The audio clip that will be played when the player walks
audioSource	Audio source	Private variable referencing the Audio Source Component on the player

The `Awake()` Function

The `Awake()` function has been updated to assign the Audio Source Component on the Player GameObject to a private variable within the script. We'll be grabbing that Audio Source every time we want to play a footstep, so it's more efficient if we assign it to a variable up front, once.

The `PlayFootstepAudio()` Function

This function assigns our footstep audio clip to the Audio Source Component and then plays it.

> **Note**
>
> Later in this chapter, we'll set it up so that the audio clip is chosen at random from an array rather than the single *footStepSounds* variable. The variation in footsteps chosen will help prevent the repeating sound effect from causing listener fatigue.

Save the script and return to Unity. We have everything we need to make our character's footsteps make a sound while running, so take the following steps to finish hooking it all together:

1. Select the Player GameObject.
2. Drag a footstep sound effect from the _audio directory of the Project window into the Footstep Sounds field of the PlayerController Component.
3. Open the Animation window.
4. Select the Player_Walk animation.
5. Insert some events—shown in Figure 11.8—into the Player_Walk animation and point them to the `PlayFootstepAudio()` function. These events should be added at 0:06 and 0:15; these are the moments when the sprite's feet are completing a "step."
6. Save the changes to the animation.

Load the game up and have the player run around. You should now hear a footstep noise as the player animates their walk cycle. Having a little audio makes the character feel like they're a part of the world, doesn't it? Next up, jumping sound effects!

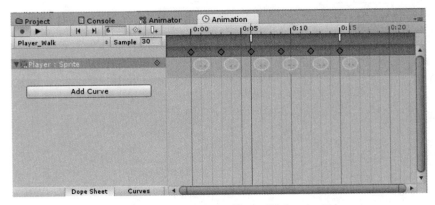

Figure 11.8   Events in the Player_Walk animation

> **Tip**
>
> On a tight budget? There are places online that sell large banks of audio files for fairly low cost. There are also selections of free ones for public (typically noncommercial) use, and there are even sites that can generate sound effects on the fly.

Adding Sound to the Jump Event

While we could also use an animation event to trigger our jump sound effect, it's important to have immediate feedback for an action like this. As the jump animation may loop based on the player's duration in the air, an event would also likely cause the sound effect to play more than once. Accordingly, we'll play the sound directly from the script, as shown in Listing 11.3.

Listing 11.3   **Adding Jump Audio to the PlayerController Script**

```
public AudioClip jumpSound;

void Update ()
{
  if(Input.GetButtonDown("Jump"))
  {
    if(isGrounded == true)
    {
      this.rigidbody2D.velocity = new Vector2(rigidbody2D.velocity.x,0);
      this.rigidbody2D.AddForce(new Vector2(0, jumpForce));
      this.anim.SetTrigger("Jump");
      this.anim.SetBool("Ground", false);
      PlayJumpAudio();
    }
```

(continues)

```
      else if(isDoubleJumping == false)
      {
        isDoubleJumping = true;
        this.rigidbody2D.velocity = new Vector2(rigidbody2D.velocity.x,0);
        this.rigidbody2D.AddForce(new Vector2(0, jumpForce));
        PlayJumpAudio();
      }
    }
  }
}

void PlayJumpAudio()
{
  AudioSource.PlayClipAtPoint(this.jumpSound, this.transform.position);
}
```

We've added a new public audio clip variable named *jumpSound*. This will be used to set the Audio Clip property of our Audio Source Component when the player jumps.

The `PlayJumpAudio()` Function

This is a simple function that tells the *jumpSound* audio clip to play at the Player GameObject's position in the world. We're doing this, rather than assigning the sound to the Audio Clip property of our Audio Source Component, because there's a chance that the audio will be lost if both the jump and footstep audios are attempting to play at the same time.

The `Update()` Function

The `Update()` function now calls the `PlayJumpAudio()` function whenever the player jumps or double jumps.

Save the script and return to Unity. Drag the jump_01 audio clip from the _audio directory to the "Jump Sound" property of the PlayerController Component. Run the game and have the player bounce around a bit. Each jump and double jump action should now play the appropriate audio, providing feedback for the player's actions.

Adding Sound to the Damage Event

The last place we're going to assign some player audio is in the player's damage event. We provide feedback for damage with the flickering of our sprite and our particle effect, but we could use a little audio as well. Similarly to how we call our jump audio, we'll call our damage audio from within a script. This will require some new code in both the PlayerController and PlayerStats scripts. Open the PlayerController script and make the changes shown in Listing 11.4.

Listing 11.4   **Changes to the PlayerController Script**

```
public AudioClip damageSound;

public void PlayDamageAudio()
{
  this.audioSource.clip = damageSound;
  this.audioSource.Play();
}
```

We've added a new public *AudioClip* variable to the script into which we can plug our damage sound effect. We've also created a new function.

The `PlayDamageAudio()` Function

This is a simple function that assigns the sound stored in our *damageSound* variable to the Audio Clip property of the player's Audio Source Component, then calls for it to play. Unlike our other recent functions, this one is specifically marked as public so that we can call it from the PlayerStats script, where our damage is normally handled.

Save the script and return to Unity. Drag the damage_01 sound into the "Damage Sound" property of the PlayerController Component.

Now we need to make some changes to our PlayerStats script so that the `PlayDamageAudio()` function is called when the player takes damage. Open the PlayerStats script and adjust the code as shown in Listing 11.5.

Listing 11.5   **Changes to the PlayerStats Script**

```
void PlayHitReaction()
{
  this.isImmune = true;
  this.immunityTime = 0f;
  this.gameObject.GetComponent<Animator>().SetTrigger("Damage");

  PlayerController playerController =
this.gameObject.GetComponent<PlayerController>();
  playerController.PlayDamageAudio();

  if(playerController.isFacingRight == true)
  {
    this.particleHitLeft.Play();
  }
  else
```

(continues)

```
    {
      this.particleHitRight.Play();
    }
  }


  void PlayerIsDead(bool playDeathAnim)
  {
    this.isDead = true;
    PlayerController controller =
  this.gameObject.GetComponent<PlayerController>();
    controller.enabled = false;
    controller.PlayDamageAudio();

    if(playDeathAnim == true)
    {
      this.rigidbody2D.velocity = new Vector2(0,0);
      this.rigidbody2D.AddForce(new Vector2(0,600));
    }

    GameObject.FindGameObjectWithTag
      ("MainCamera").GetComponent<CameraFollow>().enabled = false;
    this.gameObject.GetComponent<CircleCollider2D>().enabled = false;
  }
```

The `PlayHitReaction()` Function

We've updated the function to include a call to the `PlayDamageAudio()` function of the PlayerController script. That's all!

The `PlayerIsDead()` Function

Similarly to the `PlayHitReaction()` function, we've added a call to the `PlayDamageAudio()` function of the PlayerController script.

That's all it takes! Save the script and return to Unity. If you run the game and collide with some enemies, you'll hear the sweet, sweet sound of player injury.

Now we can move on to adding some sound effects to our collectibles.

Adding Sound to the Collectible System

We've got our player wired for sound, but we could use some in the collectible system as well. Specifically, we should provide the player with audio feedback when they strike a coin box—thus spawning a coin—and whenever they pick a coin up.

Applying Sound to the Coin Box

We'll have our sound effect play on awake, in much the same way we handled the activation of our particle effect. We'll set the sound effect to Play On Awake, causing it to play automatically when the disabled version of the coin box becomes active. Take the following steps to set it up:

1. Select an instance of the boxCoin_disabled Prefab in your Scene.
2. Click the Add Component button and select Audio > Audio Source.
3. Drag the coinBlock_01 sound file from the _audio directory into the Audio Clip field of the Audio Source Component.
4. Apply the changes to the Prefab and save it.

Play the game and try it out. Our coin boxes should now make a clear chiming noise when struck.

Applying Sound to Coin Collection

Our coins already have a script to handle their collection, so we can easily call our sound effect from there. We just need to set up the appropriate Component on our coin Prefabs first:

1. Select the coinBronze Prefab in the Project window.
2. Click the Add Component button and select Audio > Audio Source.
3. Drag the coinCollect_01 sound file from the _audio directory into the Audio Clip field of the Audio Source Component.
4. Repeat this for each of the other five coin Prefabs.

We need only one line of code to handle our audio call in the script, as shown in Listing 11.6.

Listing 11.6   **Changes to the CoinPickup Script**

```
public class CoinPickup : MonoBehaviour
{
  public int coinValue = 1;

  void OnTriggerEnter2D(Collider2D collider)
  {
    if(collider.tag == "Player")
    {
      PlayerStats stats = collider.gameObject.GetComponent<PlayerStats>();
      stats.CollectCoin(this.coinValue);
      AudioSource.PlayClipAtPoint
        (this.audio.clip, this.transform.position);
      Destroy(this.gameObject);
    }
  }
}
```

We could attempt to tell our Audio Source to play directly, but given that our GameObject will be destroyed immediately after, the sound would be cut off. Instead, we're calling the `PlayClipAtPoint()` function and providing it with the Audio Source's clip and the GameObject's location. This plays the appropriate sound at the point in space where the coin existed.

> **Note**
>
> Our audio clip is a 2D sound, so its location in space isn't particularly relevant. If it were a 3D sound, the position in space would become a lot more important. In this case, playing the audio clip at a location in space just gives us a way to play the sound without requiring that the original GameObject still be present. We could also instantiate something purely to play the sound, but this way is much cheaper and simpler.

Applying Some Extra Polish

While there are plenty more places we could add sound effects to our game, let's move on to some important polish elements: cleaning up our camera and our death sequence.

Cleaning Up the Camera

At the moment, our camera follows the player's movements perfectly. Every small movement is reflected in the camera's position, and that feels a bit harsh. To create a smoother feel, we're going to provide a bounding box within which the camera won't react to the player's movement.

Fortunately for us, Unity actually has just such a script available as part of one of their Project downloads. We're going to make use of that one here:

1. Select the Main Camera GameObject.

2. Click the Add Component button and choose New Script.

3. Name the script "CameraFollow" and ensure that the language is set to CSharp.

4. In the Project Browser, select the newly created script and move it to the _scripts folder.

5. Double-click the script to open it in MonoDevelop-Unity and enter the code shown in Listing 11.7.

Listing 11.7   **The CameraFollow Script**

```
public class CameraFollow : MonoBehaviour
{
  public float xMargin = 1;
  public float yMargin = 1;
  public float xSmooth = 4;
  public float ySmooth = 4;
```

```csharp
public Vector2 maxXAndY;
public Vector2 minXAndY;

private Transform player;

void Awake ()
{
  player = GameObject.FindGameObjectWithTag("Player").transform;
}

bool CheckXMargin()
{
  return Mathf.Abs(transform.position.x - player.position.x) > xMargin;
}

bool CheckYMargin()
{
  return Mathf.Abs(transform.position.y - player.position.y) > yMargin;
}

void FixedUpdate ()
{
  TrackPlayer();
}

void TrackPlayer ()
{
  float targetX = transform.position.x;
  float targetY = transform.position.y;

  if(CheckXMargin() == true)
  {
    targetX = Mathf.Lerp(transform.position.x,
      player.position.x, xSmooth * Time.deltaTime);
  }
  if(CheckYMargin() == true)
  {
    targetY = Mathf.Lerp(transform.position.y,
      player.position.y, ySmooth * Time.deltaTime);
  }

  targetX = Mathf.Clamp(targetX, minXAndY.x, maxXAndY.x);
  targetY = Mathf.Clamp(targetY, minXAndY.y, maxXAndY.y);

  transform.position = new Vector3(targetX, targetY,
transform.position.z);
  }
}
```

There are quite a few variables in use here! Table 11.3 breaks them down and explains their purpose.

The `Awake()` Function

This function grabs the player's Transform when the Camera GameObject initially becomes active. That Transform position will be used in calculations throughout the rest of the script.

The `CheckXMargin()` Function

This function derives the absolute value of the difference between the camera's current Transform position and the player's Transform position on the X-axis. If that value is greater than the *xMargin* value, it returns true.

The `CheckYMargin()` Function

This function derives the absolute value of the difference between the camera's current Transform position and the player's Transform position on the Y-axis. If that value is greater than the *yMargin* value, it returns true.

> **Note**
>
> The `Mathf.Abs()` function returns absolute values, which are always positive. This means that both a value of 2 and a value of -2 would return 2 via `Mathf.Abs()`. It's extremely useful for simplifying the parameters of margin tests.

The `FixedUpdate()` Function

`FixedUpdate()` just calls into the `TrackPlayer()` function. `FixedUpdate()` is used, rather than `Update()`, to create a smoother camera movement that isn't dependent on frame rate.

Table 11.3 **CameraFollow Properties**

Variable	Type	Purpose
xMargin	Float	The amount of leeway space in which the player can move on the X-axis without causing the camera to move
yMargin	Float	The amount of leeway space in which the player can move on the Y-axis without causing the camera to move
xSmooth	Float	Controls how quickly the camera moves to catch up with the player on the X-axis
ySmooth	Float	Controls how quickly the camera moves to catch up with the player on the Y-axis
maxXAndY	Vector 2	The maximum X-axis and Y-axis values the camera can have
minXAndY	Vector 2	The minimum X-axis and Y-axis values the camera can have

The `TrackPlayer()` Function

Let's walk through this function, one step at a time:

1. Two variables are created to store the camera's current X and Y location.
2. If `CheckXMargin()` returns true, it calculates where the camera's new X-axis position will be using `Mathf.Lerp()`, a function used for smoothing into/out of movements.
3. If `CheckYMargin()` returns true, it calculates where the camera's new Y-axis position will be using `Mathf.Lerp()`.
4. The new X-axis value (or preexisting value) is adjusted to fall between the minimum and maximum X-axis values using `Mathf.Clamp()`.
5. The new Y-axis value (or preexisting value) is adjusted to fall between the minimum and maximum Y-axis values using `Mathf.Clamp()`.
6. Finally, the camera is assigned a new position based on the adjusted X and Y values. Its Z value remains unchanged.

You may want to play around with the public properties of the script to find something that feels good to you. The following set of numbers works fairly well:

- **"XMargin"**: 1
- **"YMargin"**: 1
- **"XSmooth"**: 4
- **"YSmooth"**: 4
- **"Max XAnd Y"**: 300, 15
- **"Min XAnd Y"**: −1, 0

Not only does this script make the camera move smoothly when the player is running around, but it makes for a smoother transition when the player is teleported back to a checkpoint after falling into a pit. The visible transition also shows the player exactly where they have been relocated in relation to the pit.

> **Note**
>
> If you run the game now, you may notice that . . . nothing has changed. This is because our Main Camera GameObject is still parented to the Player GameObject. Drag the camera out from under the player so that it's no longer parented so that our script can do its job properly. Don't forget to save the changes to the Player Prefab!

Cleaning Up Player Death

At the moment, our death sequence is a bit buggy, but that's about to change. Now that our camera is divorced from the Player GameObject, we can have a little bit of fun with our death sequence.

We're going to keep the force effect, but we'll have the player fall through the world instead of colliding with it afterward. We'll also have the camera stop tracking the player during this. The force effect doesn't make sense if the player falls into a pit, so we'll address that as well.

Let's make some adjustments to the `PlayerIsDead()` function of the PlayerStats script, as shown in Listing 11.8.

Listing 11.8 **Changes to the PlayerStats Script**

```
public bool isDead = false;
private float deathTimeElapsed;

void Update()
{
  if(this.isImmune == true)
  {
    SpriteFlicker();
    immunityTime = immunityTime + Time.deltaTime;
    if(immunityTime >= immunityDuration)
    {
      this.isImmune = false;
      this.spriteRenderer.enabled = true;
    }
  }
  if(this.isDead == true)
  {
    this.deathTimeElapsed = this.deathTimeElapsed + Time.deltaTime;
    if(this.deathTimeElapsed >= 2.0f)
    {
      Application.LoadLevel(1);
    }
  }
}


void PlayerIsDead(bool playDeathAnim)
{
  this.isDead = true;
  PlayerController controller =
    this.gameObject.GetComponent<PlayerController>();
  controller.enabled = false;

  if(playDeathAnim == true)
  {
    this.rigidbody2D.velocity = new Vector2(0,0);
    this.rigidbody2D.AddForce(new Vector2(0,600));
  }
```

```
GameObject.FindGameObjectWithTag
    ("MainCamera").GetComponent<CameraFollow>().enabled = false;
  this.gameObject.GetComponent<CircleCollider2D>().enabled = false;
}

public void TakeDamage(int damage, bool playHitReaction)
{
  if(this.isImmune == false && isDead == false)
  {
    this.health = this.health - damage;
    Debug.Log("Player Health: " + this.health.ToString());

    if(this.health <= 0)
    {
      PlayerIsDead(playHitReaction);
    }
    else if(playHitReaction == true)
    {
      PlayHitReaction();
    }
  }
}
```

We've altered the *isDead* variable to be public rather than private. This will be important shortly, as we'll need to reference this variable from a different script. We've also added a private variable, *deathTimeElapsed,* to track the time that has passed since the player has been defeated.

The Update() Function
We've added a section that checks if the player is currently dead. If so, it increments the time elapsed since death until it reaches a threshold. At that point, the game is told to load the Game_Over Scene. We'll cover how that works in a moment.

The PlayerIsDead() Function
We've added an argument to the function. It now takes a bool value which we use to determine whether or not the Player GameObject will play the force effect on death. We need this option to account for death by pit trigger.

The script finds the camera and disables the CameraFollow Component, causing the camera to remain wherever it was at the time of the player's death. Last, the Player GameObject's collision Component is disabled so that the player will fall through the world.

The TakeDamage() Function
As our PlayerIsDead() function now requires a bool argument, we've updated the call to that function from within TakeDamage(). It now passes the *playHitReaction*

bool. If the damage source doesn't call for a hit reaction, death from this source doesn't warrant the force effect.

In order to load that Game_Over Scene, we need to know what number to reference. We'll set that up with the following steps:

1. Click the File menu and select Build Settings.

2. Click the Add Current button to add the current Scene to the list. If the list is currently empty, this becomes number 0.

3. Open the Game_Over Scene.

4. Add the Game_Over Scene to the Build Settings list as well. Refer to Figure 11.9 for an example of how this should look.

5. Open the PlayerStats script.

6. Make sure the Application.LoadLevel() call contains the number for the Game_Over Scene.

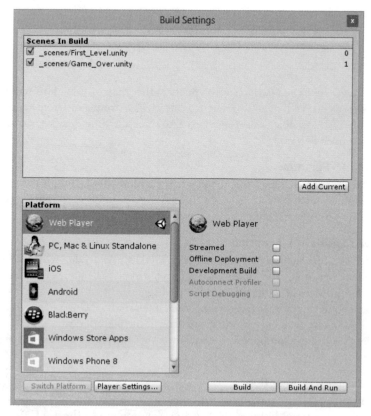

Figure 11.9   The Build Settings menu with Scenes added

All that's left now is to update the PitTrigger script so that it doesn't attempt to relocate a dead player. Open the PitTrigger script and adjust the `OnTriggerEnter2D()` function as shown in Listing 11.9.

Listing 11.9 **Changes to the PitTrigger Script**

```
void OnTriggerEnter2D(Collider2D collider)
{
  if(collider.tag == "Player")
  {
    GameObject trigger = GetNearestActiveCheckpoint();

    if(trigger != null &&
collider.gameObject.GetComponent<PlayerStats>().isDead == false)
    {
      collider.transform.position = trigger.transform.position;
    }
    else
    {
      Debug.LogError("No valid checkpoint was found!");
    }
  }
  else
  {
    Destroy(collider.gameObject);
  }
}
```

The `OnTriggerEnter2D()` Function

The IF statement that determines the closest checkpoint has been updated to include a check of the *isDead* variable—which we just made public—found in the PlayerStats Component.

Save everything and run the game to test it out. Upon death, the player will be bounced into the air and then fall through the world if the killing blow came from a creature. If the player died by falling into a pit, they'll just continue to fall. In either case, the camera ceases to follow the player.

This is now a much cleaner and clearer way to express the player's defeat.

> **Tip**
>
> If the player dies via pit trigger but still appears to teleport first, check the order of Components in the Inspector. The Contact Damage Component should be higher in the Inspector than the Pit Trigger Component, as we want that one to register first, thus dealing damage and killing the player before checking to see if the player should be teleported to a checkpoint.

Summary

In this chapter we learned about the Shuriken Particle System and used it to add some visual flair to our game. We added an effect for when the player sustains damage and an effect that plays when coin boxes are struck.

We learned about Unity's audio system and used it to apply sound effects to several of our player events as well as the collection of our coins. We also discussed the value of visual and audio feedback to the player's experience.

Finally, we took steps to polish some of the game's other elements. We created a smoother follow-cam and tidied up the death sequence in order to make the game more presentable and provide a better gameplay experience.

In Chapter 12, "Organization and Optimization," we'll go over some final tips and recommendations for game optimization, organization, and file handling.

Exercises

Our footstep audio is likely going to be the most commonly heard sound effect in the game. The constant repetition can wear on the player, causing listener fatigue. In order to help mitigate that, let's create an array of footstep sound effects to draw from.

1. Open the PlayerController script. Make the changes shown in Listing 11.10.

Listing 11.10   **Changes to the PlayerController Script**

```
public AudioClip[] footstepSounds;

void PlayFootstepAudio()
{
  this.audioSource.clip = footstepSounds[(Random.Range(0,
footstepSounds.Length))];
  this.audioSource.Play();
}
```

2. Select the Player GameObject.
3. Set the size of the Footstep Sounds array to 3.
4. Assign a different footstep sound to each field in the array.
5. Update the Prefab and save changes.
6. Run the game and try it out! You should now be hearing a randomized arrangement of footstep noises when the player is walking.
7. Save the Scene and Project files.

On to the next chapter!

Organization and Optimization

We have come so far, and our little game Project is almost complete! But before we put the final pieces in place and deploy our game for others to admire, we should look at a few ways to make it run as smoothly and efficiently as possible.

In this chapter we will take a look at some means for organizing and optimizing our game. We have done a good job so far of trying to be on top of our Project and the content we add, but having an understanding of project management will help you in any project you might be a part of in the future.

Another big polish task is with optimization. Optimizing game assets, scripts, and even our Project Browser can go a long way toward making sure our game is playing the way we intend it to. We will dig into the level we have designed to look for ways in which we can reduce build size, improve performance, and clean up the code. Reducing draw calls, optimizing collision, and building cleaner sprite atlases are a few areas that will help our game run optimally.

So with that, let's get to it!

Organizing Assets

For the most part we have managed the organizational aspects of our Project fairly well. Our Project has a root folder called Assets. Underneath that we have specific folders to break up the assets, and each folder is named to clarify this. Figure 12.1 shows the Project Browser folder structure up to this point.

Our folders also have an underscore before their names. This helps clarify what they are used for, and it helps you or anyone else using the Project to find things quickly and easily. The underscore tells us that this folder houses additional content; for example, we know that the _animations folder will have assets dealing with animations inside of it.

Figure 12.1   Our Project folder structure

> **Warning**
>
> While naming a folder with an underscore as the first character is absolutely fine in Unity, there are development environments where it can be problematic. Be aware of this if you find yourself moving over to other environments.

The underscore also lets us know that this name should not be used for anything else, meaning that the term *animations* is a pretty general term. You want to avoid naming things with a broad term that could confuse you or others later on. A good rule of thumb is to not be general enough that something could be construed as something else or cause you to run into issues with naming later on. If you named an animation "animation1," you might not remember later on what the contents are.

You might be able to continue to use the name, simply appending a number and counting up. But what if later on you needed to have something else named "animation1"? Now you have the problem of renaming everything to make the name you want available. One or two animations might be OK to rename and remember, but imagine 100 or more of them!

Inside the _animations folder we have all of the animations and animator states for our different GameObjects. We could easily add two additional folders to split off these different files, but we chose not to in this case. Having a single place for both of these asset types makes sense when they work together. Since the Animator uses the animations, we can easily tell that the Player Animator state will use the Player_Idle, Player_Jump, and Player_Walk animations.

Organizing Our Prefabs

Take a look at the _prefabs contents, and prepare to scream (or laugh—some people handle pressure better than we do)! This folder has no organization to speak of and it shows. While the names of all the assets indicate fairly clearly what they are, we can organize this folder a lot better.

All of the assets were pulled from the _sprites folder, which luckily does contain folders to break up the individual sprites. Let's set up the _prefabs folder to match this:

1. In the Project Browser, right-click on the _prefabs folder and select Create > Folder.
2. Rename this new folder to match the first one under _sprites. Call it "enemies."

Now that we have a folder for any of the enemy Prefabs, all of them can be moved there. This seems easy enough, but there has to be a better way. This is where labels come in. We briefly covered labels in Chapter 1, "Setting Up the Unity Development Environment," and maybe this should have been explained a lot sooner than the end of the Project. Better late than never!

Labels

Labels are for earmarking individual assets so that you have a way of filtering and keeping track of them even within their own folder. We added a label for all of our enemy Prefabs when we created them, called simply "Enemy." Makes sense, right?

From the Project Browser, select the icon just to the left of the star, the one that looks like a garment tag. This is a drop-down of all of our labels. By clicking on a label, you make it active, and it shows just those assets with the label name. Figure 12.2 shows our list of premade labels.

1. From the Label list, left-click the Enemy label to make only those assets with this label visible.
2. Highlight all of these by selecting the first one, and then Shift and left-click the last one.
3. Drag and drop all of these into the enemies folder under the _prefabs folder.

Figure 12.2   The list of labels from the Project Browser

Hierarchy

One last place you might want to do some organizing is with the Hierarchy of your Scene. This can become messy and convoluted, even more so than the Project Browser. This is because when you drag things into your Scene, there is no real structure for them. If you have an asset called "myAsset," and then drag in multiple copies, they will all keep the same name. Having 20 of these with the same name makes it hard to tell which one is which!

A good way to keep this structured is by placing things in their own containers. Unity does not really provide a clean way to do this, but we can use empty GameObjects to act as containers. Let's walk through the steps for our level design.

> **Note**
>
> We briefly touched on this concept in Chapter 4, "Building the Game World," when we were creating our first level. The following is basically a more detailed explanation with the theory behind it.

1. Start a new Scene file by going to the File Menu and selecting New Scene.
2. From the Project Browser, find the _backgrounds folder, and inside this should be a file called "levelDesign_background.png." Left-click and drag this into your Hierarchy.
3. With levelDesign_background still selected, make sure the coordinates are all positioned at 0 for X, Y, and Z in the Transform Component.
4. In the Inspector, change the Sorting Layer for the background from Default to Background.

> **Tip**
>
> This background matches the dimensions of our game. We made this as a guide for knowing the bounds that the camera could see, and how the Scene and GameObjects were framed. But we also used this as a guide for breaking up assets in the Hierarchy. By isolating GameObjects to this space of the Scene, we can create a container for just this section.

5. From the GameObject menu, choose Create Empty. Rename this "Screen1," and hit Enter to accept.
6. Again, let's check that we are at the center of the world. Make sure this new GameObject's Transform values are all set to 0 from the Inspector. By doing this we know that any child GameObjects for this will have correct world space values when we place or reposition them.
7. From the Project Browser > _prefabs folder, drag the grassMid Prefab into the Hierarchy and drop it into the new Screen1 group we made. If by accident you dropped it into the Scene View or just in the Hierarchy, make sure its world space values are set to 0, 0, 0. This is our first piece.

8. Drag another one of the grassMid Prefabs into the Screen1 group.

9. Now with this selected, set its Transform X value to 1.0. This should move it one place to the right of the first one.

10. Keep doing this for a total of 16 grassMid GameObjects running across the Scene. You have created your first game screen, as well as a master GameObject with grassMid child GameObjects.

Tip

We came up with exactly 16 pieces by their size in relation to the dimensions of the screen. Each screen is 960 units across. In Chapter 3, "Creating 2D Sprites," we set the initial Pixels To Units size for the GameObject to 60. With our sprites equal to the Pixels To Units size, and our snapping set to 1, we can easily position these one by one, or move them 1 unit to the right. Sixteen pieces each defined to 60 Pixels To Units: $16 \times 60 = 960$.

There are a few positives to this approach, the first being that we have created the start of a game level that is organized. Another positive is that we can duplicate this and easily make a second screen. Let's do this now to get an idea of how modular and iterative this process can be:

1. From the Project Browser, open the _backgrounds folder again, and once again drag a copy of it into our Hierarchy.

2. Once again, we need to set the Sorting Layer for this background. In the Inspector, change the Sorting Layer to Background.

3. In the Inspector, set its X Transform to 16. This will move it to the right exactly 16 units, placing it next to the first background we have.

4. Select the Screen1 parent object from the Hierarchy. Selecting the parent will affect all of the underlying children as well.

5. Duplicate this by going to the Edit menu and then choosing Duplicate. You could also use the shortcut Ctrl + D.

6. It will keep the same name in the Hierarchy, so you will have two copies of Screen1. Choose the second one and name it "Screen2."

7. Just as we have two backgrounds and we moved the Transform to a value of 16 in X, let's do this for our Screen2 parent. With Screen2 selected, set the X value to 16. It should now be moved exactly 1 screen or 16 units over. Figure 12.3 shows our current design.

Using this approach, we can keep our Scene easily manageable and our Hierarchy organized. The only drawback is maintaining this as the design changes or elements are added, but we find the effort to be worthwhile. Figure 12.4 shows the final Hierarchy layout.

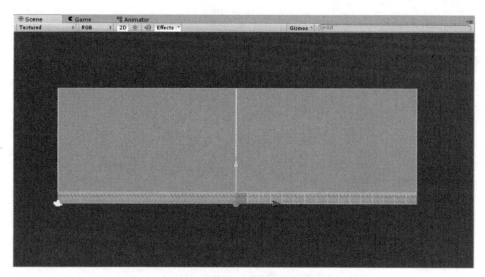

Figure 12.3   Scene View with grouped GameObjects

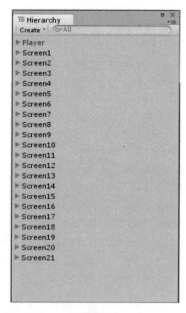

Figure 12.4   Our Hierarchy, organized into groups for easy management

There are plenty of ways to keep your Scene clean and your Hierarchy organized. You could also have turned the screen into a Prefab that would update the clones you added, but we will see shortly why we chose not to do that.

Organizing Scripts and Code

As your game grows, so too will your collection of scripts and the amount of code contained within many of them. It will become imperative that you are able to quickly and easily find the materials that you are looking for in order to continue working efficiently. Let's take a look at a few ways that we can better organize and manage our Project's code materials.

Organizing the Script Files

There are two key ways to organize any type of file content, and scripts are no exception:

1. Folder structure
2. File names

For obvious reasons, a combination of the two is typically employed. We've been only loosely organizing our script files in the previous chapters based on some very general naming conventions and the use of a single _scripts folder. As you can see, it's starting to look a bit messy, so let's consider some ways in which we could improve.

At the moment, our scripts typically fall into a handful of categories:

- Player data and control scripts
- Enemy data and control scripts
- Collectible scripts
- Level hazard scripts
- Game system scripts

We could easily add appropriately named subfolders to our _scripts folder and move the relevant scripts into them. This would greatly speed up searches for specific scripts and would make it easier to tell at a glance what areas of the game a script most likely affects.

In addition to some structural changes, we could consider some changes to our naming schemes for the scripts themselves. However, we've generally been prefacing the names of our scripts in such a way as to make them easily identifiable. All scripts related to our coin collectibles, for instance, start with the word *Coin*, and all of our player management scripts begin with the word *Player*. That said, there is always room for improvement.

Naming schemes become extremely important for assets, so it's a good idea to have a general scheme in mind at all times. Try to keep it relatively simple, consistent, and, most importantly, clearly descriptive. You—and possibly other developers down the road—should be able to identify the likely purpose of a script at a glance.

There is no set folder structure or nomenclature scheme to adhere to, nor is there a "best" way to do it. What we have provided here are only suggestions; the best way is whatever way works most effectively for you (and your team, if you have one).

Organizing the Code

While all of our code is functional, there are potentially numerous ways in which we could better organize it. We'll look at a pair of ways that will help us both reduce the visual clutter of working with a large script and reduce the odds of introducing bugs by centralizing some of our important data.

Using Regions in Code

Use of the #region and #endregion keywords would allow us to break our code up into collapsible sections. Let's take a look at one of our largest scripts—PlayerController—and see how we could break it down using regions. Open the script and adjust it as shown in Listing 12.1.

Listing 12.1 **Regions in the PlayerController Script**

```
public class PlayerController : MonoBehaviour
{
  #region VARIABLES
  #region PUBLIC HIDDEN VARIABLES

  [HideInInspector]
  public bool isFacingRight = true;
  [HideInInspector]
  public bool isGrounded = false;
  [HideInInspector]
  public bool isDoubleJumping = false;

  #endregion
  #region PUBLIC VARIABLES

  public float maxSpeed = 7.0f;
  public float jumpForce = 850.0f;
  public PhysicsMaterial2D jumpMaterial;

  public Transform groundCheck;
  public LayerMask groundLayers;

  public AudioClip[] footstepSounds;
  public AudioClip jumpSound;
  public AudioClip damageSound;

  #endregion
  #region PRIVATE VARIABLES
```

```csharp
private float groundCheckRadius = 0.2f;

private AudioSource audioSource;
private Animator anim;

private float deathTimeElapsed;

#endregion
#endregion

#region INHERENT METHODS [Awake, Update, FixedUpdate]

void Awake()
{
  // code snipped out
}

void Update ()
{
  // code snipped out
}

void FixedUpdate()
{
  // code snipped out
}

#endregion
#region UTILITY METHODS [Flip]

void Flip()
{
  // code snipped out
}

#endregion
#region AUDIO METHODS [PlayFootstepAudio, PlayJumpAudio, PlayDamageAudio]

void PlayFootstepAudio()
{
    // code snipped out
}

void PlayJumpAudio()
{
  // code snipped out
}
```

(continues)

```
public void PlayDamageAudio()
{
  // code snipped out
}

#endregion
}
```

We've now separated our code into several major collapsible regions:

- Variables with subregions for our public non-Inspector, public Inspector, and private variables
- Inherent methods for functions that can exist on any Unity GameObject
- Utility methods for general-purpose functions that assist the script
- Audio methods for functions that specifically call or interact with player audio

We can quickly reduce our script to a less cluttered, more legible state by collapsing the regions, as shown in Figure 12.5. There are a variety of ways in which you can use regions—for instance, you can also use regions within a function—and it's up to you to find the ways that you feel are most helpful.

> **Tip**
>
> As a personal preference, we list the names of the functions contained within each region so that we can see what they contain without having to expand them. This approach does require that you be diligent in updating your region names in the event that you relocate, remove, or rename a function, however.

Using Constants in Code

A **constant** is a piece of data whose value will never change. Unlike a variable, the initial value assigned to a constant is permanent and immutable in nature. We can certainly make use of that, given the number of variables we use that are never assigned new values, such as

- The player's maximum speed
- The player's jump force
- The ground check radius
- The names of Animator variables
- The names of our inputs

We're going to create a Constants script that will store values for these variables, allowing us to reference them from a centralized location. This will help reduce potential bugs that can result from typos. It can also help prevent bugs that could occur in the

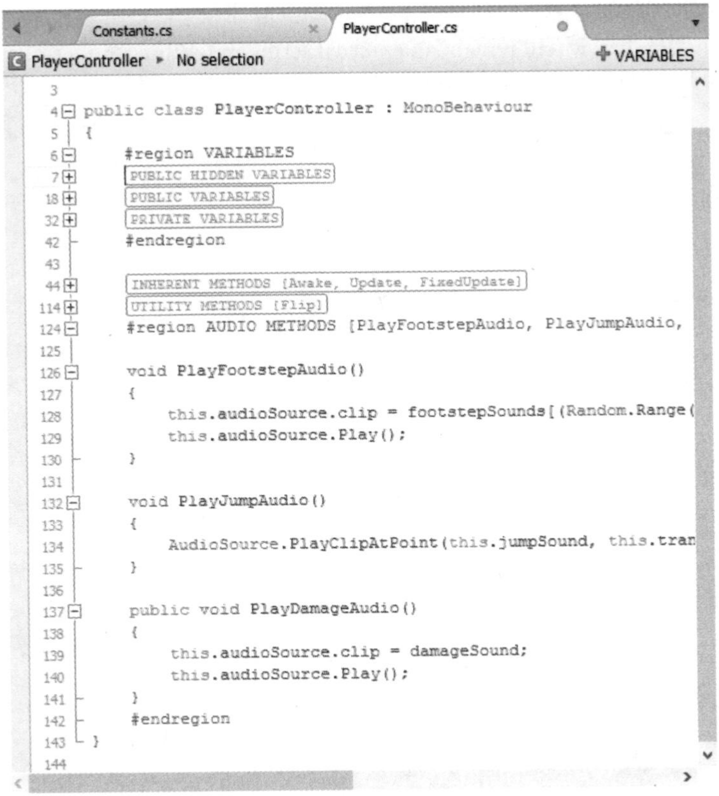

Figure 12.5   Partially collapsed regions in the PlayerController script

event that one of these values (e.g., speed) is temporarily altered and later reverted. It even makes renaming your inputs relatively painless, as you'll no longer have to update the string references in every script that has them!

Tip

We're going to lock the player's speed and jump strength as a way to show how these constants work. However, if you're still tinkering with those values, you're better off leaving them as public variables so that you can quickly adjust and test them during runtime. Once we swap them for constants, we won't be able to do that as easily anymore. The trade-off for increased security is often decreased flexibility.

Let's create our new script:

1. Navigate to the _scripts folder in the Project View.

2. Create a new C# script and name it "Constants."

3. Open the newly created script.

Unlike previous scripts, this one won't exist on any specific GameObject as a Component. Rather, it will remain an external script and will not inherit from the MonoBehaviour class. Set the Constants script up as shown in Listing 12.2.

Listing 12.2 **The Constants Script**

```
public class Constants
{
  #region PLAYER MOVEMENT VALUES

  public const float playerMaxSpeed = 7;
  public const float playerJumpForce = 850;
  public const float playerGroundCheckRadius = 0.2f;

  #endregion
  #region ANIMATOR VARIABLE NAMES

  public const string animSpeed = "Speed";
  public const string animJump = "Jump";
  public const string animDie = "Die";
  public const string animDamage = "Damage";

  #endregion
  #region INPUT NAMES

  public const string inputMove = "Horizontal";
  public const string inputJump = "Jump";

  #endregion
}
```

Any future changes to these values will occur from within this script rather than via the Inspector window. Now we need to update the PlayerController script to make use of our new constants, as shown in Listing 12.3.

> **Tip**
>
> It can be helpful, particularly in a language such as JavaScript that has no natural concept of a constant, to name constants using all capital letters in order to make them more identifiable. As an example, we could change the name `inputMove` to `INPUT _ MOVE`.

Listing 12.3 **Updated PlayerController Script**

```
public class Constants
{
  #region PUBLIC VARIABLES
  public float maxSpeed = Constants.playerMaxSpeed;
```

```
public float jumpForce = Constants.playerJumpForce;
public PhysicsMaterial2D jumpMaterial;

public Transform groundCheck;
public LayerMask groundLayers;

public AudioClip[] footstepSounds;
public AudioClip jumpSound;
public AudioClip damageSound;

#endregion
#region PRIVATE VARIABLES

private float groundCheckRadius = Constants.playerGroundCheckRadius;

private AudioSource audioSource;
private Animator anim;
private float deathTimeElapsed;
#endregion
#endregion

#region INHERENT METHODS [Awake, Update, FixedUpdate]

void Awake()
{
  anim = this.GetComponent<Animator>();
  audioSource = this.GetComponent<AudioSource>();
}

void Update ()
{
  if(Input.GetButtonDown(Constants.inputJump))
  {
    if(isGrounded == true)
    {
      this.rigidbody2D.velocity = new Vector2(rigidbody2D.velocity.x,0);
      this.rigidbody2D.AddForce(new Vector2(0, jumpForce));

      this.anim.SetTrigger(Constants.animJump);
      PlayJumpAudio();
    }
    else if(isDoubleJumping == false)
    {
      isDoubleJumping = true;
      this.rigidbody2D.velocity = new Vector2(rigidbody2D.velocity.x,0);
      this.rigidbody2D.AddForce(new Vector2(0, jumpForce));
```

(continues)

```
                PlayJumpAudio();
              }
          }
      }


      void FixedUpdate()
      {
        isGrounded = Physics2D.OverlapCircle
          (groundCheck.position,  groundCheckRadius, groundLayers);
        PhysicsMaterial2D material =
          this.gameObject.GetComponent<CircleCollider2D>().sharedMaterial;

        if(isGrounded == true)
        {
          this.isDoubleJumping = false;
        }
        if(isGrounded == true && material == this.jumpMaterial)
        {
          CircleCollider2D collision =
  this.gameObject.GetComponent<CircleCollider2D>();
          collision.sharedMaterial = null;
          collision.enabled = false;
          collision.enabled = true;
        }
        else if(isGrounded == false &&
  this.gameObject.GetComponent<CircleCollider2D>().sharedMaterial == null)
        {
          CircleCollider2D collision =
  this.gameObject.GetComponent<CircleCollider2D>();
          collision.sharedMaterial = this.jumpMaterial;

          collision.enabled = false;
          collision.enabled = true;
        }
        try
        {
          float move = Input.GetAxis(Constants.inputMove);
          this.rigidbody2D.velocity = new Vector2
            (move * maxSpeed, rigidbody2D.velocity.y);
          this.anim.SetFloat(Constants.animSpeed, Mathf.Abs(move));

          if((move > 0.0f && isFacingRight == false)
            || (move < 0.0f && isFacingRight == true))
        {
          Flip ();
        }
      }
```

```
  catch(UnityException error)
  {
    Debug.LogError(error.ToString());
  }
 }
}
```

We've now replaced variable values with references to our Constants script. Similarly, we've also replaced the string references to our inputs and Animator variables. If you run the game, everything should still play out exactly as it did before!

If we were to rename a string reference, or wanted to change the player's maximum speed, we could now update our reference in a single location—the Constants script—and every script referencing it would receive the change. This can save a lot of time and hassle down the line.

Using Shorthand Code

We stated in Chapter 5, "The Basics of Movement and Player Control," that for the purposes of syntactical clarity for the new user, this book would not use shorthand code. As you become more comfortable with coding, however, it is highly recommended that you learn to write everything in shorthand. It's a de facto standard in game development, and as you learn it, you'll find that you can get the same amount of coding done with less actual material in the script. This is an important skill that will help you become a more efficient programmer.

Additional Thoughts on Organizing Code

As the scripts grow, the `Update()` and `FixedUpdate()` functions are likely to get particularly messy. Chunks of these functions can be packed up into their own functions and then called. The various player inputs in the PlayerController script, for example, could be managed by an input controller function to reduce clutter. Making an effort to keep the major functions concise will help you manage your code in the long term.

Optimizations

Optimizing your game is a very vital piece of game development and should be addressed early on. It's something you should continually be thinking about as your Project begins to take shape. Optimizations can often be overlooked as being something of a burden or addressed only toward the end, but ignoring them will cause more headache later on as things begin to bottleneck.

Good optimization boils down to the performance of your game and how smoothly it is able to run. Just as with most things, the fewer complicated moving parts it contains, the less likely it is to have problems or break down. Creating a game works the same way. While we want to have an entertaining experience, we have to find ways of doing so without the cost to gameplay.

Optimizations can be in all areas of your Project, from art assets and scripting all the way down to the platforms for which you build your game. The more experience you have with Unity and game design, the easier it becomes to develop an "eye" for optimization and know what to prepare for from the beginning of your Project.

Prefabs

Creating prefabbed GameObjects is a great way to keep your game organized, but it is also an important step for optimizing your game. Since Prefabs are "master" GameObjects that are reused throughout your game, using them lets you know there isn't unnecessary data being added to them.

Prefabs can also be instantiated—spawned—at runtime. This means that they are not drawn, and therefore not used, until they are added into the game. This can help reduce the number of draw calls in a Scene because the Prefabs are loaded only when they are needed.

Physics

Using the physics engine adds a great deal of overhead to the CPU you are using. While we want to have physics for our game, we must take into account when, how, and why we are using them. Using fewer Rigidbodies and physics simulations is always good, but there are ways we can optimize them on top of this.

Time Manager

One method of controlling demand on the CPU is with the Time Manager. This controls Time Scale, which affects how things react in real time, but it also controls how often to check for physics calculations. You can find the Time Manager in the Project Settings rollout (Edit > Project Settings > Time). Figure 12.6 shows the Time Manager settings.

> **Note**
>
> The Time Manager handles both physics simulations as well as `FixedUpdate()` functions. Both of these can lead to frame rate slowdowns if used continuously and in multiple occurrences at one time. Keep this in mind when adding these to your scripts and your GameObjects.

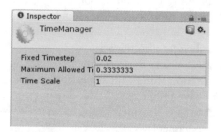

Figure 12.6   Time Manager settings

- **Fixed Timestep:** Determines how often per frame the engine calculates physics simulations. The lower the value, the more times it will check.

- **Maximum Allowed Timestep:** Determines the maximum allotted time in which to run a physics simulation per frame. Calculations and `FixedUpdate()` events that take more than the time allotted will be curtailed so as not to further affect frame rate.

- **Time Scale:** Handles the value of time for your game. A value of 1.0 is equal to 1 second in real time.

For our little game, the default values should work fine. We are not running a large number of `FixedUpdate()` calls or physics simulations, but it's always good to know where this feature is and how to use it for your next game.

Number of Physics Objects

The number of Rigidbodies and colliders you are using in your Scenes will play a role in the performance and frame rate, as the physics engine has to calculate all of these. Obviously not using any would have no hit on the physics engine, but what fun would that be? Again, keeping the numbers reasonable and dynamically loading them will help with this.

> **Note**
>
> Static Collider will also help with the physics calculations, since they do not move and do not require a Rigidbody with them. The physics engine can collectively find these within the Scene and store their data at the beginning. To make a GameObject static, from the Inspector, set the "Static" flag as checked. This is located next to the GameObject's name field.

Rigidbody Attributes

The Rigidbody Components hold a few attributes that can tax the CPU and slow down performance. We discussed these a little in Chapter 7, "Setting Up Player Physics and Colliders," but let's look at how we can change them to affect our playback:

- **Interpolate:** Determines how the object moves through a physics simulation. No Interpolation will run faster, but the animation may tend to play back jerky.

- **Sleeping Mode:** Determines if the GameObject's collision is calculated at the start or once contact is made. Setting this to Sleep lets the physics engine wait until it needs to check this.

- **Collision Detection:** Lets the physics engine determine how it collides with other objects. Setting this to Discrete means it will check less often, but at the expense of possibly missing a collision.

Draw Calls

Draw calls are the rendering "calls" that the graphics API has to perform. What this means is that for every GameObject that Unity cannot batch together, it has to perform a draw call. Although it would be pretty tough to not have any, the fewer Unity has to process, the better the performance. A good number is around 20 when working with mobile platforms.

Sprites

As we are dealing with 2D sprites, this is a big area for controlling draw calls. If each sprite had to use its own draw call, we would easily kill our frame rate trying to load our Scene. Luckily, we can use sprite atlases to manage multiple sprites on one sheet. This way, we are using only a single draw call to render them.

Sprites can also be set to "Static" and then batched together. Unity does this to some extent, but by ensuring that they are static, we can make sure we are using all available resources.

We also affect the draw calls for sprites based on their sorting. Using the Sorting Layer and the Order in Layer attribute will affect how the draw calls work.

The Sorting Layer will draw the sprites based on their sorting order listed in the Layer Manager. With this you can determine what sprites the camera will draw in front of or behind other sprites. This is useful for having objects appear in the foreground and background of the Player GameObject.

The graphics API draws the bottommost layer and then works its way up, so objects on different layers have to be rendered separately. Keeping sprites that share an atlas to the same layer is beneficial. Sorting Layers will not cause a draw call as long as all of the sprites use the same atlas.

> **Note**
>
> Order in Layer does not affect the draw call number, contrary to belief. The Sorting Layer will take priority and draw the sprites based on that. It is after this that the Order in Layer is checked. The order will just set which one is drawn first based on the atlas sheet. Keep this in mind when layering your sprites and try to keep them in the same atlas and Sorting Layer.

Materials

Materials are another factor you must consider when trying to reduce your draw calls. Since the graphics API has to account for the individual shading attributes of a Material, it has to draw each of them to produce the correct rendering for that object. This comes into play a lot more with 3D objects, but it is something to take note of even for 2D GameObjects. Using different Materials might be something you want to do to give a specific look to your game. Just remember that doing so comes with a price. Even if you are batching your sprites, using a different Material for some of them will require a second draw call.

Warning

Unity uses a standard default Material for 2D sprites. This should be sufficient in most cases for 2D games. Just remember that changing the Material of any sprite will allocate an additional draw call.

Triangle Count

Triangle count refers to the unique number of polygon triangles that are being drawn in a game. Everything being rendered in the engine is using some variation of polygons, and the engine has to take these into account. Even the 2D sprites we are using are placed on some sort of polygonal mesh, usually a plane made up of two triangles.

Polygons affect the CPU (processor) side of the engine more than draw calls (graphics side), so you should try to keep them within a reasonable budget. Take into account the platform and the number of polygons you should be shooting for. There are a ton of resources on the Net for these budgets.

Colliders also use polygon counts to build their mesh. Whenever you use colliders, it's recommended to try to use the primitive ones rather than a polygonal mesh one, simply because the mesh collider uses more points to match the object, and therefore adds more triangles. Figure 12.7 shows two examples of a collider for an object, one using simple primitive colliders and the other a polygonal mesh one. Both will most likely do the job. You may even be able to get away with just the rectangular primitive one in a lot of cases.

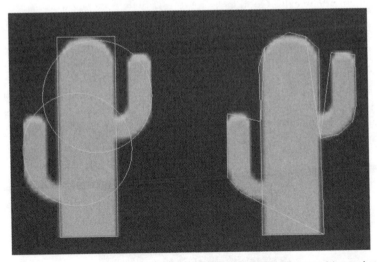

Figure 12.7   Cacti, one with three primitive colliders and the other with a polygonal collider. The polygonal may be more accurate but will be more expensive.

> **Tip**
>
> Think about the use of colliders and the precise detection that is needed. In a lot of cases you would be better off using the prefabricated colliders instead of the polygonal one, even if you are using more than one. A Circle Collider for a character head and a Box Collider for the body will still most likely result in a lower triangle count than a collider that conforms more to the sprite.

Batching

One final place we can manually control some of the draw call count is when we are building and batching our assets.

Batching means taking the assets and trying to combine them into single render calls to reduce the number needed. By combining a series of sprites that use the same atlas, along with the same Material and Sorting Layer, Unity can batch (process) them all at once to create a single draw call. So in theory, if you could keep all of your 2D sprites to a single atlas and Sorting Layer, you could create a game with one draw call! Crazy, right?

We have just scratched the surface when it comes to optimizing collision and meshes and reducing draw calls and batching. What we did learn will be helpful for building a 2D game, but there is a ton more to optimizations with Unity.

The 3D side of Unity and Unity Pro offers more resources and tools for getting the best performance out of your game, such as mesh baking and texture baking. Use the Unity documentation and scour the Web. There are thousands of forum posts and tutorials on reducing draw calls. Good luck!

Rendering Statistics Window

The Rendering Statistics window (Figure 12.8) will give us a more accurate representation of how we are sitting with our optimizations and frame rates. This feature is really handy because it is included in the Unity free version. It is also viewable as the game is running, so you can keep an eye on where your resources are being pulled from.

You can find the Render Statistics window in the Game View. From the top menu bar, simply click the Stats button to toggle it on.

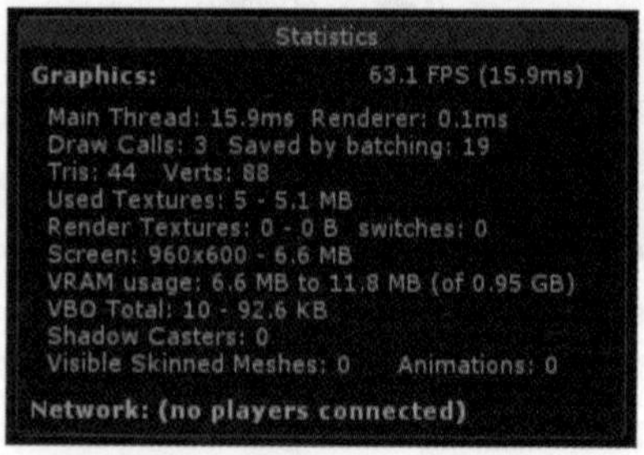

```
                         Statistics
Graphics:                    63.1 FPS (15.9ms)

Main Thread: 15.9ms  Renderer: 0.1ms
Draw Calls: 3   Saved by batching: 19
Tris: 44    Verts: 88
Used Textures: 5 - 5.1 MB
Render Textures: 0 - 0 B  switches: 0
Screen: 960x600 - 6.6 MB
VRAM usage: 6.6 MB to 11.8 MB (of 0.95 GB)
VBO Total: 10 - 92.6 KB
Shadow Casters: 0
Visible Skinned Meshes: 0     Animations: 0

Network: (no players connected)
```

Figure 12.8   Rendering Statistics window from our game

- **FPS:** Frames per second. This is how many frames per real-time second our game is able to render. The higher the FPS, the smoother and more accurate your game will be. You should strive for 30 FPS or more.
- **Draw Calls:** Number of draw calls our GPU has to process after any batching has occurred.
- **Saved by batching:** Number of draw calls reduced due to batching.
- **Tris/Verts:** Total number of triangles and vertices being drawn for the Scene.
- **Used Textures:** Total number of textures being used, and their size to save to memory.
- **Render Texture:** Number of textures rendered to the graphics engine. These are things that are processed in real time, such as water, holograms, or video monitors.
- **Screen:** Size of the game screen resolution and overall memory usage.
- **VRAM usage:** Average amount of video RAM being used, and the total VRAM available from the graphics card.
- **VBO Total:** Vertex buffer object, the total number of mesh objects that are pushed to the graphics card.
- **Shadow Casters:** Total number of GameObjects that cast shadows. Usually these are lights in the Scene.
- **Visible Skinned Meshes:** Number of skinned GameObjects in the Scene.
- **Animations:** Number of animations in the Scene.

Summary

Well, we covered a great deal in this chapter about organizing your Project as well as some tips for optimizing your game. We looked at ways to keep your folders and Hierarchy clean, and using layers and labels to more easily locate assets. We also looked at Prefabs and how they can be really beneficial.

We also looked at a few ways to organize and clean up our scripts to make them simpler, easier to manage and read, and maybe a little lighter on the CPU as well. The script files themselves can be small, but the slightest leak or loop can cause a great deal of heartache.

Last, we looked at some ways to optimize our game and reduce calculations on the graphics API. We also learned a great deal about draw calls and how to get the most out of our sprite atlases, colliders, and Materials.

In the next chapter we will add the last few elements to our game. We will add the finishing touches for our menus and Game_Win and Game_Over Scenes. We will then build and publish our game for all the world to see! Let's get to it!

Exercises

Our Scene needs a lot of love to reduce triangle counts and draw calls and to be optimized. Start by looking at our Screen1 group and GameObjects, and try to find areas where you can reduce some of these counts.

1. Try removing the colliders attached to the sprites and create a single collider that encompasses them all. Maybe use an Edge Collider that has only two points instead of a Box Collider with four.

2. Try to locate where all of the draw calls originate. Are there ways to optimize some of them and reduce the total number? Does the problem lie in the Sorting Layers?

3. Do this throughout the Scene, looking for areas that could be improved. Remember that you can always hop over to the Game View (even without running it) to see how the Render Statistics look.

13

Bringing It All Together

The end approaches and we have built quite the game! Our hero has animations, physics, scripts, and even a double jump! We have enemies, platforms, and dynamic bridges! We even have our menus and a GUI with all of its relevant information. Whew! It was a lot of work, but it shows what you can get out of a 2D game.

Let's put the finishing touches on our game now. We will start by adding a trigger that will end the level after we have completed it. We will then put some functionality into our game to restart a level when the player dies, and one for when the game is complete. We will add a few small scripts so our levels will run in order from the first one to the last, along with a Game Win scenario.

Last, we will look at what is involved in building our game. We will go over some of the setup for building a game for various platforms. Finally, we will build and deploy our game to the Unity Web Player. After all this hard work, won't it be exciting to show off your own version of the game?

So with that, let's take this game home!

Tying the Levels Together

We've tied our level into a Game Over screen in the event that the player perishes, but what happens when the player clears a level? For that matter, how do we even tell the player that they've cleared a level in the first place? In order to properly wrap this up, we're going to need to fill in some small—but crucial—gaps in our game. These include

- Adding a victory trigger to the level
- Loading the next level after victory
- Restarting a level after Game Over
- Restarting the game after winning

Preparing the Victory Trigger Prefab

In order for a player to advance through the game, we need to create a trigger that will load the player into the next map. This should be something visible, providing the player with an obvious goal to reach. With that in mind, let's create a flag to mark the end of our levels:

1. Create an empty GameObject and name it "triggerVictory."
2. Click the Add Component button and select Rendering > Sprite Renderer.
3. Set its Sprite property to "flagBlue."
4. Click the Add Component button and select Physics 2D > Box Collider 2D.
5. Set the "Is Trigger" property to true.
6. Set the Box Collider 2D's Size values to X: 1, Y: 1.
7. Set the Box Collider 2D's Center values to X: 0, Y: 0.

You should now have a new GameObject that looks similar to Figure 13.1.

The trigger is the same length and width as the flag, which makes the collision feel sensible but also allows players to jump over it. Unlike our checkpoints, what the player is touching is obvious so we don't have to worry as much about players accidentally missing it. Whether or not you keep it that way is entirely up to you; just consider it within the context of the experience you're designing, as always!

> **Tip**
>
> Try adding some minor animation to the flag, as we did with our enemies. It will stand out more against the background that way.

Before we create the actual script that we'll use to transition the player between levels, we need to add some new values to our Constants script, as shown in Listing 13.1.

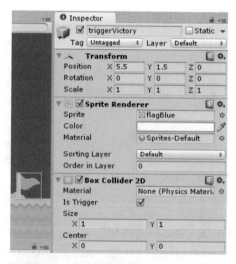

Figure 13.1   The triggerVictory GameObject

Listing 13.1   **New Values in the Constants Script**

```
public class Constants
{
  #region PLAYER PREFS

  public const string PREF_COINS = "Coins";
  public const string PREF_CURRENT_LEVEL = "CurrentLevel";

  #endregion
  #region SCENE NUMBERS

  public const int SCENE_LEVEL_1 = 6;
  public const int SCENE_LEVEL_2 = 2;
  public const int SCENE_LEVEL_3 = 3;
  public const int SCENE_GAME_OVER = 1;
  public const int SCENE_GAME_WIN = 4;
  public const int SCENE_TITLE = 5;

  #endregion
}
```

The constants that we've just added to the script represent the names of variables in the `PlayerPrefs` class—which we will discuss later in this chapter—and the numeric IDs of Scenes that can be found in our Build Settings.

- **PREF _ COINS:** The name of the `PlayerPrefs` variable that tracks coin collection between levels
- **PREF _ CURRENT _ LEVEL:** The name of the `PlayerPrefs` variable that tracks what level the player is currently on
- **SCENE _ LEVEL _ 1:** The ID of our first level in the Build Settings
- **SCENE _ LEVEL _ 2:** The ID of our second level in the Build Settings
- **SCENE _ LEVEL _ 3:** The ID of our third level in the Build Settings
- **SCENE _ GAME _ OVER:** The ID of our Game_Over Scene in the Build Settings
- **SCENE _ GAME _ WIN:** The ID of our Game_Win Scene in the Build Settings
- **SCENE _ TITLE:** The ID of our Title_Screen Scene in the Build Settings

> **Note**
>
> Your constant values may not match those of the code provided, so be sure to check your Build Settings and adjust as necessary. Whenever a Scene is added, it takes the next available integer value as an ID. You can also load Scenes by name, in which case you could point the constants to the Scene name using a string value rather than an integer. Use whichever way you feel is least likely to cause you to have to edit the values in this script!

These new Scene ID constants will be extremely useful if anything ever causes the order of our Scenes to be shuffled around. We will always refer to the levels in code by their Constants value names rather than discrete integers, reducing any potential confusion when the inevitable decision is made to swap one level for another in the game's progression.

Creating the Victory Trigger Script

Now that we have our constant values prepared, we can create a Component that tells our trigger how to end the level when the player enters it:

1. Select the triggerVictory GameObject.
2. Click the Add Component button and select New Script.
3. Name the script "VictoryTrigger" and ensure that the language is set to CSharp.
4. Drag the triggerVictory GameObject to the _prefabs directory to save it as a Prefab.
5. In the Project Browser, select the newly created script and move it to the _scripts folder (or an appropriately named subfolder if you've been organizing!).
6. Double-click the script to open it in MonoDevelop-Unity.

We'll set up something relatively simple that waits briefly and then loads a provided Scene. We'll carry forward the number of coins that the player has from level to level as well so that they can continue to rack up their score.

> **Note**
>
> Be aware that the actual Player GameObject is being lost between levels. This is why each level has its own Player GameObject present. We are transferring only certain bits of data forward to give the appearance that it is the same GameObject.

Fill out the newly created script as shown in Listing 13.2.

Listing 13.2   The VictoryTrigger Script

```
public class VictoryTrigger : MonoBehaviour
{
  public int sceneToLoad;
  public float delay = 1;

  private float timeElapsed;
  private bool isTriggered;

  void Update ()
  {
    if(isTriggered == true)
```

```
    {
      timeElapsed = timeElapsed + Time.deltaTime;
    }

    if (timeElapsed >= delay)
    {
      Application.LoadLevel(sceneToLoad);
    }
  }

  void OnTriggerEnter2D(Collider2D collider)
  {
    if(collider.tag == "Player")
    {
      timeElapsed = 0;
      isTriggered = true;

      collider.GetComponent<PlayerController>().enabled = false;
      collider.rigidbody2D.velocity = new Vector2(0,0);
      collider.GetComponent<Animator>().SetFloat(Constants.animSpeed, 0);

      PlayerPrefs.SetInt(Constants.PREF_COINS,
        collider.GetComponent<PlayerStats>().coinsCollected);
    }
  }
}
```

Let's take a look at the variables this script is using:

- **sceneToLoad**: The ID (in Build Settings) of the Scene to be loaded.
- **delay**: The time (in seconds) to wait before loading the next Scene. This allows you to polish the event with fireworks visual effects, sound effects, or similar down the road.
- **timeElapsed**: The time (in seconds) that has elapsed since touching the trigger.
- **isTriggered**: Tracks whether or not the trigger has been activated by a player.

The `OnTriggerEnter2D()` Function

When an object enters the trigger, we first test to see if it's the player. We wouldn't want an enemy randomly ending the level, now would we? Or would we? That could be an interesting mechanic, if the player were manipulating the way in which enemies moved, but those are thoughts for another time and place.

Once the player contacts the trigger, we set the *timeElapsed* variable to a value of 0 and mark the trigger as activated via the *isTriggered* bool. These will be put to use in the `Update()` function.

We also remove control from the player by disabling the PlayerController Component, zero out their X and Y velocity, and set the Animator Component's speed to 0 so that the Player GameObject doesn't still think it's trying to move.

Finally, we grab the `PlayerPrefs` class and store the number of coins the player has within it. `PlayerPrefs` is a class that is intended for storing and accessing player preference data between game sessions. We're piggybacking on it for our purposes as a quick and simple way of storing data without delving into data storage structures, which are outside the scope of this book.

> **Note**
>
> For more information on the `PlayerPrefs` class, try this link: http://docs.unity3d.com/ScriptReference/PlayerPrefs.html.

The `Update()` Function

Once the *isTriggered* bool is true, this function measures the time that elapses until it reaches or exceeds the delay variable. At that time, the game is told to load the Scene provided by the *sceneToLoad* integer.

Save the scripts and try running the game. If the player touches the flag, they should be sent to the next level you provided, but you'll notice that the coin count has been reset to 0. We've saved the data but we aren't retrieving it yet. Let's take care of that next.

Retrieving the Coin Value

In order to retrieve the player's coin value from `PlayerPrefs`, we need to make some adjustments to our PlayerStats script, as shown in Listing 13.3.

Listing 13.3   **Changes to the PlayerStats Script**

```
public class VictoryTrigger : MonoBehaviour
{
  void Start()
  {
    spriteRenderer = this.gameObject.GetComponent<SpriteRenderer>();
    if(Application.loadedLevel != Constants.SCENE_LEVEL_1)
    {
      coinsCollected = PlayerPrefs.GetInt(Constants.PREF_COINS);
    }
    PlayerPrefs.SetInt(Constants.PREF_CURRENT_LEVEL,
Application.loadedLevel);
  }
}
```

The `Start()` Function

The `Start()` function now tests whether or not the level being loaded is the first game level, and if it is, nothing new happens. If any other level is being loaded, however, we set the *coinsCollected* variable to match the value found in `PlayerPrefs`. This conditional check is necessary to prevent a fresh run of the game from starting the player off with however many coins they had the last time they played.

We also grab the ID of the currently loaded level and store it in `PlayerPrefs` so that we can reload the current level later on if the player dies and wishes to retry it.

Save the script and try running the game once again. You should find that the coins are now carried between levels but the value is reset whenever you start the game over (or load the first level).

Hooking Up the Intro Screens

We created a splash screen and a title screen in Chapter 10, "Creating the Menus and Interface Elements," but at the moment they aren't doing anything for us. We need to add them to our Scenes In Build list in the Build Settings. You may recall that we opened the Build Settings window in Chapter 11, "Applying Effects to the GameObjects," in order to get numeric assignments for our Scenes, but here's a quick refresher on where to find it:

1. Open the File menu.
2. Select Build Settings to open the window.
3. Alternatively, you can use the Ctrl + Shift + B hotkeys.

You should now be looking at the Build Settings window, as shown in Figure 13.2. The Scene at the top of the list—carrying an ID value of 0—is the Scene that will start when the game is launched. If we want our splash screen to display, we need to add it to that list and give it the top spot. Take the following steps:

1. Open the Splash_Screen Scene.
2. Open the Build Settings window if you closed it already.
3. Click the Add Current button.
4. Click and drag the Splash_Screen Scene entry in the list up to the top so that it has an ID value of 0.
5. Open the Title_Screen Scene.
6. Click the Add Current button.

Now that the splash screen has the right value, it will be the first Scene loaded when the game is launched. You may have to juggle numbers either in the list or in the Constants script in order to get everything to line up correctly again.

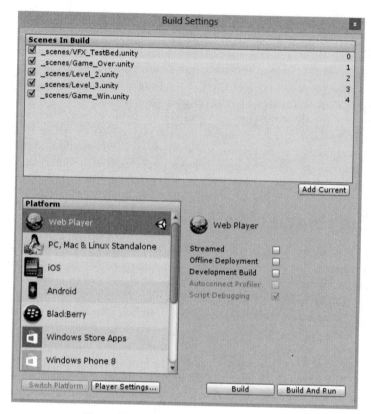

Figure 13.2   The Build Settings window

The splash screen still needs to connect to the title screen, and similarly, the title screen needs to connect to the first level. Fortunately, we have all of the necessary materials to make that happen. Open the SplashScreenDelayed script and add the highlighted code in Listing 13.4.

Listing 13.4   **SplashScreenDelayed Script**

```
public class SplashScreenDelayed : MonoBehaviour
{
  public float delayTime = 5f;

  void Start()
  {
    StartCoroutine("Delay");
  }

  IEnumerator Delay()
```

```
  {
    yield return new WaitForSeconds(delayTime);
    Application.LoadLevel(Constants.SCENE_TITLE);
    Debug.Log("Time's Up!");
  }

  void Update()
  {
    if (Input.anyKeyDown)
    {
      Application.LoadLevel(Constants.SCENE_TITLE);
      Debug.Log("A key or mouse click has been detected");
    }
  }
}
```

We've added an `Application.LoadLevel()` call to both the `Update()` and `Delay()` functions. This will load the Title_Screen Scene, which we now need to hook to the game's first level. Open the TitleScreenScript script and make the change to it as noted in Listing 13.5.

Listing 13.5   **TitleScreenScript's `Update()` Function**

```
void Update()
{
  if (Input.anyKeyDown)
  {
    Application.LoadLevel(Constants.SCENE_LEVEL_1);
  }
}
```

Our Title_Screen Scene will now load directly into the first level of the game once any key is pressed. Our Project is becoming more and more like a real game, but it's still missing something important, which we'll get to now.

Win or Lose: Getting Back into the Action

We've created Scenes for our Game Over and Game Win scenarios, but we need to get the player back into the action. Game Over offers the player a chance to retry the level, restart the game, or quit, while Game Win offers the player a chance to restart the game or quit.

Neither of those buttons does anything right now, so we're going to tie some small bits of code to them to make them fully functional.

Recovering from Game Over

When a player has been defeated one way or another, it typically results in a Game Over screen in platformer titles, and ours is no different. If you're developing the kind of game in which the player has the option of retrying or reloading, you'll want to keep this Scene as succinct as possible. The longer you keep them here, the less likely it is that a player is going to feel like diving back in. Let's give players the functionality to get back into the game now:

1. Open the Game_Over Scene.
2. Locate the GameOverScript script.
3. Open it in MonoDevelop-Unity.

Make the adjustments to the script shown in Listing 13.6.

Listing 13.6   **Changes to the GameOverScript Script**

```
public class GameOverScript : MonoBehaviour
{
  public GUISkin Skin;
  public float gapSize = 20f;

  void OnGUI()
  {
    GUI.skin = Skin;
    GUILayout.BeginArea (new Rect ((Screen.height / 2) - Screen.height /
      4,(Screen.width / 2) - Screen.width / 4,
      Screen.height, Screen.width));
    GUILayout.BeginVertical();
    GUILayout.Label( "Game Over" );
    GUILayout.Space( gapSize );

    if(GUILayout.Button ("Retry!"))
    {

Application.LoadLevel(PlayerPrefs.GetInt(Constants.PREF_CURRENT_LEVEL));
    }
    GUILayout.Space( gapSize );

    if(GUILayout.Button("Restart!"))
    {
      Application.LoadLevel(Constants.SCENE_LEVEL_1);
    }

    GUILayout.Space( gapSize );
```

```
#if UNITY_STANDALONE
    if(GUILayout.Button("Quit!"))
    {
      Application.Quit();
    }
#endif
    GUILayout.EndVertical();
    GUILayout.EndArea ();
  }
}
```

The `OnGUI()` Function

If the player elects to retry the level where they died, we tell the game to load a Scene based on a `PlayerPrefs` variable that we store at the start of each level. Due to the way we set up our handling of coins, this will also return the player's coin value to what it was when they first tried the level.

If the player elects to restart the game, we explicitly load the first level of the game, whereas we tell the application to terminate if the player chooses to quit.

You may have noticed that there's something a bit different around the script for quitting the game. As a Web Player version of the game won't need a Quit button—quitting is just closing the tab in the browser—we'd really rather not have that button be present. The `#if UNITY_STANDALONE` tag tells the script to use that portion only if the game is built for a standalone platform. When you run this on any other platform, you won't even see the button!

> **Note**
>
> Be aware that quitting won't actually close the application when tested from Play mode.

Starting Over from a Win

Once the player has completed the game, what do they do? In our case, we're going to give them the option to restart or quit out of the application. There is very little difference between how we're handling this and how we handled the Game_Over Scene.

1. Open the Game_Win Scene.
2. Locate the GameWinScript script.
3. Open it in MonoDevelop-Unity.

Make the adjustments to the script shown in Listing 13.7.

Listing 13.7   **Changes to the GameWinScript Script**

```
public class GameWinScript : MonoBehaviour
{
  public GUISkin Skin;
  public float gapSize = 20f;

  void OnGUI()
  {

    GUI.skin = Skin;

    GUILayout.BeginArea (new Rect ((Screen.height / 2) - Screen.height /
      4,(Screen.width / 2) - Screen.width / 4,
      Screen.height, Screen.width));
    GUILayout.BeginVertical();
    GUILayout.Label( "You Won!" );
    GUILayout.Space( gapSize );

    if(GUILayout.Button ("Restart Game"))
    {
      Application.LoadLevel(Constants.SCENE_LEVEL_1);
    }

    GUILayout.Space( gapSize );

#if UNITY_STANDALONE
    if(GUILayout.Button("Quit!"))
    {
      Application.Quit();
    }
#endif

  GUILayout.EndVertical();
  GUILayout.EndArea ();
  }
}
```

The OnGUI() Function

If the player elects to restart the game, we explicitly load the first level of the game, whereas we tell the application to terminate if the player chooses to quit. As with the previous script, we've nested the Quit button scripting within #if UNITY_STANDALONE to prevent it from showing up in other platforms. That's really all there is to it!

Be sure to save the scripts and test various successes and failures in your game.

Building and Deploying the Game

We've been creating a game this entire time but the question remains: how do we share it with other people? Fortunately for us, Unity has an excellent system for compiling all of the code and assets into an executable format (building) so that they can be published to a server or other delivery mechanism (deploying). The list of platforms supported by Unity is incredibly diverse. It has your standard PC/Mac/Linux options, but it also includes a selection of major consoles and mobile operating systems as potential deployment platforms.

Open the Build Settings window now so that we can take a closer look at what it offers. There should be a small Unity logo next to one of the platforms in the Platform list. This means that the tools will attempt to build for this specific platform whenever you use the Build or Build And Run buttons. Let's take a moment to discuss what the various buttons on this window can do for you:

- **Switch Platform:** Changes the platform for the build process to whatever is currently selected in the Platform list window.
- **Player Settings:** Displays a number of options in the Inspector panel relevant to the selected platform, including resolution, icon, and splash screen settings, as shown in Figure 13.3.

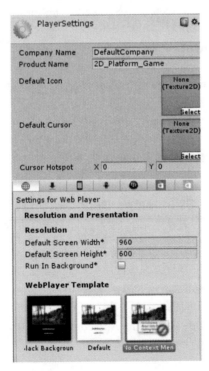

Figure 13.3   Player Settings window for cross-platform and Web Player

- **Build:** Builds the current platform selection.
- **Build And Run:** Builds the current platform selection and runs it immediately.
- **Add Current:** This adds the current Scene to the Scenes In Build list and assigns it a numeric ID.

> **Note**
>
> While many of the build options are available with standard Unity, there are a handful of platforms that require special licenses that can be obtained at an additional fee. Some licenses may also require approval, and others may require that specific development hardware be used to set up the game for that platform.

As you've seen, there are also several options related specifically to the selected platform available in the Build Settings window. We'll be building our game for the Unity Web Player platform, but let's also examine the settings for PC, Mac, and Linux standalone computers, as they are common platforms for Unity Project deployment.

Web Player's Build Settings

The following properties control some of the basic elements of a Web Player build:

- **Streamed:** If true, the Web Player content is meant to be streamed rather than entirely loaded up front.
- **Offline Deployment:** If true, the Web Player will not reference any online resources.
- **Development Build:** If true, the Autoconnect Profiler and Script Debugging options become available.
- **Autoconnect Profiler (Unity Pro only):** If true, enables Profiler functionality that can be used to gather valuable information about your game as it runs.
- **Script Debugging:** If true, debugging options such as MonoDevelop-Unity will be able to attach to the game's process to provide debug functionality.

PC, Mac, and Linux Standalone Build Settings

The following properties control some of the basic elements of a standalone build:

- **Target Platform:** Selects which Operating System type you are specifically building for.
- **Architecture:** Allows you to choose between 32-bit (x86) and 64-bit (x86_64) architecture types.
- **Development Build:** If true, the Autoconnect Profiler and Script Debugging options become available.

- **Autoconnect Profiler (Unity Pro only):** If true, enables Profiler functionality that can be used to gather valuable information about your game as it runs.
- **Script Debugging:** If true, debugging options such as MonoDevelop-Unity will be able to attach to the game's process to provide debug functionality.

Cross-Platform Player Settings

These settings are shared among all possible platforms that you can build for. Click the Player Settings button to show them in the Inspector panel.

- **Company Name:** The name of your company. The preferences file's location is based on this information.
- **Product Name:** The title of the game that will be shown in the menu bar when running. This also determines where the preferences file is located.
- **Default Icon:** The icon that the application will show when running on every platform. This can be overridden on a per-platform basis.
- **Default Cursor:** The default cursor that the application will have on every platform that uses one.
- **Cursor Hotspot:** A hotspot is the active pixel of the pointer that is used to target a click. This property determines the hotspot and is measured in pixels from the top left of the default cursor.

Web Player's Player Settings

Last, let's take a look at the Player Settings that are available when you build for the Unity Web Player platform.

Resolution and Presentation

- **Resolution:** These options determine the screen height and width that the game will occupy in the browser window.
- **Run In Background:** If true, the game will continue to run when the window does not have focus.
- **Web Player Template:** These are options for the basic Web page that is created at build time. The game window will be embedded into this page.

> **Note**
>
> Build Settings will differ depending on the platform you select. Some give you the ability to define an application icon or splash screen to show when the game launches. Other settings such as rendering options or publisher settings will also show up if applicable.

Other Settings

- **Rendering Path:** The type of rendering that will be used by default. Deferred Lighting is best used if you have many real-time lights, but it requires Unity Pro. Forward Rendering is a shader-based path that supports per-pixel lighting and real-time shadows from one directional light. Vertex Lit rendering has the lowest visual quality and does not support real-time shadows. This is best used on older machines or platforms with limited power, such as certain mobile systems.
- **Use Direct3D 11:** If true, enables the use of Direct3D 11 for rendering. This won't do anything if your card isn't capable of supporting DirectX 11.
- **Static Batching (Unity Pro only):** If true, the engine attempts to reduce draw calls for geometry of any size that does not move and shares the same Material. This is more effective than dynamic batching and requires less processing power. Only items with the "Static" property flagged will be batched in this way.
- **Dynamic Batching:** If true, automatically batches moving objects that share Material and certain other criteria into the same draw call. This is done automatically and does not require that objects be flagged in any special way.
- **GPU Skinning (Unity Pro only):** If true, causes the GPU to handle skinning rather than the CPU. This applies only to certain platforms, such as those that use DirectX 11.
- **First Streamed Level:** This is the index of the first level that should be loaded if you are publishing to a Streamed Web Player.
- **Scripting Define Symbols:** These are custom compilation flags. There are a fair number and you can find details for each on Unity's site.
- **API Compatibility Level:** Controls how compatible the software is with certain libraries. Lower compatibility tends to equate to smaller file sizes.
- **Optimize Mesh Data:** If true, any data on meshes that is not required by their applied Material will be removed.

The Right Settings for the Job

If it seems like a lot to take in, don't worry. To get our game built and deployed, we're really going to have to delve into only a small fraction of these options. We've been preparing for a Web Player build since the beginning, so take the following steps to bring this game on home:

1. Open the Build Settings window.
2. Make sure that Web Player is the selected platform. If it isn't, click on it and click the Switch Platform button to select it.
3. Make sure that none of the settings boxes are checked.
4. Click the Player Settings button.

5. Expand the Resolution and Presentation settings.

6. Set the Default Screen Width to 960.

7. Set the Default Screen Height to 600. These are the default values used by the Web Player and should suit our purposes just fine.

8. If you're using a black background for the camera, or something very close to black, select the Default Web Player template. If you're using a brighter color, select the Black Background template. The contrast will make it very clear to players where the borders of the game window are in the Web page's layout.

We can't give the game an icon, nor can we give it a splash image, and we don't need to tinker with any of the other settings, so that's it! With that, our game is ready for the build process.

Building the Game for the Web Player

Take the following steps in order to build and run the game immediately so that we can test to be sure it's functioning correctly:

1. Click the Build And Run button in the Build Settings window.

2. Create a new directory in which the built game will be stored. This does not need to be under the same directory as the game's assets. Put it wherever you like!

3. Give your browser permission to run the Unity Web Player, if it requests it.

4. Play your game in a browser window.

That's it—you can actually play your game! Pretty fantastic, isn't it?

Deploying the Game to the Web

Deploying the game means putting it someplace where other people can access it. In the case of a Web Player game, that means uploading it to a Web server and handing out the URL to prospective players. Getting you onto a Web server is a little outside the scope of this book, but suffice it to say, there are a number of hosting services out there and even sites that support posting games for players to purchase or play for free.

All you have to do is upload the folder that you created during the build process and hand out that URL!

> **Note**
>
> If you want to deploy to a standalone format, it's actually quite straightforward. In fact, we even made provisions for it in the GUI code so that we'd have a Quit button, so give it a try! If you want to build for other platforms, such as mobile, make sure to consider how users will interact with your game. The simple controls of this game would be easy to replicate on a touchscreen, but the loss of precise control could make it quite a bit more difficult. A platform with controller inputs, on the other hand, would suit it quite well.

Post-Deployment

Once the game is out there, however, be prepared to support it. No game is perfect; players will find bugs you never dreamed of and will want to see them fixed. Some people will encounter technical issues and may need your assistance. Getting a game out to other users is just the beginning, but a well-supported game is likely to do much better in the long run.

Consider creating e-mail addresses specifically for bug reports and support requests, and make sure that information is readily available to your players. Forums can be another excellent way to manage post-deployment support as your users can help one another rather than leaving everything entirely on your shoulders.

If you plan to release additional content down the road, a mailing list, social media account, or dedicated news section on a Web site can be helpful for generating additional interest. These also serve as ways to let people know that the game is being supported so that players don't feel like they're playing abandonware.

Moving Forward

While the game is finished—inasmuch as any game is ever considered to be done—there are still plenty of things that could be done with this game or with new Projects. We've discussed ways to make a platformer with Unity's 2D tools, but those can easily be used for other game types. Of course, Unity also supports 3D games, so there's an entire other dimension of development waiting out there!

Polish Considerations

There are still further ways you could polish the game, if you are so inclined. Here are a few suggestions to consider:

- Use flag sprites for checkpoints and have them change color.
- Alternatively, have the flags rise and begin fluttering when activated.
- Add visual effects such as fireworks to the victory trigger.
- Add an audio stinger to the victory trigger.
- Add a fade-out to the victory trigger.
- More enemy types!
- More hazard types!
- Add a timer to the level.
- Carry health forward from level to level to make the game more difficult.
- Carry the player's score forward when they restart after beating the game so that they can rack up even higher scores.

You can probably think of a few other bits and pieces that you'd like to add in order to make the game shine. A little polish in the right place can go a long way. As you work on a game in progress, it's very easy to let minor bugs and small visual errors—such as tiny hitches or quirks in the animations—slide because the game is "in progress." In order to effectively polish a game for release, you need to start looking at it as though the game were done and ask yourself, "Would I be willing to accept that in a finished title?"

By the same token, it's easy to get caught up with trying to polish everything forever, aiming for a level of shine that's implausible due to limited time. Find the balance between polish and schedule that works best for you, and remember that sometimes, cutting something from the game may be better than leaving it in half-done. It's a hard lesson to learn, but it will serve you well.

Monetization

Monetization can be a sticky subject and a deep rabbit hole in which to dive, but assuming you want to continue making games in the future, it's possible that you may want to make some money off of the ones you've created. Some people find the idea that game development is "business" to be unpalatable, but the simple fact remains that a career as a developer means you are in the business of making games.

Common Purchase Models

There are numerous approaches to monetization. These are the most common of the purchase models:

- **Pay once:** An initial amount is paid up front for the game and its content. This one-time payment could be made before the game is played, or it could be made to unlock the rest of the game after a demo section is played. This model sometimes employs downloadable content (DLC) or expansion packs in order to provide additional content later on. The barrier to entry is the cost of the game.

- **Subscription:** This is typically the domain of the MMORPG (massively multiplayer online role-playing game) genre, though many of those have abandoned it in favor of free-to-play models. In a subscription model, a set payment is required every so often, usually once per calendar month. Subscription-based games often include a pay-once initial cost as well, giving them a high barrier to entry.

- **Free to Play:** The free-to-play—or F2P—model provides a core set of gameplay for free that can be extended through additional in-game purchases known as micro-transactions. Examples of F2P purchases would be items and gear to make the game easier (often known as the "pay to win" approach) or vanity items that are used to customize and personalize elements of the game. There is no real barrier to entry in this case, as players can try the game for no cost.

Choosing the "Right" Monetization Strategy

This is the stuff of dissertations, but let's try to examine it a bit more briefly than that. There are a lot of factors to consider when attempting to monetize your game, some of which are more esoteric than others.

- **Pay once:** Does your game work best in one bundled package? Will you be adding content in larger chunks later? If so, this model may work best for you, particularly if your game doesn't break down into smaller, discrete parts (e.g., story-based games tend to be better suited to pay-once models). If your game is map-structured (i.e., it has levels that aren't tied together by a story), you may be able to sell or give away additional content as DLC.

- **Subscription:** Does your game have constant upkeep costs, such as server hosting? Will you be providing frequent support and patch updates? Realistically, a subscription model isn't likely to be the optimal choice and should be used at your own risk. It does not enjoy even a fraction of the popularity it once did among games, though it has become a prevailing model for major utility software suites.

- **Free to play:** Can your game be broken down into a number of parts? If so, you may be able to sell some of those parts using the F2P model. You need to consider your audience, though. If the game has any sort of competitive element, the "pay to win" approach can create major disparities between the power levels of your player base and potentially drive people away. If you have character customization, a vanity approach may work better for you. If your game is based on lots of individual maps, you could potentially sell packs of additional maps and levels, similarly to the pay-once model.

> **Note**
>
> Content that is available for download on the same day a game is released—otherwise known as "Day 1 DLC"—has an often undeservedly bad reputation because people assume that it was completed along with the core game and then sold separately. Often, that content is completed after the core game has already gone to gold master and is finished before release. That said, we would still be wary of using Day 1 DLC due to its "shady" reputation.

When choosing your purchase model, you need to consider not only the game that you're making but the effect your plan will have on your players. Will they want to buy in? Will buying in make them feel regret? A great game with a poorly chosen/executed purchase model is still going to find itself doomed to failure.

> **Tip**
>
> If you pursue a "pay to win" version of the F2P model, we recommend that you make the purchasable materials also available through in-game effort. This means that impatient people or people who just want to pay can get the materials more easily, while those who are playing your core game will still be able to close the disparity gap through hard work and/or time.

What If This Game Were . . . ?

As an experiment, let's take a moment to examine what we could potentially do with our game if we were to apply each of the aforementioned purchase models to it.

Our Game: Pay-Once Edition

- Players would receive the entire game when purchased, including all levels, enemies, and so on.
- The price would need to be commensurate with the size of the game and the platform; for a small game with moderate replay value, you'd want to go quite cheap.
- If we were to add online leaderboards for both score and time, we could command a slightly higher price and make it more appealing to the speed run audience and achievers.

Our Game: Subscription Edition

This is not an appropriate model for the game, but let's try for the sake of the experiment!

- We would need to add content and patch updates with incredible frequency to warrant a subscription—every two to four weeks, most likely.
- We would almost certainly need to add online leaderboards in order to create a sense of persistence that would help warrant a subscription.
- We would almost certainly need to add unlockable content to the game in terms of character visualization changes to improve persistence and add a visible way for players to show off their progress.
- The subscription price would need to be incredibly low.

Our Game: F2P Edition

- The first few levels of the game would be free for download.
- Additional levels would be purchasable in challenge packs, probably based on a prevailing theme for the pack (e.g., the Physics Challenge pack or the Hard-Core Challenge pack).
- If we wanted to make it "pay to win," we could allow players to purchase larger health bars. We do not recommend this.
- We could add purchasable content that changes the way the character looks. This would be only cosmetic in nature.
- We could add online leaderboards and include an image of the player's character with their time/score. This would add value to the aforementioned cosmetic purchases.

There are many ways to approach monetization, as you can see. Consider your audience, consider your game, and consider your platform; only then will you have an idea of what the "right" way to proceed may be.

Final Words

Let's take a moment to reflect upon what you've accomplished over the course of this book.

You created levels out of nothing and filled them with hazards, enemies, and challenges befitting the platformer genre. You created a player character and gave it life through animation and audio, then wrote scripts to control it. You added visual flair and collectibles. You bundled the whole thing together into a game that can be played on the Web.

You did all of that, and you should give yourself a well-deserved pat on the back. Many people who set out to build a game stop long before they accomplish even a fraction of what you've done. The game may be simple, but we firmly believe that simplicity is at the core of many great games. Our hope is that you can continue to use these building blocks to create something even better.

We'd like to impart some advice that has served us well over the years:

- Always start with something small that you can build upon. This keeps things manageable and will help prevent you from becoming overwhelmed.

- A single small, completed project will teach you more than a dozen incomplete ones will, no matter how epic you thought they could be.

- Complexity and simplicity are not mutually exclusive. Great systems and puzzles often employ a simple core that is woven into something that appears more complicated. The simple core makes them readily understandable and accessible.

- Test your work at every given opportunity, and remember not to play the game as you intend it to be played, but as it is more likely to be played. Aim to break it.

- Watch other people playtest your material and see how they handle it without your inherent meta-knowledge of the game.

- When receiving feedback from playtesters, remember that the issue expressed is not necessarily the problem but rather a symptom. Read between the lines and find the root of the issue so that you can provide a real solution.

- Love your work but never fall in love with it. Be passionate, but remember that nothing is sacred or above being tweaked, reworked, or cut entirely if it makes the game better overall.

Game development is a vast ocean of possibility, and you've only just broken the surface. Take a breath, dive deep, and plumb the depths. There has been no better time to join the game development community, so our final words to you are simply this:
Welcome to the fold!

14

UGUI

Shipping with Unity version 4.6 and above will be a new Unity GUI system that offers a much wider ability to create highly interactive and complex interface systems. The new tools are built with the idea of visually creating and laying out all of the elements for the GUI instead of trying to create them through code and GUI Styles, which can be daunting and rather limiting.

The new system uses a lot of rules similarly to the native Unity GUI, though. It still uses a CSS approach to laying things out within an area, and then uses that to define how the other elements are placed. The biggest difference is that you can create scalable interfaces that allow you to shift and scale elements in real time, and not have to deal with continually editing code and checking your results to achieve the same thing.

UGUI (Unity GUI) also uses a lot of the same OnGUI-type controls, such as images, text, scroll bars, and buttons, but with a few additional features such as masks, shadows, and outline effects. Let's get into how to set up a UGUI system and see all of the controls and their attributes, and how you can very easily create a personal interface or menu to your liking.

UGUI Components

As mentioned previously, the new Unity GUI is still structured like the native OnGUI system, or like a standard Web CSS style of adding elements to build a UI. What that means is that by "layering" a series of elements, you are able to build a complex interface with backgrounds, images, sliders, buttons, and so forth. The biggest difference with the UGUI is that you can create these with premade UGUI components and scripts, which enables you to more easily and quickly create interfaces and test things more rapidly. Figure 14.1 shows the UGUI GameObjects from which you can start.

- **Panel:** A Panel is set up using the Image Component with its anchors and bounds stretched to match the parent GameObject.
- **Button:** The UGUI works the same as the native GUI Style, calling a button with position and size, only visually. The one nice advantage of the UGUI Button Component is that all of the different states for the button exist with the Component. Changing the color for a hovered or clicked state is much easier this way.

Figure 14.1   The new UGUI GameObjects

- **Text:** A Text Component works just like the native GUI Text control would. You can easily change font, colors, and size from the Inspector of the Component rather than having to hard-code or use a GUI Style.

- **Image:** The Image Component allows you to attach a sprite asset to render on screen. You can also control the size and aliasing with an Image Component.

- **RawImage:** RawImage works just like the Image Component but uses a texture asset rather than a sprite. You also cannot control the size and aliasing other than using standard 2D scaling.

- **Slider:** The Slider is made up of multiple Image Components to create a background, Slider, and Slider handle elements. These are just children of the parent Slider UI object that can then control position, size, and rotation for the entire Component. The main Slider object also acts like the button, allowing you to control the different looks for the states when it is being used.

- **Scrollbar:** Similar to the Slider Component, the Scrollbar uses a Slider area with a Slider handle. The only difference is that it does not have the fill element that the Slider uses. A good example for use of a Scrollbar would be Web-page-type scrolling.

- **Toggle:** A Toggle is a checkbox UI element used for checking something on or off, commonly used for equipping a weapon, toggling an option on or off, or making selections in an inventory. The Toggle uses two Image Components for the background graphic and then the toggle image. It also has a Text UI Component attached to it to be used as a label.

- **InputField:** The InputField allows you to input some sort of value or text over your image. It uses a single Component that holds both text and an image. InputFields are good for games where you need to enter a name or value.

- **Canvas:** The base of the UI system. This controls the size and screen space for the UI Components, as well as rendering to the camera and allowing interaction via raycasting.

- **Event System:** The Event System acts as the controller for your GUI. It works hand-in-hand with the Layout System to drive all of the controls you might use in your GUI. We will discuss the Event System a little more later in this chapter.

Creating Our Example Interface

Let's create an interface example to give you an idea of how you can create your own. Our example is not in any way connected to our 2D platform Project, but by the time you read this you will have the new UGUI in your hands and can add it if you so choose! To begin, let's create a new Scene.

> **Note**
>
> We assume you are running the Unity 4.6 Beta or later. While Unity 4.5.1 does include a basic Canvas and Rect Transform Component, they are merely shells of themselves from version 4.6. And besides, you should be running the latest and greatest anyway, right?

1. Start a new Unity Scene by using the shortcut Ctrl + N hotkeys.
2. Create a Canvas GameObject by going to the GameObject menu > UI > Canvas.
3. Set the Render Mode to Screen Space Camera.
4. From the Render Camera attribute, select the target icon to the right and select your Main Camera. This will position and scale your Canvas to match the Aspect Ratio of the camera.

Before moving on, let's find out exactly what the Canvas Component does and how we can use it for the various GUIs we might want to create.

Canvas Component

The Canvas Component serves three main functions for the GUI display. First, it acts similarly to a parent object, controlling the overall layout of the GUI controls connected to it. Since the Canvas Component must be attached to render GUI displays, think of it like an actual canvas; without it you would not be able to use your paints and realize your idea on screen.

Second, the Canvas Component controls the GUI display in 3D space. Setting the Render Mode for the Canvas gives us a few options. It will help determine whether the GUI is used as an overlay to the camera, or if the canvas is set to World Space, and then used as an element in the game world. We will look at this in more detail shortly.

Last, the Canvas Component determines if the GUI will receive events for actions to happen, such as a button press or being used interactively, like a map that you can pan around. We will look at the Event System a little later. Figure 14.2 shows the default Canvas Component.

Figure 14.2   A Canvas GameObject with its attributes

Render Mode

The Render Mode determines how the GUI will be displayed in the Game View. Your interface style and needs will determine the setting for your Canvas.

- **Screen Space Overlay:** The Canvas is essentially attached to the Main Camera. A good example for using this is a third-person shooter where you need to continually relay information to the player.

- **Screen Space Camera:** Similar to the Screen Space Overlay, this one keeps elements on screen by using a secondary camera to render the Canvas elements. Our initial GUI setup using the native GUI approach was similar to this setup.

- **World Space:** This style uses the Canvas and GUI in true 3D space. A good use of this is when you need to display text or visual elements to the player, but they are fixed to a point in 3D space. A speech bubble above a 3D character would be a good use of the World Space setting.

- **Pixel Perfect:** When this box is checked, Unity will try to render the GUI elements as accurately as possible to the nearest pixel. In some cases this may sharpen the UI to give it a really solid, crisp appearance.

- **Receives Events:** If checked, this allows the Canvas to react to interactive actions, such as button presses. By default, this will assign the Main Camera as the camera with which you can use the GUI interactively.

> **Note**
>
> By default, if the Scene does not contain a Canvas GameObject, one will be automatically added when you create a UI GameObject. You can also use more than one Canvas in your Scene, if needed.

Now that we have our Canvas set up, let's create the background image for our UI. For this we will need to add an Image Component for the UI and add an image to it:

1. With the Canvas GameObject selected, add an Image Component by going to Component > UI > Image.

2. From the Project Browser, find the UGUI_bgExample image under the Chapter14_projectFiles folder.

3. Drag and drop the image into the Source Image slot of the Image Component.

4. Make sure Image Type is set to "simple" and that Preserve Aspect is checked.

Figure 14.3 shows the UI with the border graphic in place.

Now that we have our UI border, let's add our mini-map graphic. This will be used like an interactive map that the user could possibly pan around. The idea is that the map graphic is bigger than the actual map border area and requires a little setup to make it work for our interface. Most games that allow for any amount of extensive traveling usually have some type of mini-map for the player to know where they are, or need to get to.

We need to apply another image, but this time using a new GameObject.

1. With the Canvas GameObject selected, add a new GameObject > UI > Image to your Scene. The Image will automatically become a child of the Canvas.

Figure 14.3   Image graphic for the initial UI look

2. Rename this new Image GameObject "Mask."

3. In the Inspector, click the target icon next to the Image Source and assign the UGUI_maskExample image.

With our image attached, we now need to define the Rect Transform for the new GameObject. The Rect Transform controls the position of the individual GUI elements as well as their relationship with the parent GameObject, in this case the camera. Before we go into adding a mask to our UI, let's get a thorough understanding of exactly what the Rect Transform is.

Rect Transform

The main component of the UGUI system is the Rect Transform. All other GameObjects have the basic Transform Component, but the Rect Transform works solely for the UGUI setup.

The Rect (short for rectangular) Transform is used to control the size and positioning of the UI elements in your Scene. Even in 3D space, all the UI elements are two-dimensional, so by using rectangular values for position and size, we can get a good idea of their look and placement. Figure 14.4 shows the Rect Transform for a Canvas GameObject.

Note

By default, all UGUI components have a Rect Transform attached to them. A UI element needs a Rect Transform in order to be used. You can parent a regular 3D GameObject to a UI element and it will maintain its 3D positional Transform. But as soon as a UI Component is attached to it, the Transform will change to the Rect Transform.

Screen Space

The Rect Transform serves many purposes for displaying your UI GameObject, and many factors affect this. The first is the position in relation to its parent. When a camera is linked to the Canvas Component, it in essence becomes the parent, driving the

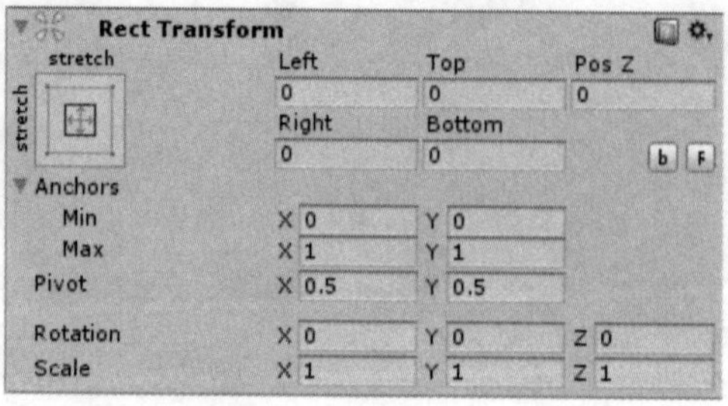

Figure 14.4   The Rect Transform with 2D position spacing

GameObject. This makes sense, as the Screen Space is in relation to the camera, and the camera's position and Aspect Ratio drive the UI bounds.

When the UI GameObject is set to World Space, the Rect Transform can be used. Since World Space uses X, Y, and Z positioning and you must also set the size of the UI sprite, the Rect Transform will change to reflect this. Figure 14.5 shows the Rect Transform with World Space attributes. Notice that the Left and Top attributes have been replaced with Pos X and Pos Y respectively. Also notice that Right and Bottom have changed to Width and Height for the element.

> **Note**
>
> Rect Transform still allows Z positioning, though this is practically irrelevant unless you're using Screen Space Screen or Screen Space Camera. Also, X, Y, and Z rotation and scale are possible, no matter what Screen Space the GameObject is set to.

Pos X and Pos Y indicate the distance of the pivot point in relation to the Anchors.

Anchors

Anchors control the bounds, size, and orientation of the UI element in relation to its parent GameObject. As we mentioned before, with the camera driving the Canvas GameObject, that camera controls the dimensions of the Rect Transform. When you add a second UI GameObject, such as an Image or Button, the anchors are dependent upon its parent.

Anchors work by taking the bounds of the parent object and allowing you to anchor, or constrain, the UI element to positions on the parent object. By doing this, you can justify where the UI element pivots and transforms from if the GUI is moved or scaled. This is very handy for building your game to different platforms, where the screen size is different between a tablet and a smartphone.

Anchors use a Minimum and Maximum value (seen in Figure 14.5) to position one of four anchors on the GUI. Each anchor is symbolized by a small outlined triangle and starts in the top right corner. At Maximum with all four anchors to the bottom left, they will all have a value of 1.0.

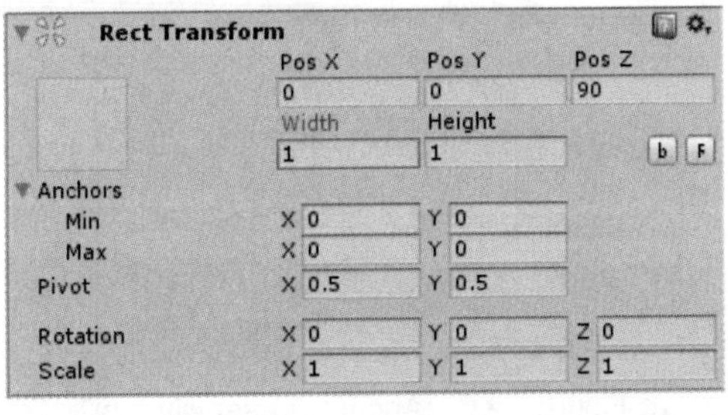

Figure 14.5   Rect Transform with World Space attributes displayed

The Pivot values are for the center axis of the UI element. This value is based on the position of the anchors and also uses a 0-to-1 scale. What this means is that wherever the anchor points are placed, the Pivot for X and Y will be based on the bounds of the UI element. Let's look at the placement for our Mask GameObject and setting its anchors:

1. Make sure you have the Mask GameObject still selected.

2. The Mask should be at 0, 0, 0 position, with a width and height of 100 each. If this is not the case, that's OK as we will be adjusting it anyway.

3. From the Inspector, in the Rect Transform, set the Anchor Min X to a value of 0.641, and Y to a value of 0.15.

4. Set the Anchor Max X and Y values to 0.875 and 0.83 respectively.

Unity provides us with some presets for our anchors. They can be accessed by clicking on the rectangle icon just above the Anchor Min and Max values. Left-clicking will reveal the Anchor Presets. Figure 14.6 shows the Anchor Preset window with all of the available presets.

UI Rect Tool

With the new UI toolset, Unity has also given us a new UI Rect tool. It can be found in the upper left of the Unity interface, now positioned alongside the other Transform icons. Figure 14.7 shows the Transform toolbar with the additional UI Rect tool.

With the UI Transform tool selected, you will now find four points along the edge of the UI Image for the Mask GameObject. This will allow you to move the Image Component as well as affect its size by grabbing one of the points and dragging it around.

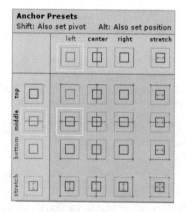

Figure 14.6   Anchor Preset window

Figure 14.7   Transform toolbar with the new Rect Tool highlighted

> **Tip**
> The UI Transform tool works exactly the same as if this were just a sprite element. Click one of the corners to drag and scale. Click and drag just outside the corner to rotate the image. Scale from a corner will scale that direction, and holding Shift will scale the image uniformly.

Another handy feature is moving and scaling the image over the anchors. Unity assumes the anchors will encompass the UI element and allows you to snap the edge and corners of the UI components to them. Let's do this for our UI pieces:

1. Make sure you still have the Mask image selected.
2. Click to select the new UI Transform tool.
3. Drag one of the corners of the image and move it toward its comparable corner, until it snaps into place.
4. Do this for all corners of the Image Component to match them to their anchors.

Adding the Mask

We didn't rename this GameObject "Mask" without having a reason! Let's add a Mask Component so we can get this working correctly. With the Mask GameObject selected, add the Mask by going to Component > UI > Mask. This will add the Mask Script Component to the GameObject.

Our Mask is now set up correctly, but we need an image for it to mask correctly. Let's add the elements we need to create our example mini-map:

1. Select the Mask GameObject.
2. Add a new Image GameObject by going under the GameObject Menu and then UI. Select the Image from this menu.
3. From the Hierarchy, select the new Image GameObject.
4. Rename this from "Image" to "miniMap."
5. Left-click and drag this onto the Mask GameObject, making it a child object.

The Event System and Event Triggers

When we originally created our Canvas GameObject, you may have noticed that an Event System GameObject was also created in our Scene. Unity assumes your UI will have some type of interactivity to it and uses a built-in script to help drive this. Of course, all of this might need to be done in your own scripts, but this method is a quick way of setting up some simple GUI elements. Figure 14.8 shows the default Event System that was created.

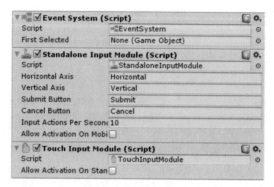

Figure 14.8   Our default Event System Components

Event System

The Event System script itself has one variable slot for First Selected. This lets you place an initial GameObject that will automatically be selected when the Scene starts. A good use for this would be on a series of menus that the user may want to bypass quickly. Having these Event Systems within each Scene, you could add an initial selection so that they could quickly execute them and get through the menus faster. After all, no one likes staring at menus!

Standalone Input Module

The Standalone Input script sets a few default actions for when the game is deployed and then used with either a keyboard or controller. These are the same input defaults available from the Input Manager.

Touch Input Module

The Touch Input script allows you to activate touch input for a device that uses touch actions and gestures. By clicking the Allow Activation on Standalone toggle, you are telling Unity to add touch parameters in your build.

Summary

We touched on a few of the features and components of the new Unity UGUI system and how it works. We gave a brief overview of building a simple Options menu with some text elements, buttons, and graphics. We also looked at building a mask to hide images behind.

The new UGUI has a lot more to it, and you can only grow by digging deeper into the Components and anchoring systems. Try building your own complex interfaces, and remember the various resources and tutorials provided by Unity.

With that, good luck. We hope this has been an informative guide and valuable learning experience, and that this guide has gotten you off on the right foot so that you can build your own exciting worlds and gameplay that we will all get to experience!

Appendix

JavaScript Code Samples

Herein are JavaScript versions of all final scripts used in the Project, in case that's your preferred language. The differences between C# and JavaScript are relatively minute at times, and the bulk of the code remains unchanged, so you should still be able to follow along with the book. Fully commented versions are available through this book's companion site.

Register your book at informit.com/title/9780321957726 to access assets, code listings, and video tutorials on the companion website.

Player Scripts

This section contains the final scripts that are used to control the player's movement along with tracking health, coins, and similar values. You'll find the following scripts here:

- **Listing A.1:** The PlayerController Script
- **Listing A.2:** The PlayerStats Script

Listing A.1   **The PlayerController Script**

```
#pragma strict
private var Constants : Constants = new Constants();

@HideInInspector
public var isFacingRight : boolean = true;
@HideInInspector
public var isGrounded : boolean = false;
@HideInInspector
public var isDoubleJumping : boolean = false;

public var maxSpeed : float = Constants.playerMaxSpeed;
public var jumpForce : float = Constants.playerJumpForce;
public var jumpMaterial : PhysicsMaterial2D;
```

(continues)

```
public var groundCheck : Transform;
public var groundLayers : LayerMask;

public var footstepSounds : AudioClip[];
public var jumpSound : AudioClip;
public var damageSound : AudioClip;

private var groundCheckRadius : float = Constants.playerGroundCheckRadius;
private var audioSource : AudioSource;
private var anim : Animator;
private var deathTimeElapsed : float;

function Start()
{
  anim = this.GetComponent(Animator);
  audioSource = this.GetComponent(AudioSource);
}

function Update ()
{
  if(Input.GetButtonDown(Constants.inputJump))
  {
    if(isGrounded == true)
    {
      this.rigidbody2D.velocity = new Vector2(rigidbody2D.velocity.x,0);

      this.rigidbody2D.AddForce(new Vector2(0, jumpForce));

      this.anim.SetTrigger(Constants.animJump);
      PlayJumpAudio();
    }
    else if(isDoubleJumping == false)
    {
      isDoubleJumping = true;

      this.rigidbody2D.velocity = new Vector2(rigidbody2D.velocity.x,0);
      this.rigidbody2D.AddForce(new Vector2(0, jumpForce));
      PlayJumpAudio();
    }
  }
}

function FixedUpdate()
{
  isGrounded = Physics2D.OverlapCircle
    (groundCheck.position,  groundCheckRadius, groundLayers);
```

```
var material : PhysicsMaterial2D =
  this.gameObject.GetComponent(CircleCollider2D).sharedMaterial;
var collision : CircleCollider2D;

if(isGrounded == true)
{
  this.isDoubleJumping = false;
}
if(isGrounded == true && material == this.jumpMaterial)
{
  collision = this.gameObject.GetComponent(CircleCollider2D);
  collision.sharedMaterial = null;
  collision.enabled = false;
  collision.enabled = true;
}
else if(isGrounded == false &&
  this.gameObject.GetComponent(CircleCollider2D).sharedMaterial == null)
{
  collision = this.gameObject.GetComponent(CircleCollider2D);
  collision.sharedMaterial = this.jumpMaterial;
  collision.enabled = false;
  collision.enabled = true;
}
try
{
  var move : float = Input.GetAxis(Constants.inputMove);
    this.rigidbody2D.velocity = new Vector2
    (move * maxSpeed,    rigidbody2D.velocity.y);
  this.anim.SetFloat(Constants.animSpeed, Mathf.Abs(move));

  if((move > 0.0f && isFacingRight == false)
    || (move < 0.0f &&  isFacingRight == true))
  {
    Flip ();
  }
}
catch(error : UnityException)
{
  Debug.LogError(error.ToString());
}

}
function Flip()
{
  isFacingRight = !isFacingRight;
```

(continues)

```
    var playerScale : Vector3 = transform.localScale;
    playerScale.x = playerScale.x * -1;
    transform.localScale = playerScale;
    }


function PlayFootstepAudio()
{
  this.audioSource.clip = footstepSounds[(Random.Range(0,
footstepSounds.Length))];
  this.audioSource.Play();
}


function PlayJumpAudio()
{
  AudioSource.PlayClipAtPoint(this.jumpSound, this.transform.position);
}


public function PlayDamageAudio()
{
  this.audioSource.clip = damageSound;
  this.audioSource.Play();
}
```

Listing A.2 **The PlayerStats Script**

```
#pragma strict

private var Constants : Constants = new Constants();

public var health : int = 6;
public var coinsCollected : int = 0;
public var isImmune : boolean = false;
public var immunityDuration : float = 1.5f;

private var immunityTime : float = 0f;
private var flickerDuration : float = 0.1f;
private var flickerTime : float = 0f;
private var spriteRenderer : SpriteRenderer;

public var isDead : boolean = false;
public var particleHitLeft : ParticleSystem;
public var particleHitRight : ParticleSystem;

private var HUDCamera : GameObject;
private var HUDSprite: GameObject;
private var deathTimeElapsed : float;
```

```
function Start ()
{
  spriteRenderer = this.gameObject.GetComponent(SpriteRenderer);
  if(Application.loadedLevel != Constants.SCENE_LEVEL_1)
  {
    coinsCollected = PlayerPrefs.GetInt(Constants.PREF_COINS);
  }
  PlayerPrefs.SetInt(Constants.PREF_CURRENT_LEVEL,
    Application.loadedLevel);
  HUDCamera = GameObject.FindGameObjectWithTag("HUDCamera");
  HUDSprite = GameObject.FindGameObjectWithTag("HUDSprite");
}

function Update ()
{
  if(this.isImmune == true)
  {
    SpriteFlicker();
    immunityTime = immunityTime + Time.deltaTime;
    if(immunityTime >= immunityDuration)
    {
      this.isImmune = false;
      this.spriteRenderer.enabled = true;
    }
  }
  if(this.isDead == true)
  {
    this.deathTimeElapsed = this.deathTimeElapsed + Time.deltaTime;
    if(this.deathTimeElapsed >= 2.0f)
    {
      Application.LoadLevel(Constants.SCENE_GAME_OVER);
    }
  }
}

public function CollectCoin(coinValue : int)
{
  this.coinsCollected = this.coinsCollected + coinValue;
  this.HUDSprite.GetComponent(CoinCounter).value = this.coinsCollected;
}

public function TakeDamage(damage : int, playHitReaction : boolean)
{
  if(this.isImmune == false && isDead == false)
```

(continues)

```
   {
     this.health = this.health - damage;
     Debug.Log("Player Health: " + this.health.ToString());
     this.HUDCamera.GetComponent(GUIGame).UpdateHealth(this.health);

     if(this.health <= 0)
     {
       PlayerIsDead(playHitReaction);
     }
     else if(playHitReaction == true)
     {
       PlayHitReaction();
     }
   }
}
function PlayHitReaction()
{
  this.isImmune = true;
  this.immunityTime = 0f;
  this.gameObject.GetComponent(Animator).SetTrigger(Constants.animDamage);

  var playerController : PlayerController =
    this.gameObject.GetComponent(PlayerController);
  playerController.PlayDamageAudio();

  if(playerController.isFacingRight == true)
  {
    this.particleHitLeft.Play();
  }
  else
  {
    this.particleHitRight.Play();
  }
}


function SpriteFlicker()
{
  if(this.flickerTime < this.flickerDuration)
  {
    this.flickerTime = this.flickerTime + Time.deltaTime;
  }
  else if (this.flickerTime >= this.flickerDuration)
  {
    spriteRenderer.enabled = !(spriteRenderer.enabled);
    this.flickerTime = 0;
  }
}
```

```
function PlayerIsDead(playDeathAnim : boolean)
{
  this.isDead = true;
  this.gameObject.GetComponent(Animator).SetTrigger(Constants.animDamage);
  var controller : PlayerController =
this.gameObject.GetComponent(PlayerController);
  controller.enabled = false;
  controller.PlayDamageAudio();

  if(playDeathAnim == true)
  {
    this.rigidbody2D.velocity = new Vector2(0,0);
    this.rigidbody2D.AddForce(new Vector2(0,600));
  }
GameObject.FindGameObjectWithTag("MainCamera").GetComponent
  (CameraFollow).enabled = false;
  this.gameObject.GetComponent(CircleCollider2D).enabled = false;
}
```

Collectible Scripts

This section contains the final scripts that are used to control the game's coin collectibles. These scripts manage the act of spawning coins, collecting them, and activating the coin boxes. You'll find the following scripts here:

- **Listing A.3:** The CoinBox Script
- **Listing A.4:** The CoinPickup Script
- **Listing A.5:** The CoinSpawner Script

Listing A.3   **The CoinBox Script**

```
#pragma strict
public var poppedStatePrefab : GameObject;

function OnTriggerEnter2D(collider : Collider2D)
{
  var heading : Vector3 = this.transform.position -
    collider.gameObject.transform.position;
  var distance : float = heading.magnitude;
  var direction : Vector3 = heading / distance;

  if((direction.x < 0.1 && direction.x > -1.1) && (direction.y < 1.1
    && direction.y > 0.4) && collider.tag == "Player")
```

(continues)

```
    {
       CoinPop();
    }
}

function CoinPop()
{
  poppedStatePrefab.SetActive(true);
  this.gameObject.SetActive(false);
}
```

Listing A.4   **The CoinPickup Script**

```
#pragma strict
public var coinValue : int = 1;

function OnTriggerEnter2D(collider : Collider2D)
{
  if(collider.tag == "Player")
  {


    var stats : PlayerStats =
collider.gameObject.GetComponent(PlayerStats);
    stats.CollectCoin(this.coinValue);
    Destroy(this.gameObject);
  }
}
```

Listing A.5   **The CoinSpawner Script**

```
#pragma strict
public var coinSpawnPoint : GameObject;
public var coinPrefabs : Transform[];

function Start()
{
  this.SpawnCoin();
}

function SpawnCoin()
{
  var random : int = Random.Range(0, coinPrefabs.Length);
  var coin = Instantiate(coinPrefabs[(Random.Range(0,
    coinPrefabs.Length))], coinSpawnPoint.transform.position,
```

```
        coinSpawnPoint.transform.rotation);
    coin.rigidbody2D.AddForce(new Vector2((Random.Range(-120, 120)), 700));
}
```

Enemy Scripts

This section contains the final scripts that are used to control the game's enemies. Note that it does not include the FlightPoints script used by the Fly enemy type; that is located in the "Game System Scripts" section under Listing A.11. You'll find the following scripts here:

- **Listing A.6:** The EnemyController Script
- **Listing A.7:** The EnemySlime Script
- **Listing A.8:** The FlyController Script

Listing A.6   **The EnemyController Script**

```
#pragma strict
@HideInInspector
public var isFacingRight : boolean = false;
public var maxSpeed : float = 1.5f;

public function Flip()
{
    isFacingRight = !isFacingRight;
    var enemyScale : Vector3 = this.transform.localScale;
    enemyScale.x = enemyScale.x * -1;
    this.transform.localScale = enemyScale;
}
```

Listing A.7   **The EnemySlime Script**

```
#pragma strict
class EnemySlime extends EnemyController
{
    function FixedUpdate()
    {
        if(this.isFacingRight == true)
        {

            this.rigidbody2D.velocity = new Vector2
                (maxSpeed, this.rigidbody2D.velocity.y);
        }
```

(continues)

```
    else
    {
      this.rigidbody2D.velocity = new Vector2
        (maxSpeed * -1,    this.rigidbody2D.velocity.y);
    }
  }

  function OnTriggerEnter2D(collider : Collider2D)
  {
    if(collider.tag == "Wall")
    {
      Flip ();
    }
    else if (collider.tag == "Enemy")
    {
      var controller : EnemyController =
collider.gameObject.GetComponent(EnemyController);
      controller.Flip();
      Flip ();
    }
  }
}
```

Listing A.8   **The FlyController Script**

```
#pragma strict
class FlyController extends EnemyController
{

}
```

Game System Scripts

This section contains the final scripts that are used to control the game's core systems. It includes scripts for the camera, flight paths, and most trigger-related systems. You'll find the following scripts here:

- **Listing A.9:** The CameraFollow Script
- **Listing A.10:** The CheckpointTrigger Script
- **Listing A.11:** The FlightPoints Script
- **Listing A.12:** The SpawnTrigger Script
- **Listing A.13:** The VictoryTrigger Script

Listing A.9   **The CameraFollow Script**

```
#pragma strict
public var xMargin : float = .01f;
public var yMargin : float = .01f;
public var xSmooth : float = 8f;
public var ySmooth : float = 8f;
public var maxXAndY : Vector2;
public var minXAndY : Vector2;

private var player : Transform;

function Awake ()
{
  player = GameObject.FindGameObjectWithTag("Player").transform;
}

function CheckXMargin()
{
  return Mathf.Abs(transform.position.x - player.position.x) > xMargin;
}

function CheckYMargin()
{
  return Mathf.Abs(transform.position.y - player.position.y) > yMargin;
}

function FixedUpdate ()
{
  TrackPlayer();
}

function TrackPlayer ()
{
  var targetX : float = transform.position.x;
  var targetY : float = transform.position.y;

  if(CheckXMargin())
  {
    targetX = Mathf.Lerp(transform.position.x, player.position.x,
      xSmooth * Time.deltaTime);
  }

  if(CheckYMargin())
  {
    targetY = Mathf.Lerp(transform.position.y, player.position.y,
      ySmooth * Time.deltaTime);
  }
```

(continues)

```
    targetX = Mathf.Clamp(targetX, minXAndY.x, maxXAndY.x);
    targetY = Mathf.Clamp(targetY, minXAndY.y, maxXAndY.y);
    transform.position = new Vector3(targetX, targetY, transform.position.z);
}
```

Listing A.10   **The CheckpointTrigger Script**

```
#pragma strict
public var isTriggered : boolean;

function OnTriggerEnter2D(collider : Collider2D)
{
  if(collider.gameObject.tag == "Player")
  {
    isTriggered = true;
  }
}
```

Listing A.11   **The FlightPoints Script**

```
#pragma strict
public var waypointA : GameObject;
public var waypointB : GameObject;
public var speed : float = 1;
public var shouldChangeFacing : boolean = false;
private var directionAB : boolean = true;

function FixedUpdate()
{
  if(this.transform.position == waypointA.transform.position
    && directionAB == false || this.transform.position ==
    waypointB.transform.position && directionAB == true)
  {
    directionAB = !directionAB;
    if(this.shouldChangeFacing == true)
    {
      this.gameObject.GetComponent(EnemyController).Flip();
    }
  }
  if(directionAB == true)
  {
    this.transform.position = Vector3.MoveTowards
      (this.transform.position, waypointB.transform.position,
      speed * Time.fixedDeltaTime );
  }
```

```
  else
  {
    this.transform.position = Vector3.MoveTowards
      (this.transform.position, waypointA.transform.position,
      speed * Time.fixedDeltaTime );
  }
}
```

Listing A.12   The SpawnTrigger Script

```
#pragma strict
public var gameObjects : GameObject[];
public var isTriggered : boolean = false;

function OnTriggerEnter2D(collider : Collider2D)
{
  if(collider.tag == "Player" && this.isTriggered == false)
  {
    this.isTriggered = true;
    for(var gameObject : GameObject in gameObjects)
    {
      gameObject.SetActive(true);
    }
  }
}
```

Listing A.13   The VictoryTrigger Script

```
#pragma strict
var Constants : Constants;

public var sceneToLoad : int;
public var delay : float = 1;

private var timeElapsed : float;
private var isTriggered : boolean;

function Start()
{
  Constants = new Constants();
}
function Update ()
{
  if(isTriggered == true)
```

(continues)

```
  {
    timeElapsed = timeElapsed + Time.deltaTime;
  }

  if (timeElapsed >= delay)
  {
    Application.LoadLevel(sceneToLoad);
  }
}

function OnTriggerEnter2D(collider : Collider2D)
{
  if(collider.tag == "Player")
  {
    timeElapsed = 0;
    isTriggered = true;

    collider.GetComponent(PlayerController).enabled = false;
    collider.rigidbody2D.velocity = new Vector2(0,0);
    collider.GetComponent(Animator).SetFloat(Constants.animSpeed, 0);

    PlayerPrefs.SetInt(Constants.PREF_COINS,
collider.GetComponent(PlayerStats).coinsCollected);
  }
}
```

GUI Scripts

This section contains the final scripts that are used to control the game's GUI. It includes scripts for the in-game health and coins GUI as well as scripts for the various menu and title screens. You'll find the following scripts here:

- **Listing A.14:** The CoinCounter Script
- **Listing A.15:** The GameOverScript Script
- **Listing A.16:** The GameWinScript Script
- **Listing A.17:** The GUIGame Script
- **Listing A.18:** The SplashScreenDelayed Script
- **Listing A.19:** The TitleScreenScript Script

Listing A.14 **The CoinCounter Script**

```
#pragma strict
public var spriteDigits : Sprite[];
public var value : int = 0;
```

```
public var spacing : float = 0.4f;
private var displayValue : int = -1;

function Update ()
{
  if (displayValue != value)
  {
    var digits : String = value.ToString();
    var renderers = GetComponentsInChildren(SpriteRenderer);
    var numRenderers : int = renderers.Length;
    if(numRenderers < digits.Length)
    {
      while(numRenderers < digits.Length)
      {
        var spr : GameObject = new GameObject();
        spr.AddComponent(SpriteRenderer);
        spr.transform.parent = this.transform;
        spr.transform.localPosition = new Vector3
          (numRenderers * spacing, 0, 0);
        spr.layer = 5;
        numRenderers = numRenderers + 1;
      }
      renderers = GetComponentsInChildren(SpriteRenderer);
    }
    else if(numRenderers > digits.Length)
    {
      while(numRenderers > digits.Length)
      {
        (renderers[numRenderers-1] as SpriteRenderer).sprite = null;
        numRenderers = numRenderers - 1;
      }
    }
    var rendererIndex : int = 0;
    for(var digit : char in digits)
    {
      var spriteIndex : int = int.Parse(digit.ToString());
      (renderers[rendererIndex] as SpriteRenderer).sprite =
        spriteDigits[spriteIndex];
      rendererIndex++;
    }
    displayValue = value;
  }
}
```

Listing A.15   **The GameOverScript Script**

```
#pragma strict
var Constants : Constants;;

public var Skin : GUISkin;
public var gapSize : float = 20f;

function Start()
{
  Constants = new Constants();
}

function OnGUI()
{
  GUI.skin = Skin;
  GUILayout.BeginArea (new Rect ((Screen.height / 2)
    - Screen.height / 4,(Screen.width / 2) - Screen.width / 4,
    Screen.height, Screen.width));
  GUILayout.BeginVertical();
  GUILayout.Label( "Game Over" );
  GUILayout.Space( gapSize );

  if(GUILayout.Button ("Retry!"))
  {
   Application.LoadLevel(PlayerPrefs.GetInt(Constants.PREF_CURRENT_LEVEL));
  }
  GUILayout.Space( gapSize );
  if(GUILayout.Button("Restart!"))
  {
    Application.LoadLevel(Constants.SCENE_LEVEL_1);
  }
  GUILayout.Space( gapSize );

#if UNITY_STANDALONE
  if(GUILayout.Button("Quit!"))
  {
    Application.Quit();
  }
#endif

  GUILayout.EndVertical();
  GUILayout.EndArea ();
}
```

Listing A.16   The GameWinScript Script

```
#pragma strict
var Constants : Constants;

public var Skin : GUISkin;
public var gapSize : float = 20f;

function Start()
{
  Constants = new Constants();
}

function OnGUI()
{
  GUI.skin = Skin;

  GUILayout.BeginArea (new Rect ((Screen.height / 2)
    - Screen.height / 4,(Screen.width / 2) - Screen.width / 4,
    Screen.height, Screen.width));
  GUILayout.BeginVertical();
  GUILayout.Label( "You Won!" );
  GUILayout.Space( gapSize );

  if(GUILayout.Button ("Restart Game"))
  {
    Application.LoadLevel(Constants.SCENE_LEVEL_1);
  }

  GUILayout.Space( gapSize );

#if UNITY_STANDALONE
  if(GUILayout.Button("Quit!"))
  {
    Application.Quit();
  }
#endif

  GUILayout.EndVertical();
  GUILayout.EndArea ();
}
```

Listing A.17   **The GUIGame Script**

```
#pragma strict
public var heart1 : GameObject;
public var heart2 : GameObject;
public var heart3 : GameObject;
public var heartFull : Sprite;
public var heartHalf : Sprite;
public var heartEmpty : Sprite;

public function UpdateHealth(health : int)
{
  switch(health)
  {
  case 0:
    heart1.GetComponent(SpriteRenderer).sprite = this.heartEmpty;
    heart2.GetComponent(SpriteRenderer).sprite = this.heartEmpty;
    heart3.GetComponent(SpriteRenderer).sprite = this.heartEmpty;
    break;
  case 1:
    heart1.GetComponent(SpriteRenderer).sprite = this.heartHalf;
    heart2.GetComponent(SpriteRenderer).sprite = this.heartEmpty;
    heart3.GetComponent(SpriteRenderer).sprite = this.heartEmpty;
    break;
  case 2:
    heart1.GetComponent(SpriteRenderer).sprite = this.heartFull;
    heart2.GetComponent(SpriteRenderer).sprite = this.heartEmpty;
    heart3.GetComponent(SpriteRenderer).sprite = this.heartEmpty;
    break;
  case 3:
    heart1.GetComponent(SpriteRenderer).sprite = this.heartFull;
    heart2.GetComponent(SpriteRenderer).sprite = this.heartHalf;
    heart3.GetComponent(SpriteRenderer).sprite = this.heartEmpty;
    break;
  case 4:
    heart1.GetComponent(SpriteRenderer).sprite = this.heartFull;
    heart2.GetComponent(SpriteRenderer).sprite = this.heartFull;
    heart3.GetComponent(SpriteRenderer).sprite = this.heartEmpty;
    break;
  case 5:
    heart1.GetComponent(SpriteRenderer).sprite = this.heartFull;
    heart2.GetComponent(SpriteRenderer).sprite = this.heartFull;
    heart3.GetComponent(SpriteRenderer).sprite = this.heartHalf;
    break;
  case 6:
    heart1.GetComponent(SpriteRenderer).sprite = this.heartFull;
    heart2.GetComponent(SpriteRenderer).sprite = this.heartFull;
```

```
    heart3.GetComponent(SpriteRenderer).sprite = this.heartFull;
    break;
  }
}
```

Listing A.18 The SplashScreenDelayed Script

```
#pragma strict
var Constants : Constants;
public var delayTime : float = 5f;

function Start()
{
  Constants = new Constants();
  StartCoroutine("Delay");
}

function Delay()
{
  yield WaitForSeconds(delayTime);
  Application.LoadLevel(Constants.SCENE_TITLE);
}

function Update()
{
  if (Input.anyKeyDown)
  {
    Application.LoadLevel(Constants.SCENE_TITLE);
  }
}
```

Listing A.19 The TitleScreenScript Script

```
#pragma strict
var Constants : Constants;
public var Skin : GUISkin;

function Start()
{
  Constants = new Constants();
}

function Update()
{
  if (Input.anyKeyDown)
```

(continues)

```
    {
       Application.LoadLevel(Constants.SCENE_LEVEL_1);
    }
}

function OnGUI()
{
  GUI.skin = Skin;
  GUILayout.BeginArea (new Rect (300, 480, Screen.width, Screen.height));
  GUILayout.BeginVertical();
  GUILayout.Label("Press Any Key To Begin", GUILayout.ExpandWidth(true));
  GUILayout.EndVertical();
  GUILayout.EndArea ();
}
```

Hazard Scripts

This section contains the final scripts that are used to control the game's hazards. It includes the following scripts:

- **Listing A.20:** The ContactDamage Script
- **Listing A.21:** The PitTrigger Script

Listing A.20   **The ContactDamage Script**

```
#pragma strict
public var damage : int = 1;
public var playHitReaction : boolean = false;

function OnTriggerEnter2D(collider : Collider2D)
{
  if(collider.tag == "Player")
  {
    var stats : PlayerStats =
collider.gameObject.GetComponent(PlayerStats);
    stats.TakeDamage(this.damage, this.playHitReaction);
  }
}
```

Listing A.21   **The PitTrigger Script**

```
#pragma strict
function OnTriggerEnter2D(collider : Collider2D)
{
  if(collider.tag == "Player")
```

```
    {
      if(collider.GetComponent(PlayerStats).health > 0)
      {
        var trigger : GameObject = GetNearestActiveCheckpoint();

        if(trigger != null)
        {
          collider.transform.position = trigger.transform.position;
        }
        else
        {
          Debug.LogError("No valid checkpoint was found!");
        }
      }
    }
    else
    {
      Destroy(collider.gameObject);
    }
  }

function GetNearestActiveCheckpoint()
{
  var checkpoints : GameObject[] =
GameObject.FindGameObjectsWithTag("Checkpoint");
  var nearestCheckpoint : GameObject = null;
  var shortestDistance : float = Mathf.Infinity;

  for(var checkpoint : GameObject in checkpoints)
  {
    var checkpointPosition : Vector3 = checkpoint.transform.position;
    var distance : float =
      (checkpointPosition - transform.position).sqrMagnitude;
    var trigger : CheckpointTrigger =
      checkpoint.GetComponent(CheckpointTrigger);
    if(distance < shortestDistance && trigger.isTriggered == true)
    {
      nearestCheckpoint = checkpoint;

      shortestDistance = distance;
    }
  }
  return nearestCheckpoint;
}
```

System Scripts

This section contains the final script, the Constants Script, which is used to store our constant values.

Listing A.22   **The Constants Script**

```
#pragma public class Constants
{
// PLAYER PREFS
public var PREF_COINS : String = "Coins";
public var PREF_CURRENT_LEVEL : String = "CurrentLevel";

// SCENE NUMBERS
public var SCENE_LEVEL_1 : int = 6;
public var SCENE_LEVEL_2 : int = 2;
public var SCENE_LEVEL_3 : int = 3;
public var SCENE_GAME_OVER : int = 1;
public var SCENE_GAME_WIN : int = 4;
public var SCENE_TITLE : int = 5;

// PLAYER MOVEMENT VALUES
public var playerMaxSpeed : float = 7.0;
public var playerJumpForce : float = 850.0;
public var playerGroundCheckRadius : float = 0.2f;

public var animSpeed : String = "Speed";
public var animJump : String = "Jump";
public var animDie : String = "Die";
public var animDamage : String = "Damage";

// INPUT NAMES
public var inputMove : String = "Horizontal";
public var inputJump : String = "Jump";
}
```

Note

JavaScript does not actually have any concept of "constants" in the way that C# does, so these values could potentially be manipulated at runtime. Be cautious accordingly.

Index

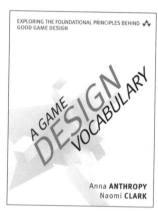